CYRENIUS CHAPIN

CYRENIUS CHAPIN

Buffalo's First Physician
and
War of 1812 Hero

THOMAS C. ROSENTHAL

excelsior editions
State University of New York Press
Albany, New York

Painting by Raymond Massy depicting Dr. Chapin lighting the cannon aimed at British forces marching towards Buffalo on Black Rock Road. Courtesy of The Buffalo History Museum.

Published by State University of New York Press, Albany

EU GPSR Authorised Representative:
Logos Europe, 9 rue Nicolas Poussin, 17000, La Rochelle, France
contact@logoseurope.eu

Excelsior Editions is an imprint of State University of New York Press

For information, contact State University of New York Press, Albany, NY
www.sunypress.edu

Library of Congress Cataloging-in-Publication Data

Name: Rosenthal, Thomas C., author.
Title: Cyrenius Chapin : Buffalo's first physician and War of 1812 hero / Thomas C. Rosenthal.
Description: Albany : State University of New York Press, 2025. | Includes bibliographical references and index.
Identifiers: LCCN 2024038239 | ISBN 9798855801804 (hardcover : alk. paper) | ISBN 9798855801811 (pbk. : alk. paper) | ISBN 9798855801828 (ebook)
Subjects: LCSH: Chapin, Cyrenius, 1769–1838. | Buffalo (N.Y.)—History—19th century. | Niagara Frontier (N.Y.)—History—War of 1812. | Physicians—New York—Buffalo—Biography. | New York (State). Militia—Officers—Biography. | Buffalo (N.Y.)—Biography.
Classification: LCC F129.B853 C437 2025 | DDC 974.7/9703092 [B]—dc23/eng/20250203
LC record available at https://lccn.loc.gov/2024038239

To Georgia

Contents

Illustrations

Timeline

1600s	Iroquois (Haudenosaunee) Confederation (People of the Longhouse) unites five (later six) Native American nations. Erie and Neuter Tribes are assimilated as Seneca Nation becomes 'Keepers of the Western Gate."
1650	Dutch claimed all New York lands west of the Hudson River, but French trappers dominate frontier interaction with Native Americans.
1725	French build Fort Niagara where the Niagara River empties into Lake Ontario.
1754–1763	The French and Indian War between France and Britian ends a century of French dominance in Canada.
1769	On February 7, Cyrenius Chapin is born in Bernardstown, Massachusetts.
1792	Shays Rebellion: Cyrenius Chapin (age sixteen) accompanies his father, a captain in the Massachusetts State militia.
1793	Cyrenius Chapin (age twenty-four) completes an apprenticeship with his brother.
1794	Cyrenius Chapin marries Sylvia Burnham, also from Bernardstown.
1795	Dr. Benjamin Rush promotes heroic bloodletting.
1798–1802	Edward Jenner introduces a vaccination using cowpox.
1801	Joseph Ellicott conducts an intense three-year survey of the Holland Land Company's vast Western New York holdings.

| 1801 | Dr. Chapin makes an offer to buy the entire New Amsterdam (Buffalo) township. |

1801 Dr. Chapin makes an offer to buy the entire New Amsterdam (Buffalo) township.

1803 Publication of the first American medical textbook by Samuel Stearns.

1803 Louisiana Purchase moves the United States boundary westward to the Rocky Mountains.

1803 Dr. Chapin receives the deed for Lot 41, Township 11, range 8, overlooking Buffalo Creek Seneca village.

1805 Dr. Chapin builds a combined home and office in New Amsterdam, the sixteenth frame structure in the village.

1805 Dr. Chapin is elected regional chair of the Federalist party.

1807 Dr. Chapin and Samuel Pratt establish Franklin Square Cemetery.

1808 Dr. Daniel Chapin becomes New Amsterdam's second physician. Soon, five physicians are practicing in the village.

1808 The New York State Legislature creates Niagara County. It includes the future Erie County.

1812 Dr. Chapin and Syliva's only son dies. The funeral is attended by Chief Red Jacket.

1812 Dr. Dan Chapin and Dr. Cyrenius Chapin compete to form the first Niagara County Medical Society.

1812 President Madison signs declaration of war with Britain in June.

1813 Buffalo incorporates as a village, formally adopting the name Buffalo.

1813 Dr. Chapin's Forty Thieves burn Canadian government buildings and plunder anything they deem official Canadian property. Laura Secord becomes a Canadian hero. In September, Dr. Chapin is captured by the British after the Battle of Beaver Dams, for the first time.

1813 Britain defeats Napoleon at the Battle of Leipzig on December 10.

1813 On December 30, British soldiers backed by Indian mercenaries begin a destructive march south along the Niagara River to Buffalo, which they burn. Cyrenius Chapin is taken as a prisoner of war for the second time.

1819   Dr. Chapin receives a government pension of $250 annually for his services during the War of 1812.

1821   Dr. Chapin starts the Niagara County Agricultural Society and organizes the first county fair. He later starts an Erie County Agricultural Society.

1825   Dr. Cyrenius Chapin is elected the president of the Erie County Medical Society.

1832   Millard Fillmore draws up papers to incorporate Buffalo as a city. The *Buffalo Patriot* prints the first public notice of the cholera epidemic.

1837   The Canadian Patriot Wars (aka Hunters Wars) consists of skirmishes from the St. Lawrence River to Michigan. William Lyon Mackenzie appears in Buffalo in the company of Dr. Cyrenius Chapin.

1838   Dr. Cyrenius Chapin (aged sixty-eight) dies on February 20, George Washington's birthday.

Chapter 1

Dr. Chapin and the Niagara Frontier

Aspirations Are the First Step of Engagement

As new snow fell on a frigid December 30, 1813, the British army and several hundred Algonquin mercenaries pillaged the New York villages along the Niagara River shoreline, burning everything in their path. From the village of Black Rock, they continued marching toward Buffalo. Descriptions of scalping and rape preceded them, horrifying 5,000 Buffalonians into a hasty retreat through the snowdrifts of the Western New York wilderness. In the chaos, Cyrenius Chapin, a physician and lieutenant colonel in the New York volunteer militia, pressed five men and boys to join with him to stall the British advance. Affecting his usual bravado, Dr. Chapin commandeered a small six-pound cannon and shouted orders to mount it on a barrier of stone and lumber his boys had erected across the village's northern perimeter at Niagara Street. As the British closed in, Chapin fired his cannon, blowing a hole in the leading ranks of redcoats. A second attempt to fire the cannon shattered its makeshift carriage and Chapin ordered his boys to run, shouting, "Every man for himself and the devil for us all!" He then tied a white handkerchief to his sword and rode out to parley with the advancing Redcoats. Claiming authority far exceeding his rank, Chapin negotiated the village's surrender in exchange for saving its homes. The proposed surrender passed up the British chain of command to General Riall, who vetoed it. Riall knew Dr. Chapin by reputation and considered him a scoundrel who had escaped British detention once before. By nightfall, all of Buffalo was in flames (Aigin, 1814; Goldman, 1983).

∽

Twelve-year-old James Aigin was one of those boys at Dr. Chapin's side trying to hold off the British torching of Buffalo in the War of 1812. Cyrenius Chapin was Buffalo's first physician, described by neighbors and patients as "that irascible stalwart old soldier, Colonel, as well as Doctor" (Welch, 1891). Canadian historians offer a different take. They describe Dr. Chapin as a man whose "too free use of ardent spirits . . . hindered his usefulness, both as a physician and citizen." Drunk or sober, Cyrenius Chapin was a popular man in Buffalo who made audiences shout patriotism (Graves, 2001). Like the heroes of many frontier villages, he was a populist with little influence on the national scene, tremendous influence on his neighbors' lives, and a frustrating knack for being intense regardless of whether he was right or wrong. Chapin secured his place among those who stacked the cultural bricks that built America.

This is the story of Dr. Chapin's Buffalo and the Western New York frontier he helped forge in the early nineteenth century. It is presented mostly chronologically, starting in 1801 with Chapin's first visit to Buffalo, or New Amsterdam, as the Holland Land Company hoped it would be called. Ambition drove him to propose buying a township worth of land from surveyor Joseph Ellicott, but denied that, he returned in 1803 with his family and established a large medical practice that spanned both sides of the Niagara River, crossing the porous Canadian and New York border at will. Most Western New Yorkers were squatters, trappers, or subsistence farmers, and the more established Canadians paid his fees in hard cash: British pounds and shillings. However, Chapin was a steadfast American Federalist with a forceful personality and an infuriating gall, surpassed only by his caring nature. He involved himself in building the foundation of frontier Buffalo society over a career that spanned an age of enlightenment for medicine, Western New York, and the Niagara Frontier (Hill, 1923).[1]

~

In 1801, Chapin must have seen Buffalo as a promising hamlet on the shore of Lake Erie near where the 36-mile-long Niagara River flows northward in its swift 335-feet descent over rapids and the falls at Niagara to Lake Ontario. Just down the river, a couple miles from Lake Erie and nearly

---

1. Throughout the text, Niagara Frontier is used to describe an area spanning the Niagara River, including the Niagara Peninsula of Canada and Western New York. Western New York is used to designate the portion of the Niagara Frontier within New York State.

Figure 1.1. Western New York road map, 1804. *Source:* Devoy, 1896. Public domain.

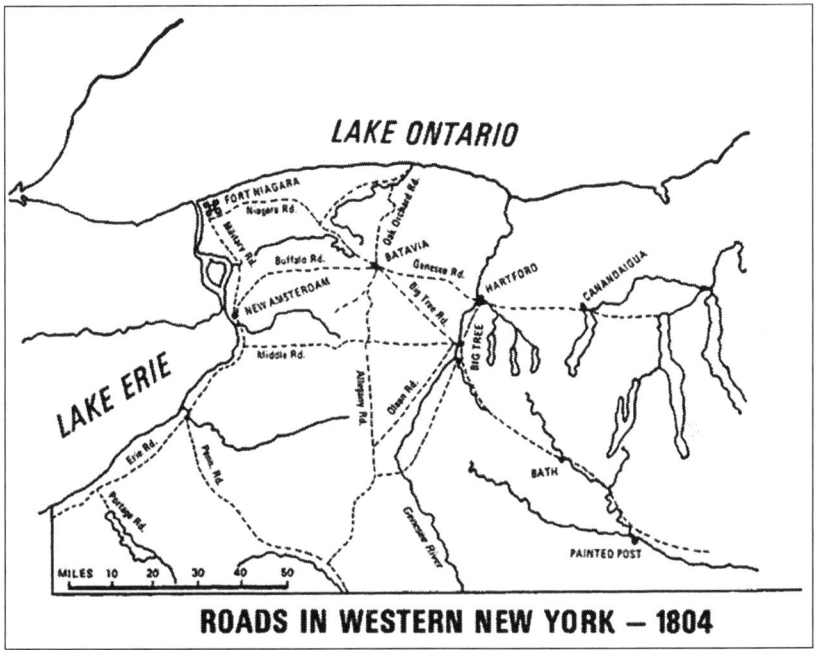

equal in size, the village of Black Rock grew around a small harbor. Native Americans had already built an extensive history in the region, but now the entire area—and most of the land west of the Genesee River—was owned by the Holland Land Company, and Native Americans made up most of the region's 4,000 residents.

Since time unknown, Niagara Falls has captured the imagination of Native American and European white men alike. An Englishman, John Maude, visited the Falls in 1800 and in his journal he wrote, "I crept upon my hands and knees to a projection of the rock, which, by a sudden curve at this place, was directly opposite to a huge column of falling water, if water it could now be called; for the velocity of the current, the resistance of massy (sic) rocks in the Rapids, and the present resistance and admixture of another element, had lashed it into foam, white as the drifted snow, and so compact as to resemble a falling body of pure vegetable cotton" (Maude, 1826).

Figure 1.2. Early nineteenth-century painting of Niagara Falls by John Maude, a Western New York tourist, in the year 1800. *Source:* Maude, 1826. Public domain.

Buffalo was on the Lake Erie shore near where the lake released its waters into the Niagara River. Throughout the nineteenth century, Buffalo typified the trajectory of America. The 1803 Louisiana purchase abruptly moved the western boundary of the United States to the Rocky Mountains, nearly doubling America's land mass and changing Buffalo from the frontier's edge to being a transit and supply center. Almost as quickly, immigration tripled the US population and Buffalo grew exponentially (Goldman, 1983). Eleven states were added in the first four decades of the nineteenth century: Ohio (1803), Louisiana (1812), Indiana (1816), Mississippi (1817), Alabama (1819), Illinois (1819), Maine (1820), Missouri (1821), Arkansas (1836), and Michigan (1837). Agriculture was the economic backbone of New York, which, with 2.5 million citizens by 1840, was becoming America's most populated state. At the federal level, America was toying with a two-party political system. The Alexander Hamilton/George Washington Federalist favored a strong central government. The Thomas Jefferson Democrat-Republicans championed a vision of powerful agrarian individualism governed locally with little federal interference (Chazanof, 1970).

In America's frontier towns, development was driven by the personalities of early settlers. Success depended on navigating the clashing cultures of back woodsmen—white European farm families and Native Americans—while challenged by the capricious nature of weather and land. By the time it arrived, news of the outside world was old, but men like Dr. Chapin paid attention. From the isolation of his world's window, he supported the new American government while charting his own semiautonomous interpretation of what the American experiment meant. Pioneers like Dr. Chapin acted in the interest of the people with whom he interacted, though to a large extent he interpreted his needs and wants as their needs and wants. He was of a generation that projected their idiosyncrasies onto their villages. Without them, American society would be different today.

~

History sets the stage for understanding the role Dr. Chapin played in Buffalo's earliest launch. In the mid-seventeenth century, the Dutch claimed all New York lands west of the Hudson River and traded with the Native American Haudenosaunee (also known as Iroquois) for furs, but they did little to encourage settlement. The first Europeans to exploit the riches of the Niagara Frontier region, including the falls of the Niagara, Black Rock harbor, and the many creeks emptying into Lake Erie, were French trappers. These fiercely independent French freebooters traveled by canoe or on foot paths Native Americans had forged throughout Western New York and around Niagara Falls (Morgan & Lloyd, 1904).

The first French trappers encountered Aboriginal tribes who were mostly peaceful, particularly the Neuter Indians[2] living along both sides of the Niagara River and the Eries occupying the southern shores of the lake bearing their name. The more aggressive and suspicious Algonquin and Huron Nations occupied the lands north of Lakes Erie and Ontario, extending as far west as Lake Huron. Letters from French priests called Lake Erie "Lake du Chat" because to the French ear, "erie" meant cat. Their descriptions convinced King Louis XIV that the Niagara Frontier could be the epicenter of an expansive fur trade (Munro, 1799). France promoted settlement but

---

2. Throughout the text, the outdated term "Indian" is used when directly representing how whites referred to Native Americans in the early nineteenth century. The more respectful, and accurate, "Native American" reference is preferred today.

closely monitored immigration up the Saint Lawrence and encouraged only French Catholic colonists (Borneman, 2006).

As seventeenth-century French trappers were exploring access to the Niagara Frontier, the Seneca Nation defeated and then assimilated the Neuter and Erie tribes. The Senecas were now established as the dominant people on the Niagara Frontier, earning the title "Keepers of the Western Gate" from the Haudenosaunee confederacy. With the Seneca's success, the Iroquois secured their dominance of upstate New York from Lake Erie to the Mohawk Valley. Also known as the Five Nations and later the Six Nations, the Haudenosaunee confederation included the Iroquoian-speaking Seneca, Cayuga, Onondaga, Oneida, and Mohawk Nations, later adding the Tuscarora Nation.

Relations between early Europeans and the Seneca waxed and waned as both sides alternately traded, cheated, and fought over the lucrative fur trade. By 1687, the English claimed Massachusetts and much of New York and Ohio, the French claimed Montreal and most of Canada, and French Jesuit priests dominated interactions with Native Americans on both sides of the Niagara River (Livingston, 1910). The largest Seneca village grew along one of the creeks flowing into Lake Erie, the name of which sounded like "Buffalo" to the European ear. (Alternatively, the name comes from "beau fleuve," French for a beautiful river. The exact origin is uncertain.) As the population of Senecas grew, the French became nervous about securing the critical portage route around Niagara Falls and protecting it from Seneca or British interruption. In 1725, they built a fort on the New York side of the Niagara River on a rocky promontory just east of where the Niagara emptied into Lake Ontario. The fort was nearly surrounded by water, with Lake Ontario to the north and the river curving around its western and southern sides (Borneman, 2006). Known as Fort Niagara today, it will change hands several times over the next 150 years (R. S. Allen, 2006).

Between 1754 and 1763, a series of conflicts between the French and the English on the Niagara Frontier mirrored their near-perpetual wars in Europe. Known to Americans as the "French and Indian Wars," a force of 600 British troops, 100 New York militia, and 1,000 Native Americans laid siege to Fort Niagara, capturing it in July 1759. A century of French dominance in Canada and the Niagara River passed to the English with the signing of the *Treaty of Paris* in February 1763. (*Treaty of Paris* is also the title given to the 1783 treaty ending the American Revolutionary War.) To appease the Haudenosaunee, 1763 also saw King George III sign a proclamation declaring that all lands west of the Appalachians would be off-limits for settlement without royal approval. One year later, April 1764, Sir William Johnson concluded a treaty with the Seneca chiefs conveying ownership of a four-mile-wide track of land along the Niagara River to the King of England and securing the portage route around Niagara Falls from Fort Niagara to Buffalo Creek. The British would control Fort Niagara and would continue to, until signing *Jay's Treaty* in 1795, finally abandoning the fort twelve years after the Revolutionary War (R. S. Allen, 2006).

In the first year of America's Revolutionary War, the Seneca Nation took a position of neutrality. However, by 1777, the Haudenosaunee saw little chance for an American victory and signed a treaty declaring their allegiance to England. For the rest of the war, rumors of Indian attacks halted further settlement on the Niagara Frontier (Devoy, 1896).

It would take until 1795 for a new treaty (*Jay's Treaty*), ratified by a bare two-thirds majority of United States senators), to clarify the borders agreed to in the 1783 revolutionary war *Treaty of Paris*. The British army finally abandoned Fort Niagara, and the United States extended "favored-trading" status to England (J. W. Pratt, 1925).

~

Permanent white European settlement in Western New York began with the Dutchman, Cornelius Winney. After migrating west from the Hudson River, Winney built a small log store in 1790 overlooking Buffalo Creek and made his living trading with the Senecas. In 1794, William Johnston took up residence in a block house he built near Winney's store. Soon Martin Middaugh, a Dutch cooper, and his son-in-law, Ezekiel Lane, settled near Johnston in a log house. John Palmer then opened a tavern, increasing the number of New Amsterdam buildings to five, all within a quarter mile of the Seneca village on Buffalo Creek and Lake Erie.

The Holland Land Company started buying up land in 1792, much of it from Robert Morris, who owned four million acres in New York he purchased from Massachusetts owners in 1791 (Goldman, 1983). The Holland Land Company was a consortium of six Dutch banking houses backing a handful of American citizens who acted as their agents. The Company eventually purchased 3.3 million acres, nearly all the land in New York west of a line extending from Pennsylvania to Lake Ontario that roughly followed the Genesee River. Their holdings included the present site of Buffalo, or New Amsterdam, as the company hoped it would be called. Surveying and land sales began in earnest once the federal government and the Haudenosaunee

Nation signed the treaty at Geneseo's Big Tree in 1797. The treaty set aside tracts for the Haudenosaunee Nation called reservations, including the Seneca village on the shores of Buffalo Creek (Chazanof, 1970).

Through the first decade of the 1800s, most New Yorkers still considered the area of New York between the Genesee River and Lake Erie to be a great western wilderness controlled by Native Americans, or Indians as the tribes were then called. Families were generally distrustful of Indians whose societal traditions were misrepresented in tall tales and cheap novels. By setting aside land for European settlement and restricting the Senecas to defined reservations, the Big Tree Treaty addressed many of these concerns and opened up Western New York for European settlers. Most were subsistence farmers willing to carve a homestead out of dense forest at a reasonable price. Still, it would be years before the area's economy no longer depended on trading whiskey, knives, and rifles for Seneca furs. During that time, the Senecas' Buffalo Creek reservation thrived as a meeting point for the Haudenosaunee Nations (Chazanof, 1970).

∾

When thirty-two-year-old Dr. Cyrenius Chapin first visited New Amsterdam in 1801, the only white men wearing European dress were employees of the Holland Land Company. The village had yet to be surveyed and would not formally be called Buffalo until 1813. The youngest of five children was born in Bernardstown, Massachusetts, on February 7, 1769; Cyrenius Chapin married Sylvia Burnham from his hometown shortly after completing his medical studies in 1793. For several years, he practiced medicine in Winhall, Vermont; then he and Sylvia moved to Sangerfield in Oneida County, New York.

Chapin was a stubborn man who made friends and enemies with equal aptitude. His childhood role models likely included some of America's first heroes, such as Daniel Boone and Ethan Allen. In 1784, John Filson published a book with somewhat exaggerated accounts of Daniel Boone's (1734–1820) settlement of Kentucky that became very popular. Filson's hero made all things seem possible, given enough courage and fortitude (Filson, 1784). Ethan Allen (1738–1789) was a New England farmer, patriot, land speculator, and politician who is credited with founding Vermont. Allen published several accounts of his exploits that were widely read at the turn of the nineteenth century (McWilliams, 1976). No doubt men like Boone and fellow New Englander Allen stirred Cyrenius to seek his own wilderness experience. Western New York was a wild frontier where he could carve out his own prospects. The lingering spirit that inspired the American revolution continued to empower many self-directed men, confident that their own potential was unlimited (C. Johnson, 1876).

Cyrenius's great-great-grandfather was Deacon Samuel Chapin, a Puritan who arrived in Massachusetts in 1643. Cyrenius's father, Captain Caleb Chapin (1736–1815), was a Bernardstown farmer who supplemented his income by making and installing millstones. His mother was the former Rebecca Bascom (1740–1825). Captain Chapin fought in both the French and Indian Wars and in the Revolutionary War. In 1786, he led a Massachusetts State militia to put down anti-tax riots known as the Shays Rebellion. Led by Daniel Shays, in protest of paying state duties in hard currency, nearly 4,000 New England farmers attempted to seize weaponry from the federal armory in Springfield. Seventeen-year-old Cyrenius served as his father's personal aide throughout the Shays campaign in a firsthand experience that would define his view of leadership, personal responsibility, and the role of government and community (G. F. Pratt, 1869).

Cyrenius studied medicine as an apprentice to his eldest brother, Dr. Caleb Chapin, a highly respected doctor in Bernardstown. There is no evidence that either of the Chapin brothers attended lectures at a medical college or received a formal academic degree. They both learned medicine by serving guild-style apprenticeships that focused on the composition and compounding of medicines and on a comprehensive knowledge of remedies based on patient symptoms. There was little attention paid to theory, and studying under just one preceptor limited one's perspective about medicine's potential. Knowledge was acquired in an atmosphere of "see-it-once, then do-it-yourself." Textbooks included the US Dispensatory, a medical dictionary, an anatomy book, and whatever other books the preceptor had on his shelf (G. F. Pratt, 1869; Stephens, 1847; Wood, 1875).

Both Chapin brothers subscribed to the romantic idea that payment was secondary to a physician. They both could be aggressive when seeking payment from those with the means to pay, yet they both accepted barter from the less fortunate. As medical men, the Chapins viewed themselves more like clergymen than businessmen. Throughout his career, Cyrenius stayed focused on sustaining a medical practice, and despite his humble training, he gained a reputation for continually reading and staying current. All the while, he sought opportunities to upgrade his economic status through nonmedical enterprises (G. F. Pratt, 1869).

We shall see how Dr. Cyrenius Chapin would manifest his faith in the future of Buffalo by moving his family to New Amsterdam in 1803, where, other than the chief agent of the Holland Land Company, Joseph Ellicott, he exercised more influence than anyone in the region's development. Like all those who succeeded on the frontier, Cyrenius was bold, resolute, and energetic. He could be generous and freehearted with his fellows, reckless about the conventions of society, and occasionally blind to the consequences of his acts. Driven by self-confidence and a strong will, the only direction he knew was forward. He counted his close friends warmly and his enemies with bitter assertions. But as a physician, Dr. Cyrenius Chapin never lost the confidence of his community (C. Johnson, 1876).

One visitor to Buffalo would later ask what sort of man this Dr. Cyrenius Chapin was: "I have heard so much about him." The answer: "Oh, the doc is a fine fellow, he does all the praying, swearing and shouting for this community" ("Viewed in scrapbook at Buffalo and Erie County Library without further citation.," 1909).

Chapter 2

Opportunities on a Knoll Overlooking Lake Erie

Active Individuals Find Meaningful Opportunities

It cannot be overstated: in the first decade of the nineteenth-century, Native Americans played an essential role in the white European settlement of Western New York. This, despite George Washington sending General John Sullivan (1740–1795) with 3,000 soldiers of the Continental Army to the region in 1779 to clear Western New York of Indians perceived to be cooperating with the British during the Revolutionary War. Though the Haudenosaunee were officially neutral, many clans leaned toward supporting the more established British. Sullivan's tactics were indiscriminate. His troops burned aboriginal homes, villages, and orchards located outside of Buffalo Creek (Fischer, 2007). The campaign drove some Native Americans to seek British shelter at Fort Niagara, while others moved into the Seneca village on Buffalo Creek. Some estimates suggested that 50 percent of Western New York Native Americans died of starvation and exposure that winter (Graymont, 1972). The resourceful Senecas not only adapted, but they sustained the essential elements of their culture. By 1801, Dr. Chapin found the Seneca village at Buffalo Creek to be a well-organized, self-governing community that significantly overshadowed New Amsterdam.

The Big Tree Treaty of 1797 had given formal recognition of Buffalo Creek as a reservation for the Senecas, along with several years of peace and prosperity. The little village of New Amsterdam, just a quarter mile north of Buffalo Creek, provided an opportunity for the Senecas to trade their furs for European goods. In fact, Senecas might be described as the dominant culture in Western New York through the first quarter of the nineteenth century, exerting a significant influence on Buffalo's early development and the plans of the Holland Land Company. Despite Sullivan's extirpation, the Native American population exceeded the white European population, and the two cultures competed as mutually dependent communities (Goldman, 2007). The Senecas identified with the land, understood its climate, and shared their knowledge with any new settler who was inclined to listen. White Europeans brought the concept of individual land ownership, western goods, guns, and whiskey.

The Senecas hunted, fished, trapped, and cleared land to raise crops. They not only fed their own families, but also sold their excess to white settlers at a profit. The Big Tree Treaty provided the reservation with an annual federal stipend and the Holland Land Company added another $4,000 each year for land rights (C. Johnson, 1876). The enterprise and commerce of Native American and white settlers was so integrated that the two cultures interacted daily at markets, barn raisings, and celebrations. Intermarriage was common, even among soldiers from Sullivan's army who stayed on to settle in the area.

On that first visit to the Niagara Frontier in 1801, Cyrenius Chapin rode his horse to New Amsterdam on a Native American trail that linked New Amsterdam to Batavia. The trail had been widened but was only marginally maintained as it coursed through Black Rock, through New Amsterdam, and on to the Buffalo Creek Reservation. Though it was called a road, it barely accommodated oxcarts with occasional corduroy log tracks that marginally improved travel through the many low wet spots. Black bears feasted on the nuts of beech trees. Gray wolves and panthers thrived on the plentiful deer. The woods were full of raccoons, squirrels, wild turkey, partridge, and the occasional rattlesnake. Trees along creek beds held fifty passenger pigeon nests each (C. Johnson, 1876). The primitive trails made it possible for a horse to cover twenty-five miles a day, but the most common family conveyance, the oxcart, struggled to cover twelve miles a day. In the evening, families camped together to protect their horses and oxen from poaching, which was usually blamed on Indians and only occasionally on the white robbers and thieves known to watch the roads (Letchworth, 1874).

In New Amsterdam, Chapin found little more than a collection of log cabins along muddy paths that were interrupted by occasional tree stumps. He would have met the Dutchman, Cornelius Winney, at his log-cabin store and admired Winney's view of the Seneca reservation. He noticed

Senecas frequenting the store to buy and sell goods. Chapin would have introduced himself to William Johnston at Johnson's blockhouse and met Martin Middaugh, the Dutch cooper. Haphazardly scattered nearby, there was a blacksmith shop, a silversmith, and another half a dozen cabins with no formal streets connecting them. The population was all of twenty-five whites. The doctor probably stayed in New Amsterdam's only permanent tavern, the Palmer House, which offered guests a warm space to sleep on the floor and in their clothes (Letchworth, 1874). Chapin toured both the Canadian and American shores of the Niagara River and saw potential for his family, as well as forty friends and neighbors from Oneida County who he claimed shared his interest in starting their own village on the shore of Lake Erie.

We learn more details about the New Amsterdam settlement from a Vermont fur trader, Captain Samuel Pratt (1764–1812), who also passed through New Amsterdam in 1801 and 1803. Pratt had been on an expedition to acquire furs from Native American tribes in Ohio. His trading was interrupted when he contracted smallpox and was nursed back to health by Native Americans culturally related to the Senecas. During his prolonged convalescence, Pratt gained respect for aboriginal customs, learned their language, and amassed a considerable bounty of furs. On his way home to Vermont, Pratt stopped in Buffalo Creek, where he was overwhelmed by the organization and economy of the Seneca village and its 2,100 residents. In 1804, Pratt moved his family to New Amsterdam over the objections of his thirty-eight-year-old wife, Sophia. He lured them with a promise to build what became the first frame house in New Amsterdam. Captain Pratt and Sophia later became close friends with Dr. and Sylvia Chapin. Their son, Hiram, would live with the Chapins after Samuel's death in 1812 (Letchworth, 1874).

No documents exist to confirm if Chapin's forty Oneida County neighbors formally empowered him to purchase land in western New York, but he spent considerable effort investigating the potential. He sought out Paul Busti, the Agent General hired by Wilhelm Willink, to represent the Holland Land Company's interests. A major Dutch investor, Willink owned 28 percent of the company's assets (P. D. Evans, 1924). Busti, however, spent most of his time in Philadelphia, so Chapin's only option was to meet with the surveyor and not yet designated agent, Joseph Ellicott (1760–1826). Both men were nearly six feet tall and rugged. But Ellicott was a frugal man and orderly, whereas Doc Chapin was impetuous and expeditious. Ellicott hailed from the Quakers of Bucks County, Pennsylvania, where his only formal education was several months in a rural schoolhouse. Ellicott learned surveying methods by assisting his brother, Andrew Ellicott, who, as the surveyor-general of the United States, laid out Washington, DC, for President Washington following the design of Pierre L'Enfant (Letchworth, 1874).

In 1801, Joseph Ellicott was near the end of an intense three-year survey of the Holland Land Company's lands in New York. He had grown attached to the region and liked the four-season climate. But being a perfectionist, Ellicott was not yet ready to sell large tracts of land, particularly not land that included the spot where he envisioned a grand New Amsterdam by the lake.

Dr. Chapin had his own vision. Before returning to Oneida County, Chapin made several efforts to convince Ellicott to sell him a piece of land, so large that it would have encompassed all of Ellicott's grand city. His pitch was a guaranteed, ready-made village of resettled Oneida County families who would instantly fulfill Ellicott's waterfront dream. Ellicott was not to be pushed. He wanted to put the finishing touches on his L'Enfant-like design for New Amsterdam before selling off its land. Also, Chapin had no papers to prove his backers' commitment, nor could he produce the required 10 percent down payment (Letchworth, 1874).

A month later, in November 1801, back home in Oneida County, Chapin wrote a letter to Ellicott and put his offer in writing. It read, in part: "And further I would petition you for a township of land there at the Buffalo — the one that will take in the town, for since my return a number of my friends have solicited me to petition you for a township, and for that purpose forty respectable citizens that are men of good property, have signed articles of agreement to take a township, if it can be purchased; and we will pay the ten percent when we receive the article." This letter described the desired property in detail and expanded Chapin's initial request by including the mouth of Buffalo Creek (Turner, 1849; White, 1898).

Had Chapin's offer been accepted, he and his friends would have taken title to much of today's downtown Buffalo. Ellicott stalled for several weeks before sending a polite letter informing Dr. Chapin that the answer did not favor his application. For the next two years, Chapin made several visits to Batavia to inquire about his proposal. Finally, his offer to buy a township was either definitively refused, or his investors backed out (Turner, 1849).

Chapin's interest prodded Ellicott to complete his New Amsterdam plans, lay out streets, and number lots. Ellicott wanted the village to sit on the hillock above Buffalo Creek overlooking Lake Erie. He wanted streets to radiate outward, like those of Pierre L'Enfant's Washington. It is easy to imagine the difficulties of continued bargaining between Ellicott, a detailed person, and Dr. Chapin, who was more inclined to figure things out as he went along. Both men possessed considerable egos, but the only vision for the future Buffalo that mattered was that of Joseph Ellicott, and selling off an entire township of prime land did not fit his habits of comprehensive planning.

Between 1801 and 1803, Ellicott's vision took form. He was resolute that the new town be known as New Amsterdam in honor of the conglomerate that employed him. He laid out eight primary streets that radiated from a central square he named "Niagara Square" located at the pinnacle of the Erie lakefront. In honor of the Native Americans who frequently factored into his effort, Ellicott named his radiating streets after Native American clans that regularly traveled the portage around Niagara Falls. The portage road itself he named Niagara Street and other streets he named Delaware, Chippawa, Huron, Mohawk, and Seneca. Ellicott's street names may not have provided him with much advantage, as some of the named clans only occasionally got along with the Senecas (Borneman, 2006). Ellicott's detailed planning did little to overcome the dominance of the Seneca village of Buffalo Creek. It so dominated the Niagara Frontier that settlers kept calling his prize village Buffalo Creek, or simply Buffalo.

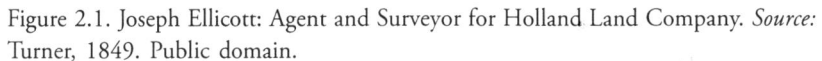

Figure 2.1. Joseph Ellicott: Agent and Surveyor for Holland Land Company. *Source:* Turner, 1849. Public domain.

Finally, on October 11, 1803, Dr. Chapin focused his petition on one of Ellicott's surveyed lots. Lot 41, Township 11, range 8, fronted on Swan Street and occupied the bluff overlooking Buffalo Creek. Chapin paid $346.50 to become Ellicott's first sale in "downtown" New Amsterdam. It was much less than his original township aspiration, but it totaled over 90 acres of prime real estate that became known as the Chapin Block. Lot 41 extended from the corner of Main and Swan streets through to Pearl Street. Within weeks, the impetuous Dr. Chapin moved Sylvia and their family to the region only to realize that New Amsterdam offered no suitable temporary housing. With winter setting in, the family was forced to rent a frame house across the Niagara River in Fort Erie, Canada (Livsey, 1991; White, 1898).

Ellicott's survey had employed over 100 surveyors, draftsmen, cooks, axmen, and camp staff. He purchased food by the barrel and bought or leased innumerable boats, ox teams, packhorses, horseshoes, blankets, tents, axes, and shoes. He used over two gross of black lead pencils to keep notes in his detailed folio books. Ellicott's employers were astonished by his accuracy and his shrewd designs for land development. No man knew the Niagara Frontier and Western New York better, and sales started as soon as Ellicott was promoted from surveyor to lead Western New York agent by Holland Land Company directors. His annual salary of $1,500 and a commission of 5 percent on all sales was about to make Ellicott a rich man. Wasting no time, Ellicott soon built new offices in the more centrally located Batavia, New York, to accommodate the monumental task ahead. The name Batavia was chosen to honor the Holland hometown of several Dutch shareholders (Chazanof, 1970; White, 1898).

Chapin's purchase marked the opening of sales for the Holland Land Company. Squatters living in the wilds of western New York were forced to purchase their land or move. New families with resources to pay for a clear title immediately improved their purchased land, but getting around Western New York was difficult. Roads were essential if Joseph Ellicott was to meet the sales quotas set by the Holland Land Company. Ellicott started by granting three families 150 acres each to settle along the Batavia/New Amsterdam Road. In exchange, the families agreed to offer rest and accommodations to travelers (Chazanof, 1970). The Army assisted by using troops stationed at Fort Niagara under the command of Major Peter Buell Porter (1773–1844) to rebuild and replace the portage trail from Lake Ontario to Lake Erie, parts of which were called Military Road. The improved road passed by Porter's home in Black Rock and did much to promote Porter's business interests. Ellicott contracted with others to survey and cut the Oak

Orchard Road from Batavia to Lake Ontario to stimulate a community Ellicott envisioned on the shores of Lake Ontario, later named Medina. A contract was also given to Jabez Warren to begin work on the Big Tree Road, also called the Middle Road, from Big Tree Reservation near Geneseo to the future village of Hamburg on Lake Erie, and today's Route 20A. Like many other contractors, Warren and members of his crew would settle in one of the broad valleys their road cut through, today known as East Aurora. Ellicott paid contractors $2.50 per mile for surveying and $10 per mile for cutting out the road, which meant removing most of the stumps from the two-rod wide paths. These projects all began in 1801 and remained in various stages of completion by the 1803 land sales (T. C. Rosenthal, 2020).

There are no records of the route Chapin took to move his family to Buffalo. However, in 1805, William Hodge (1781–1848) moved his wife and two children to Buffalo from the Albany area. He loaded all the family's possessions on a wagon, traveling overland to Utica. From Utica he joined with other families, twenty people in all, who loaded their wagons—wheels removed—on a flatboat. The flatboats traveled down the Mohawk River, through Oneida Lake, and onto the Oswego River. On the Oswego, they portaged around several rapids until arriving at Lake Ontario. There, they transferred to a lake boat for the easiest part of their trip, taking them 170 miles to the lower Niagara River at Lewiston. At Lewiston, the flatboat was lifted out of the water, loaded on a wheeled contraption, and pulled by ox teams around Niagara Falls and its rapids. Upon reentering the Niagara River, the flatboats were towed, rowed, and poled to Lake Erie and then to Buffalo Creek and the village of New Amsterdam. Hodge had been a farmer, but in Buffalo he took up carpentry and was noted for making over 300 coffins for the American and British soldiers killed in 1813 (Goldman, 1983; Hodge, 1885).

Ellicott famously used the resources of a private company, in this case the Holland Land Company, to build roads and improve property values. His effort to direct work on multiple projects gave Western New York a lead over other frontier areas. In 1806, Congress tried to follow Ellicott's road model by subsidizing construction of roads to other western territories, starting with improving Daniel Boone's Wilderness Road, later called the Cumberland Road to connect the Potomac and Ohio rivers. The Cumberland Road fell prey to the differing philosophies of Washington/Hamilton Federalist and Democrat-Republican followers of Thomas Jefferson, the latter believing that government had little business in road building. Political debates delayed the completion of the Cumberland Road to Vandalia,

Illinois, until 1837 (D. S. Brown, 2022; Faragher, 1992). In the meantime, road building and secure land titles in Western New York, driven by the energies of Joseph Ellicott, pumped the optimism of Dr. Chapin and New Amsterdam's first wave of settlers.

All of New York west of the Genesee River was initially designated Genesee County, and Batavia became its capital. It encompassed virtually all the Holland Land Company's vast holdings. Local government structure began with Governor George Clinton's appointment of Asa Ransom as the County Justice of the Peace, making Ransom the region's earliest political official. Ransom owned a section of land along Batavia Road in Clarence that offered passing accommodations to travelers.

Joseph Ellicott quickly systematized land-sale policies. He set $2.75 per acre as the standard price with a required down payment of 10 percent. It did not take long for Ellicott to realize that the down payment was too high to attract the number of settlers he needed to satisfy his superiors in the Holland Land Company. Soon, for buyers he felt to be qualified, he lowered the down payment to $1, backed up by a rigidly enforced schedule of payments.

∾

At the beginning of the nineteenth century, most Americans were farmers and there were only four common nonfarm occupations: clergy, merchants, lawyers, and doctors. Merchants thrived on selling the tools and supplies farmers needed. Lawyers did well, given the legacy of vague boundaries, forged land titles, and the rugged individualism that made for a somewhat litigious society. Doctors ranked fourth (St. John de Crevecoeur, 1793). Benjamin Rush, a signatory to the Declaration of Independence, was the nation's most famous physician, but American medicine had little structure. Eighteen-one saw the publication of the first medical textbook by an American, Boston's Samuel Stearns. Stearns was none too kind to American doctors, declaring most to be the laughingstock of refined society. Two-thirds had little education, and their knowledge base was horrid. Not one to hide behind his own modesty, Stearns claimed that his textbook corrected all the errors in previous textbooks; adding that American doctors were so poorly paid that he was forced to price his book much below its real value (S. Stearns, 1801).

Advantaged only by apprenticeship training, Dr. Cyrenius Chapin faced the challenges typical of all American doctors at the beginning of the nineteenth century. Intent on healing, but with few effective remedies, Chapin relied on a commanding, paternalistic temperament that he backed up with a stubborn willingness to tackle any affliction his patients suffered. He was not described as ostentatious, but at six feet, his height alone drew attention. His near-constant exposure to the outdoors gave him a rugged bronze complexion set off by eyebrows that arched over sharp and piercing blue eyes set on a thin face and a prominent Romanesque nose. Though no portraits exist of Dr. Chapin, a drawing was published in a Buffalo newspaper long after his death. The artist based his representation on descriptions of Dr. Chapin and personal interviews with descendants (Burr, 1927). Chapin's movements were described as quick and certain, driven by dignified authority. His partners complained he needed little sleep, rose early, and stayed active through long days that wore them out. His signature attire was a long cloak of blue cloth (Atkins, 1898). His longest tenured partner agonized over Chapin's proclivity for denouncing most anyone he did not admire and reinforcing his disapproval by issuing unnecessarily direct statements that often got him in trouble.(G. F. Pratt, 1869).

Figure 2.2. Portrait of Dr. Cyrenius Chapin created for a Buffalo newspaper in 1927. The unnamed artist based the portrait on descriptions of Dr. Chapin and the facial characteristics of his descendants. It is the only known image of Dr. Chapin. *Source:* Burr, 1927. Public domain.

Medical theories at the turn of the nineteenth century paralleled the beliefs of society as a whole. Except for the infirmities of old age, illness reflected God's will, or worse, an evil spirit. The dominant religions taught that the human soul was susceptible to manipulation by internal and external forces, and while some forces were beyond individual influence, most could be modified by behaviors or thoughts within an individual's control. The overlap between spiritual beliefs and medicine drew many religious leaders into rituals that merged medicine with various forms of exorcism intended to rebalance the influence of good and evil spirits. Preachers, being among those in the community who could read, commonly relied on textbooks to take up the practice of medicine.

Medical theories themselves were anchored in centuries of rationalizations (Whewell, 1837). Chapin's brother, Caleb, would have taught the theories of Hippocrates (fourth century BC) and Galen (second century AD) that called for rebalancing the four humors: black bile, yellow bile, blood, and phlegm. Benjamin Rush of Philadelphia amended these rationalizations by taking rebalancing to heroic extremes with the claim that he cured yellow fever victims in the 1793 epidemic. Rush wrote that the heat and redness of inflammatory conditions required an aggressive release of warm, red blood reinforced by forceful intestinal evacuation of poisonous byproducts using mercury containing calomel. The patient's symptoms were more important than the cause of disease and provided the only clue a doctor needed to select the remedy most likely to rebalance humors. Rush's heroic protocols were attractive to strong, confident men like Dr. Chapin, though not very easy on their patients (Rush, 1794). Dr. Chapin's generation was the first to witness the intrusion of experimental science on medical practice.

Descriptions of Dr. Chapin, by friends and foes alike, all include power adjectives. His partners described him as opinionated, outspoken, frank, and prone to emphasizing his viewpoint with expletives. He expected forthrightness and candor from others and valued honesty above all other qualities. Chapin could be impatient, impulsive, and easily annoyed by indecision. He enjoyed drawing people into debate and took a lively interest in his community, which, combined with his fiery nature, caused frequent confrontations. Yet, upon reflection, if he viewed himself as indiscreet, he often apologized and invested considerable effort to make amends. If he was the injured party, he never gave up the contest until his opponent either made a suitable acknowledgment or was vanquished. To patients he seemed curious, genial, and generous to a fault. He had an easy and natural empathy for the sick that prompted many families to ask Dr. Chapin to provide prayers and eulogies at funerals (G. F. Pratt, 1869).

Five men contributed the most to Buffalo's early years: Joseph Ellicott, Cyrenius Chapin, Samuel Pratt, Peter B. Porter, and Erastus Granger. They will all play prominent roles in this story. Porter and his brother built a business transporting people and goods around Niagara Falls. Granger arrived last. He was from New England and sent by President Thomas Jefferson in 1804 to be the local Indian Agent and eventually to establish Buffalo's first post office. He built a house on Flint Hill near today's Main Street entrance of Forest Lawn Cemetery on property that included over 100 acres. Many Parkside residents today find Granger's name on their deeds.

So it was that in October 1803, Ellicott signed over a dozen deeds for his New Amsterdam. It marked the launch of a great city on the shores of Lake Erie. For reasons unexplained, Chapin paid a lower amount per acre than any of the others in that first release. For Dr. Chapin, it was prime land at a good price. Joseph Ellicott got a dedicated but argumentative citizen (Turner, 1849).

Chapter 3

Religion, Home, and Practice in the Wilderness

Impetuous or Cautious, Fortune Is Fickle

Having given in to his enthusiastic and impetuous nature by moving his family to New Amsterdam and the Niagara Frontier as the days of winter shortened in 1803, Dr. Chapin and Sylvia settled for renting a home across the Niagara River in Fort Erie, Canada. Financially, it was a blessing. He quickly learned that settlements on the Canadian side were not only older, with more clapboard houses boasting solid roofs, but they were more prosperous and used hard British currency. The area was known as the Canadian peninsula, as it lay between Lakes Erie and Ontario. It boasted broad, open fields, decent roads, and mature orchards of apple and peach trees. The western end of New York was mostly tangled forest broken by a few stump-strewed roads and pastures with only abandoned sixteen-foot square log cabins with a single six-pane window and a dirt or split-log floor for accommodations. Neither side of the river had doctors, so the thirty-four-year-old Cyrenius and Sylvia made the best of it. By the summer of 1804, Dr. Chapin had developed a reputation on both sides of the river as a skilled practitioner willing to ride his horse to far reaches in the care of patients (H. P. Smith, 1884).

Though the fast-moving current of the Niagara River defined the US–Canadian border, it was a porous demarcation. Many Americans, including Dr. Chapin, believed it was only a matter of time before Canada shed its allegiance to the English monarch and joined the rebellious colonies. In fact, the twelfth article of America's first constitution, the *Articles of Confederation,* had prequalified Canadian provinces as future states in anticipation of this inevitability.

But Canada's allegiances were more complicated than most Americans appreciated. As discussed in chapter 1, the French had dominated Canada until 1763, when a *Treaty of Paris* ended the French and Indian War in North America and ceded Canada to the British (Borneman, 2006). That war had been a sentinel experience that trained much of the colonial army's leadership. It was the nature of the British empire to take a highly structured approach to managing colonies, so they brought standard colonial configuration and much-needed order to Canadian governance. They started by formally designating two provinces, an Upper Canada and a Lower Canada, as defined by the flow of the Saint Lawrence River. Each had a lieutenant-governor appointed by the British Monarch who was advised by a two-house legislature. The upper house was jointly appointed by the lieutenant-governor and the English monarch. The lower house was elected by the population (Taylor, 2010).

The French-leaning Province of Lower Canada was the most populated and spanned the areas east and northeast of the point where the Saint Lawrence River began draining the eastern end of Lake Ontario. This "Lower" Province contained all the Saint Lawrence River downstream from Lake Ontario, including Montreal and Quebec. Quebec had been founded by French explorer Samuel de Champlain as a permanent settlement in 1608. Its name was drawn from an Algonquin word meaning "the river narrows here," but the village clung to its French culture. West and upstream from Quebec, Montreal had arisen on an island where canoes had to portage around rapids (Borneman, 2006).

The Upper Province (today's Ontario Province) included all areas north of the shores of the Great Lakes and west of the St Lawrence River's origin. Upper Canada had many fewer European settlers and several small villages, including Newark (today's Niagara-on-the-Lake, across from Fort Niagara) at the Niagara River northern outflow, York (today's Toronto) where several creeks discharge on the north shore of Lake Ontario, and Fort Erie at the eastern end of Lake Erie near the origin of the Niagara River (Taylor, 2010).

Though two decades had passed since signing the *Treaty of Paris* ending the Revolutionary War, the still-reigning British King George III remained convinced it was only a matter of time before America's republican form of government failed. The British acted out their hubris by continuing to quarter British troops on American soil at several forts on the American shores of the Great Lakes. *Jay's Treaty* of 1795 required the British to abandon these forts, but it did not end the British army's gifts of guns and ammunition to Native American tribes south of the Great Lakes.

Diversity marked the population of Upper Canada. It included descendants of French trappers, refugee English loyalists from the United States, and Native Americans. Following the Revolutionary War, more Americans moved to Canada to avoid the taxes levied to pay debts the United States had assumed following the war. To boost immigration, the British offered free land, requiring little more than signing a commitment to support the English Crown. These new residents were mostly farmers who, by the first decade of the nineteenth century, only dabbled in trapping. Their priorities were working their land and feeding their families. Few had an interest in politics (Jasanoff, 2008). Barn raisings, logging bees, corn husking, and making maple syrup were the chief sources of amusement on both sides of the border. Whiskey jugs were shared without regard to which side of the border you called home.

The British empire's investments in governance and influence explain why Dr. Chapin found the Canadian Niagara peninsula and the Canadian shore of the Niagara River more developed. Established in 1780, Newark had been the first true English settlement in Upper Canada. It was positioned at the outlet of the Niagara River to encourage shipping and was designated as the official point of entry to welcome refugee English loyalists fleeing the United States. After signing a loyalty pledge to the British Crown, refugees received provisions for twelve months and seed for the first growing season. All crops above the family's needs were to be sold to the English army. In Newark's first couple of years, the outcome of the American revolution remained undecided. Records show that sixteen families, numbering sixty-eight persons, arrived in 1782. They soon cleared 236 acres of land around Newark and grew 1,178 bushels of grain and 630 bushels of potatoes. By the end of fighting in 1783, American refugees were joined by soldiers staying in the region following their discharge from the British army. They cleared nearly 1,000 acres of land. By 1800, 28,000 people had settled in Upper Canada. Only a few came from Lower Canada. A good number of Europeans new to North America and New Englanders seeking better soils also arrived. They joined Quakers, Mennonites, and other religious sects from New Jersey and Pennsylvania who came seeking the religious protections guaranteed by English law. A few were simply evading creditors (Cruikshank, 1910).

∾

Besides Hodge's travel notes in the last chapter, we get another view of Western New York from Reverend Timothy Dwight, who passed through New Amsterdam on his way west in 1803–1804. His description provides a cultural overview. He found "Buffalo Creek a worthy mill-stream whose outlet to Lake Erie was only passable by canoe due to a huge sand bar." According to Dwight, New Amsterdam's houses were modest in structure, set on a slope facing Lake Erie and Buffalo Creek. The forty-feet-wide streets crossed at right angles, giving a "beautifully boundless view of Lake Erie." The inhabitants, he thought, were a casual collection of adventurers with little regard for government or religion and typical of those living remote from regular society. He counted a near-equal number of Indians and whites roaming the village. One mile north lay the mouth of the Niagara River. A little over a mile farther north and downriver lay the slightly larger village of Black Rock, with a less formal layout but boasting a better harbor. Reverend Dwight thought the Niagara River's intense current made navigating to and from Black Rock treacherous. He noted that Canada's Fort Erie lay in full view on the opposite shore from Black Rock. Dwight also visited Fort Erie with its blockhouse, barracks, and small hamlet where he noted, "[Fort Erie] wears less the appearance of a recent settlement, and exhibits a much greater improvement than anything which we saw west of the Genesee River" (Atkins, 1898).

This is the environment Dr. Chapin found upon his arrival in 1803. His first order of business was supporting his wife and three daughters, meaning he had to find patients who could pay his fees. He identified as an American, but his Canadian patients were more established, older, and wealthier. Chapin rode dozens of miles on horseback in all directions through dense forest, often guided by markers blazoned on trees. Soon he gained a dual reputation: one for furnishing medicine and food gratuitously to needy patients, and a second for assertively collecting fees from those he considered able to pay. Each fall, after the crops were harvested, he routinely made rounds at the homes of farmers with overdue accounts. Like most frontier doctors, he accepted many a ham or produce in leu of money, but in good years he expected payment (Duffy, 1993). Chapin knew farming was risky and money was scarce. One year, when the cost of transporting wheat and corn exceeded its sales price, the well-read Chapin encouraged some of his neighbors to make potash, also called black salts, by soaking hardwood ash in water and then drying it to a powder. It was used as fertilizer and to make lye soap and window glass. Wheat sold for 25 cents a bushel, but potash brought over 3 dollars a bushel, and Chapin got paid.

Still living in Canada, Dr. Chapin was ineligible to vote in the first election for the supervisor of the large Genesee County. Most of the land was still owned by the Holland Land Company and had fewer than two white settlers per square mile. The 1803 election was held in a tavern in Batavia where the two candidates for supervisor, Peter Vandenventer and Jonathan Bemis, each took a position on the Batavia/Buffalo Road facing each other. The landowners eligible to vote lined up behind their chosen candidate. Seventy individuals lined up toward Batavia, (eastward) behind Bemis, and seventy-five lined up toward New Amsterdam behind Vandenventer, making the Dutchman Western New York's first county supervisor. The voting method left virtually no chance for fraud and avoided embarrassing anyone who could not read. It would be another year, 1804, before New Amsterdam got its first regular mail delivery arriving on horseback from Canandaigua. The local Indian Agent, Erastus Granger, took on the added responsibility of postmaster (Atkins, 1898). Also that year, Joseph Palmer, the tavern-keeper's brother, asked Mr. Ellicott to set aside a lot on which he built the first schoolhouse.

∾

Chapin's family found the four-season climate of the Niagara district quite aggregable. Moderated by the waters of Lake Erie, both winter and summer

Figure 3.1. Buffalo's Lake Erie port painted by Robert Munro, a traveler through Western New York in 1799. *Source:* Munro, 1799. Public domain.

were less severe than the hills of Oneida County. Their neighbors joked that there were really only three seasons. There was a biannual mud season that was repeated in spring and fall. The mud seasons were separated by a four-month summer and a four-month winter. Summers were moderate, with few days exceeding 80 degrees, though one might be devoured by mosquitos. During the four-month winter, you might struggle to get your nose above the snow yet be pleased that the cold didn't bite it off. Most agreed, there was seldom a day that a man could not attend to outdoor chores and enjoy healthy air. Horseback was the preferable mode of summer travel, but a wagon or a sleigh in the winter allowed the luxury of wrapping up in blankets. One resident wrote that his nose dripped less than it had when he lived in the damp air of England. Winter church services, he observed, were surprisingly free of annoying coughs (St. John de Crevecoeur, 1793).

By 1805, Dr. Chapin and Sylvia were financially ready to build a suitable home for their family on the New Amsterdam lot. Their home was the sixteenth frame structure in the village (Devoy, 1896; White, 1898). The family's new home—combination drugstore, office, and apartment—overlooked Lake Erie and was half a mile north of the Seneca village on Buffalo Creek. The move made Dr. Chapin more available, and soon he found himself filling in to lead funerals and provide sermons when none of the several itinerate clergy were in town. He seemed willing to do almost anything the community needed, leading one irreverent youth to say the doctor "did the praying and swearing for the whole community" (C. Johnson, 1876).

Soon, the Reverend Elkana Holmes was permanently assigned as a missionary to the Seneca village. Holmes made himself available most Sundays to offer a sermon at Palmer's new schoolhouse. Whenever Holmes was unavailable, Chapin substituted. Reverend Holmes and Chapin became good friends, and Holmes became a frequent visitor to the Chapin home. Later, Reverend Holmes's son would marry the Chapins' oldest daughter, Sylvia (Marquis, 1902).

While a youth in Massachusetts, Chapin had experienced the dominant Calvinist/Puritan doctrine with its strictly structured holy Trinity, in which a divine Christ was sent to atone for the sins of humankind. To a Calvinist, children were born depraved and could only achieve salvation after admitting their sin through conversion as an adult. By 1805, religious liberals countered children were born innocent, with an innate spirituality that could be preserved by following Christ's example. Dr. Chapin joined with his friend Reverend Holmes in leaning toward the more liberal view of innocence. Frontier societies, like all societies at the time, experienced more than their share of death and illness, and physicians had the dubious opportunity to observe many families confront the cycles of birth and death. Despite similar philosophies, Dr. Chapin and Reverend Holmes enjoyed debating God's role in life (Carpenter, 1823).

When not preaching, Chapin's church attendance was irregular, but he remained faithful to his Christian beliefs throughout his life and ecumenical in his philosophy. He and Sylvia are listed as contributors to building funds that initiated several denominations of Buffalo churches. In later life, Chapin embraced the views of the Scottish commonsense philosopher and physician Thomas Brown. Brown preached that human behavior could be explained as a series of rational choices contingent on circumstance, a model that describes Chapin's momentum through life (T. Brown, 1824).

Chapter 4

An Unconventional Federalist

Moral Sensibilities and Values Are Essential to Good Politics

Cyrenius Chapin was a doctor foremost, but the man cannot be understood separate from his politics, and if the measure of a man is action, Dr. Cyrenius Chapin lived large. Action was essential to his character and politics are an inherent aspect of his story. His sparse personal writings have an assertive tone, but they reveal little of his private contemplations. The records of his contemporaries make it clear that he was driven to be involved in projects and willing to accept any conflict or skirmish that followed. Shortly after arriving in New Amsterdam, he declared himself a Federalist. But he would be a unique Federalist who plotted a course that confounded rivals and allies alike.

Cyrenius's view of government authority was forged when, as a teenager, he served as his father's aide-de-camp. Chapin's father placed his responsibility as a Massachusetts militia captain over his sympathies for neighbors when he was ordered to quell the 1786 Shays's anti-tax rebellion. Central to the dispute in Shays's rebellion was federal and state taxing authority and the disparity between cash poor rural farmers accustomed to a barter economy and urban merchants dependent on a cash economy. The rebellion became one of several catalysts leading to the constitutional convention that replaced the Articles of Confederation with the United States Constitution (ratified in 1788). The new Constitution, while striving to define a more effective federal government, did little to address the issues of a maturing economy (Richards, 2003). Defining the government's role in the economy would be left to those who came to be called Federalists, like Alexander

Hamilton. For young Cyrenius, the Shays's Rebellion provided an opportunity to observe his father balance personal values, individual rights, and government authority against the risks his men faced in armed opposition with their fellow citizens.

By the nature of his medical profession, Chapin involved himself in the lives of Niagara frontier Americans and Canadians from all strata of society. His patients included both rich and poor, farmer and merchant. He spent many a night in the cabins of subsistence farmers who had little hard cash to pay his bill, pay taxes, or make mortgage payments to the Holland Land Company. Chapin also attended to the families of merchants and businessmen who thrived in a cash economy. Chapin heard the opinions of both camps. Later, his speeches at medical society meetings made it clear that he accepted barter, when necessary, but preferred cash payment for his doctoring. He understood the value of currency in sustaining a profession (Gram, 1898).

Chapin's politics were also influenced by a grudge he cultured against the Holland Land Company, and Joseph Ellicott in particular. With the passage of time, he became more upset about how little respect Ellicott had given his proposal to deliver a ready-made village of forty Oneida families to New Amsterdam. It came to seem like a rude pocket veto, and it should have received a counterproposal at the very least. State government, he believed, should not tolerate the company's heavy-handed approach to land sales and the inflexible mortgage payment demands it was making on farm families (Devoy, 1896).

As his Buffalo home and office neared completion, Dr. Chapin became convinced that his insights could improve the government. When the Federalist party sought a regional chairperson in 1805, he successfully won election to the position and remained a strong-willed, self-confident, statewide Federalist party leader for the next several decades (Devoy, 1896). His alliance paved the way for many debates with Jeffersonian Democrat-Republicans who dominated the voting philosophies of Western New York, as they did much of rural America. Throughout his life, his only break with the New York Federalist platform would be over the War of 1812 when Chapin rejected the concern of his business-oriented Federalist friends who fixated on the ruinous effect war would have on commerce. Chapin was adamant that both Canada and the United States would be better off if Canada threw off British yoke and joined the United States.

Chapin's brother and teacher had modeled a physician whose role in the community was as much preacher as healer. By identifying with the

Federalist party, Cyrenius revealed a professional self-perception that leaned toward business. More than an isolated pioneer farmer, a businessperson needed rules that a well-structured interstate government could provide. United, the states could more effectively provide a capable and protective army, defend borders, raise revenue for the common good, and facilitate commerce. For much of his career, Chapin served as a delegate to the statewide Federalist party and promoted a dominant role for Federalists in New York State politics, even as the Federalist party's influence faded in other states (Fox, 1919). Political opponents described Dr. Chapin as a fierce partisan, willing to promote his unique brand of Federalism with "uncivil enthusiasm" (C. Johnson, 1876).

America's political party arrangement was an evolving flux in 1805. The Constitution was silent on political parties, and under the Articles of Confederation, state allegiances had overshadowed any concept of party affiliation. Chapin was twenty when George Washington ran for the presidency and likely heard his merchant/farmer father argue with neighbors about the new federal government's intentions. Contemporaries of George Washington and Alexander Hamilton were the first to implement the new Constitution, and the first to confront the need for some sort of national coalition to shift authority from the states to a federal government. But there were no traditions, and every move to translate the Constitution into government structure encountered unanticipated entanglements. It was powerful urban merchants and bankers relying on interstate and international trade who stepped forward (Fox, 1919).

But early nineteenth-century Americans were individualistic and inclined to view every political change as a potential insult to their way of life. Colonial America was defined by multiple small theocracies, often Puritan in philosophy. Villages coalesced around church, often declaring compulsory days of religious observations and taxing themselves to support a pastor. The new constitution formalized a secular republic at the same time that roving lecturers and entertainers found they could make a living traveling from town to town. Their messages competed with the pulpit and delivered a broader mix of insights and understandings. Behaviors changed. Birth records from prerevolutionary Puritanical America are scant, but they suggest that fewer than one out of ten firstborn children were born fewer than nine months after a wedding. By the turn of the nineteenth century, one out of three firstborn children were conceived out of wedlock (D. S. Smith & Hindus, 1975).

Political parties, as a concept, worried George Washington. National parties or coalitions, he feared, could devalue the status of individual rights outlined in the Declaration of Independence. He puzzled over how opposing parties could be patriotic and supportive of the same constitution. Nonetheless, as early as 1790, newspapers started referring to Washington/Adams/Hamilton supporters as "Federalists." Their opponents, Thomas Jefferson and James Madison (a former coauthor of the *Federalist Papers*), were variously labeled as Democrats, Republicans, Jeffersonians, or sometimes Democratic-Republicans (Smelser, 1958).

Northern cities became Federalist strongholds while the many small villages, including the rural farm-based economy of Western New York, leaned Jeffersonian. Frontier farmers placed high value on independent, rugged individualism and a populist version of Christian morality. These were the majority of Dr. Chapin's patients, and they thought it best if the federal government stayed away from their townships. Much of America agreed, as John Adams was the only declared Federalist ever elected president (Smelser, 1958).

Federalists favored neutrality in all European conflicts. The commercial centers of Boston and New York particularly feared international entanglements that would restrict trade. When the 1793 beheading of King Louis XVI sparked another war between France and Britain, French revolutionaries sent a diplomat, Edmond-Charles Genêt, to mobilize pro-French sentiment in the United States. Genêt found an audience among Jeffersonian Democrat-Republicans and accused Federalists of fidelity to the British Crown. George Washington and his secretary of state, Thomas Jefferson, felt Genêt was purposefully sowing dissension and rescinded his diplomatic standing (Smelser, 1958). Realizing that a return to France risked his beheading, Genêt was granted asylum in the United States. Subsequently, he carved out a living by continuing to expose America's political discord in regular commentary published by the *New York Register*, often flipping sides and angering both parties.

During his second term, George Washington sent John Jay to negotiate a new treaty with England. Jay was a coauthor of several *Federalist Papers* and had served multiple roles in government, including the secretary of foreign affairs and the governor of New York. During the Washington administration, Jay had been appointed chief justice of the Supreme Court, but the court's workload was light enough to send Jay to mend relations with Britain. The resulting *Jay's Treaty* sought to settle boundary issues, cancel war debts, and force the British to fully abandon all forts within United States boundaries, including Fort Niagara. In return, the 1795 *Jay's Treaty* awarded England favored trading partner designation. Democrat-Republicans denounced the treaty as a repudiation of France's assistance during the revolution and argued that the trading designation was an insult to American prestige. Southern planters complained that the treaty failed to compensate them for slaves who fled to the British army during the Revolution. Dissent grew so intense that congress, controlled by the Federalists during John Adam's administration, passed the Sedition Act, further eroding the popularity of Adams and the Federalists (Smelser, 1958).

Thomas Jefferson, Aaron Burr, and James Madison led the policy development of the Democrat-Republicans. They promoted state rights and the idea of minimal federal power by fostering the iconic image of rugged America. They convinced their followers that Napolean's rise in postrevolutionary France showed how easily a strong central government can lead to autocracy. After Jefferson defeated John Adams in the 1800 election, only New York State and parts of New England remained Federalist strongholds. Had John Adams not appointed John Marshall as chief justice of the Supreme Court in the last few days of his administration, Federalism policies might have vanished completely. Marshall would remain chief justice until his death in 1835 (Smelser, 1958).

As a child of America's revolution, Chapin never shook his visceral dislike of the British Crown. Like most of Chapin's opinions, he held this one firmly, drawing certainty from his personal compass for judging good and evil. Chapin thought of himself as a public man. As a doctor, he prided himself on understanding people. Daily home visits made it clear that his fellow frontiersmen survived only if they remained preoccupied with their family's survival. Isolation and limited reading skills made many farmers vulnerable to rumor and hearsay that Chapin thought had contributed to Shays's Rebellion and the 1791 Whiskey Rebellion. When South Carolina's John Calhoun threatened to nullify any federal rule his home state disliked, Chapin was enraged. Chapin was certainly an individualist, but he feared anarchy, and like his fellow Federalists, believed a structured, representative central government was necessary for orderly society regulated by the ballot box (Fox, 1919).

~

This is the environment that drew Federalist Cyrenius Chapin to run for the New York State Assembly in 1805. It proved a classic contest, pitting the Hamiltonian Chapin against a Jeffersonian Democrat-Republican (Chazanof, 1970).

The Holland Land Company emerged as a major issue during the campaign. The company was still trying to sell vast amounts of land west of the Genesee River, and their resident agent, Joseph Ellicott, had carefully avoided identification with any political persuasion, fearing entanglements might limit the company's return on investment. Chapin argued for limiting the power of the Holland Land Company, using a dispute between the company and the Tuscarora Tribal Reservation as a campaign issue.

Having been pushed out of North Carolina by colonists in the early eighteenth century, the Tuscaroras settled on Seneca lands and joined the Haudenosaunee confederation. In 1802, the Holland Land Company carved out a new two-mile square Tuscarora reservation in a treaty signed by the Holland Company, New York State, and the Senecas. The Tuscarora Nation wanted more land and had resources to purchase it. However, the Holland Company held fast on a price that was far above that offered to white settlers. To Chapin, this was further evidence that the government needed to place limits on the company's power. Ellicott and his boss, Paul Busti, were livid. They began calling Chapin "the most vicious inhabitant in the county" (Chazanof, 1970).

As the 1805 election drew near, their dispute rose to a bitterly personal pitch. Ellicott attempted to discredit Chapin by raising an issue from Chapin's days in Oneida County. Before moving to Buffalo, a man by the name of Johnston stole several items, including a pair of suspenders, from Chapin's home. Chapin attempted to settle with the man for a simple confession of guilt, but court proceedings continued and Johnston was fined $25. When he could not raise the sum, Johnston was imprisoned. Ellicott claimed that continued imprisonment was costing taxpayers well more than $25. In a grand gesture that reaped many headlines, Ellicott paid Johnston's fine and claimed that Chapin was "riding through the County propagating lies and falsehoods." Ellicott paid for the distribution of a pamphlet with harsh, derogatory anti-Chapin language (Chazanof, 1970).

Chapin lost the election, but he never soured on the Federalist party. Months after the votes were counted, Ellicott admitted his pamphlet exceeded fair play and good taste, but he refused to retract a word. Though he did sour on the idea of running for elected office, Chapin enjoyed a celebrated position at festivals and parades across New York State (Chazanof, 1970).

~

Federalist and Democrat-Republican bickering continued as states and local governments explored balance with federal power. Early in the 1800s, most communities considered themselves unique, and men like Dr. Chapin were certain that the developing culture and values of their community distinguished it from every other community. Local newspapers across the nation opined that it was unrealistic to think regional interests should be sacrificed to the concerns of a national government (Kenyon, 1955). Southerners argued that "men who come from New England differ from us" (Elliot, 1896). New Englanders argued that Southerners were less industrious and little appreciated industrial-type commerce. Many in the south seemed unaware that their increasing reliance on a slave-based economy with its high value, labor-intensive crops like tobacco and cotton was making it more and more dependent upon the North for every coat, boot, hat, axe, scythe, tub, and bucket (Ayers, 2023; Olmstead, 1856).

The meaning of a *United* States continued to be debated, as South Carolina's John Calhoun declared each state had the right of nullification, a doctrine that claimed that each state could choose what national laws they might submit to on a case-by-case basis. To the Federalists' mind, nullification directly opposed the intent of America's founding fathers (Kenyon, 1955).

Chapin had just moved to the Niagara Frontier when Jefferson consummated the 1803 Louisiana Purchase. Jefferson's rationalization for the purchase depended on executive powers beyond those championed by even the most enthusiastic Federalist. Then, in 1807, Jefferson imposed an embargo on American ships. His intent was to starve France and Britain of raw materials as punishment for their interference with American trade on the high seas. Jefferson's self-imposed embargo made it illegal for any American ship to sail to any foreign port. Jefferson reasoned that demand for American raw materials, particularly cotton, would soon drive Britain and France to negotiate. He further reasoned that rugged American individuality and self-sufficiency would cause little suffering among Americans (Taylor, 2010).

By 1808, the embargo had destroyed the Boston–New York export enterprise and brought a sharp recession to the northeast. Ships rotted at the wharves of American harbors up and down the Atlantic and thousands of seamen were out of work. The embargo gave fresh life to the Federalist party, but only in the northeast. In the 1808 presidential election, another Virginian Democrat-Republican, James Madison, was swept into office, and Democrat-Republican legislators outnumbered the Federalist congressmen elected from New England and New York. Madison soon abandoned the self-inflicted embargo and began separate negotiations with France's Napoleon Bonaparte and with the English King George. Negotiations accomplished very little as a slow march to the War of 1812 began (Taylor, 2010).

In the meantime, the penchant for self-destruction returned to the Federalist party. Frustration with Madison's slow and deliberate effort to establish safe international trade prompted New England Federalists to send their own delegation to England to negotiate their own trade agreement. Madison, and most American newspapers, considered the effort to be an act of treason, and the backlash ended any hopes that the Federalist party would carry influence outside of New England and New York (Taylor, 2010).

~

The conditions that would lead to the War of 1812 were brewing. Dr. Chapin joined several New York Federalists to form a splinter group to advocate for a war with Britain, calling themselves the "American" Federalist party. Chapin began crisscrossing New York, campaigning for a slate of assembly candidates who supported the liberation of Canada from British rule. Dr. Chapin's splinter party ended up winning only one assembly seat, and the traditional New York Federalist party garnered only six assembly seats total. The election resulted in a thirty-three-seat majority for the New York Democrat-Republicans (Strum, 1980).

James Madison would be president from 1809 to 1817. His successor, James Monroe, would be the last of the Virginia presidential dynasty. More formal organization of American political parties would wait until the populist presidency of the strong-willed Andrew Jackson in 1829. Jackson's followers added structure and organization to a revised Democrat-Republican party, creating a true national party known simply as Democrats (D. S. Brown, 2022). In opposition, the Whig Party rose from the remnants of the Federalists to oppose Jackson. Taking their name from an English political caucus, the Whigs opposed the heavy-handed brand of executive power now practiced by Jackson while supporting central banking and federal-sponsored improvements to America's infrastructure. Though the Whig party closely reflected Dr. Chapin's more parochial views of power, it survived only a generation (D. S. Brown, 2022).

As the story of Dr. Cyrenius Chapin progresses, he will see the War of 1812 define the essential role of the Federal government. Democrat-Republicans will be forced to concede that waging war required central authority and power (Brands, 2018). Though his party floundered, Chapin stayed true to the rule of law under a robust Constitution that allowed for peaceful change mediated by the electoral process. Chapin considered himself a common man. Yet, the followers of Jefferson and then Jackson were convinced that they, not Federalists, epitomized the common man. Under George Washington, Americans had been willing to defer to their leaders, but by the time Andrew Jackson became president in 1829, Americans expected leaders to defer to the people (Brands, 2018).

Chapter 5

Practicing Medicine Before Science

The Success and Failures of Medicine Are Inseparable From the Doctor

Around 1835, eleven-year-old Samuel Welch woke one Sunday morning with a toothache. Still, his mother insisted he put on his Sunday-best white linen suit for church. While sitting in the family's church pew, the toothache became intolerable. Later, as an adult, Samuel wrote a memoir in which he recalled it wasn't tears but his whimpering that caused his mother to send him out of church to find Doc Chapin. As was the doctor's custom, he was sitting in his office reading. In an instant, the good doctor declared both diagnosis and solution: "Abscess, tooth must be removed." Samuel's memoir describes the remedy: "The Doctor produced his goads of torture; the keen lancet and the turnkey wrench. He placed me on the floor, between his long legs, not minding my protest of soiling my white trousers; gashing and lacerating my gums with the lancet, he applied the cold steel of that horrible instrument of barbarity, the wrench, and ground out a four-pronged double tooth, besotting my immaculate white jacket and trousers with rose [blood]." The years tempered Samuel's terror, calling Chapin a stalwart old soldier known just as the colonel or the doctor and as "an irascible rough diamond with boundless energy, who could be abrupt but with a kind heart and sterling patriotism" (Welch, 1891).

∿

Before the middle of the nineteenth century, medicine lacked the fundamentals that twenty-first-century society takes for granted. The field was just beginning to understand the nuances of human anatomy, and in some states, it was still illegal for medical colleges to allow dissections. Surgery was limited to pulling teeth, amputations, suturing lacerations, and removing superficial lumps. Surgeries were frequently complicated by postoperative infection. It would be the 1870s before Pasteur disproved spontaneous generation, Koch proved the role of bacteria, and Lister described his aseptic techniques. A belief that pus was necessary for healing dated back to ancient Greece when Hippocrates described pus as "good and laudable." Doctors' notes employed phrases like "discharge more laudable" to describe what they thought was a welcomed sign of mending (Rutkow, 2022).

General anesthesia would not be available until 1846–1847, a decade after Dr. Chapin's death. Physicians were eager to discover new cures through surgery, but besides infection, they were limited by intolerable pain. Doctors and barber/surgeons promoted pain as being essential for healing and were joined by clergy who called pain a blessing. The devout were to consider pain a welcome reminder of Christ's suffering on the cross and therefore a sacred experience that the faithful could endure. Medical textbooks declared pain an essential boost to the patient's vitality and an asset for recovery. Such notions did little to quiet the terror of being cut (Rutkow, 2022).

Demeanor was the doctor's chief tool in caring for patients. They saw a lot of disease and became skilled at sorting out which patients were going to survive and which were going to die. It was the doctor's bedside manner that helped families and patients through illness, but often there was little the doctor could do that altered the outcome. They knew how to open boils, set bones, pull teeth, suture cuts, straighten fractures, and remove necrotic fingers, toes, and bulging tumors. But it was mostly their presence that guided families through the process of illness (Hertzler, 1938; Rutkow, 2022).

~

Dr. Cyrenius Chapin's contemporaries, partners, and apprentices (which included several future Buffalo mayors) marveled at how well he kept abreast of changes in medicine. One future mayor, Orlando Allen, came to Buffalo seeking an apprenticeship with Dr. Chapin. Orlando, who will be discussed more later, discovered his talents were a better fit for business, and though he never practiced medicine, he forever credited Chapin for launching his career (Bryant, 1877).

Critics chastised Dr. Chapin for an excess of self-esteem that bordered on arrogance. Friends and foes observed that he held strong opinions and expressed his medical judgments with earnest confidence, tolerating no question about his chosen remedy. But in personal and family matters, he could be quite self-effacing. When it came to medical matters, many physician aspirants, former apprentices, and medical colleagues sought his advice and counsel (G. F. Pratt, 1869).

Though Dr. Chapin seemed to seek practice partners, in the early nineteenth century, most physicians considered solo practice to be the only ethical model of practice (Cathell, 1882). This, combined with poor roads and difficult travel, meant most physicians, particularly frontier physicians, practiced in isolation. A theory of "geographic specificity" dominated medical traditions and furthered the isolation. Geographic specificity elevated the village doctor to the status of local expert who was undeniably the best qualified person to integrate the effects of climate, geography, and season with patient-specific factors of age, gender, diet, habits, temperament, and occupation. Except for smallpox, syphilis, and pregnancy, textbooks regularly warned that remedies found successful in one region may not be successful everywhere (Burnham, 2015).

Geographic specificity was a convenient excuse for doctors wishing to ignore innovations being generated at large urban hospitals, especially those in Europe. Even as American medical literature improved, village physicians could, and usually did, claim they knew both their communities and its rugged American inhabitants best. Their experience, though anecdotal, was unassailable. As a result, doctors often fell into habits, using a few drugs repeatedly, mixing and matching them to induce defecation, perspiration, urination, vomiting, relaxation, or sleep. Their goal: rid the body of whatever poison, internal or external, causing the patient's symptoms. The records kept by most physicians focused on fees and payments, further limiting their ability to recognize patterns of illness within their own practice (Warner, 1997). Unwittingly, patients endorsed the concept of geographic specificity by consulting physicians with longstanding experience over newly minted doctors, even those with pedigrees from centers of great learning.

According to his many apprentices, Dr. Chapin was an exception. He read what he could and employed Socratic teaching methods to pepper trainees with questions (G. F. Pratt, 1869). Though rare, large hospital case studies were appearing in journals. The general medical textbooks of the early nineteenth century referenced case reports that relied on little more than the author's rationalizations and personal observations. Other than their own professional experience, frontier doctors had little else to depend on when tackling the broad range of infirmities common to the human species. Their available remedies had changed little since Dioscorides had described them in ancient Greece. The best village doctor improvised when necessary, using a mixture of common sense, tradition, and experience. It was his steady flow of apprentices, and his repeated attempts to take on a partner, that must have challenged Dr. Chapin to stay current. The frontier demanded courage in the face of calamity, and resignation in the face of tragedy (Bryant, 1877). With a life expectancy of only forty years, living in the early nineteenth century required both physicians and families to accept misfortune (Kennedy, 2023).

∾

Since Benjamin Franklin's time, it was estimated that for every 100 fevers, 92 resolved without intervention, 4 were cured with the advice of a physician, and 4 often proved fatal (Abrams, 2013). Even the mosquitos carried threats rarely seen in upstate New York today. Mosquitos transmitted an endemic form of northern malaria. Practicing without a knowledge of bacteria, viruses, or microscopic parasites, Dr. Chapin would have declared these victims to be suffering from the effects of a bad air miasma blamed for a range of illness they called ague, intermittent fever, or recurrent fever (Eberle, 1831). The word malaria is derived from an ancient Italian word for foul air. Northern malaria could debilitate, but it was much less deadly than the malaria in the southern states and was easily mistaken for any of several summer afflictions. (The South's tropical and semitropical malaria is usually caused by the more aggressive of several plasmodia parasites, *Plasmodia falciparum*, a parasite discovered in 1880 by the French army doctor, Charles Laveran. It took until 1908 for Carlos Finlay, a Cuban doctor, to discover plasmodia were transmitted by mosquitos.)

Quinine became available during Dr. Chapin's career. Discovered in the mountains of Peru, quinine was made from the bark of the Cinchona tree and revealed to Europeans in the eighteenth century by South American natives. Also known as Jesuit bark, or simply as bark, it had a miraculous effect on malaria. So curative was quinine that it was classified as a stimulant. At the time, doctors also called brandy, in which Chapin would have dissolved the quinine, a stimulant. Quinine's effectiveness, and the nearly impossible task of making a specific diagnosis, caused Dr. Chapin and his contemporaries to prescribe expensive Peruvian "Jesuit bark" for almost every summer fever. If families could not afford Jesuit bark, Chapin made a powder of the local tulip tree root that he also dissolved in brandy. Today, we know that both Peruvian bark and Tulip root contained the active ingredient artemisinin, which is still used to treat malaria (Crawford, 2021; Warner, 1997).

A lingering summer illness jeopardized a family's ability to put up stores for the winter months. Cutting a new farm out of the wilderness, working the land by hand, putting up firewood and preserves, making clothes, cooking, and raising children demanded long days of intense labor for both men and women. Few subsistence farmers in Western New York could afford a physician's fee. So, to make a living, Dr. Chapin traveled up to forty miles (roundtrip) a day on horseback making house calls. Often, he canoed across the Niagara River to visit Canadian farmers who could pay his fees in hard British currency. Cash payments allowed Chapin to discount fees for families who could only provide bartered produce or some feed for his horse. When options were few and the patient's family was facing hardship, Dr. Chapin left food and free medicine, though he admonished recipients to tell no one. Chapin gained a reputation for being eminently useful, fast and skilled with a surgical knife, always fair, and often ornery (Bryant, 1877; G. F. Pratt, 1869).

~

Dr. Chapin's medical theory dated back to Hippocrates (BC 460–370), whose writings were the first attempt to separate illness theory from religion. More accurately called rationalizations than science, Hippocrates's *Corpus Hippocraticum* presented disease as a disruption of an individual's natural balance usually set in motion by troubles in the gut. His limited understanding of physiology or anatomy (Greek law forbid human dissection) led him to conclude that illness had everything to do with the peculiarities of the individual and little to do with any outside agent. To heal, one had to deduce which of the four humors (black bile, yellow bile, blood, and phlegm) were out of balance. Evidence of excessive black bile could be found in dark stool or vomit. Yellow bile excess revealed itself through yellow-to-green vomit or jaundice. Phlegm was most commonly produced by the lungs, and an excess of blood caused the painful, warm, red swellings of inflammation (F. Adams, 1886; Arabaci, 2023).

Later, another Greek, Galen of Pergamon (AD 129–200), expanded Hippocrates's ideas by expounding on the role of the liver's production of bile and, as wrongly alleged by Galen, blood. He assigned each humor a particular temperament: blood made one extroverted and social; yellow bile contributed to passion and charisma; black bile made one melancholic; and phlegmatic people were kind and dependable but restrained (Arabaci, 2023). But, like Hippocrates, Greek and Roman law prevented the dissection of human bodies, forcing Galen to make assumptions based on his dissection of pigs.

Fast forward to Dr. Chapin's career, and physicians still lacked any way to see inside the body. Beyond being good listeners and observers, and feeling for subtle changes in the patient's pulse, physicians had to link the patient's description of symptoms with what their body revealed externally. For this, the body's fluids were critical. That meant urine, sweat, mucus, vomit, feces, and blood provided clues about the body's invisible inside. The doctor's selection of remedy depended on his analysis of these fluids.

Chapin's job was to use these clues to readjust the patient's stock of humors using diet, intestinal purging, vomiting, fluid pushes, sweating, and Galen's favorite, bleeding. Blood, being warm, red, and moist, seemed to be the substance that caused fever, inflammation, and pain. Galen's writings were so convincing that nineteenth-century Western physicians commonly used venesection (bleeding), leeching, and cupping in ways that remained little changed until the second half of the 1800s (Arabaci, 2023).

Bloodletting came under some challenge when William Harvey (1578–1657) proved that blood was pumped by the heart and circulated through the body. But with few effective therapies, Harvey's discovery ended up reinforcing bloodletting as circulating blood became the likely agent that transported the other three humors around the body (J. R. Johnson, 1816). Bloodletting persisted as a mainstay of medical treatment for three reasons: (a) it was dramatic; (b) it made both patient and doctor feel like something was being done; and (c) it was supported by years of rationalized tradition. Loss of blood was associated with renewal as in menstruation, childbearing, and the warm redness of inflammation. As Dr. Chapin entered medicine, Benjamin Rush was near the peak of his celebrity. He was a signatory to the Declaration of Independence and a prolific physician writer. Rush's widely distributed pamphlet in 1794 claimed that his patients survived the 1793 yellow fever epidemic in Philadelphia, provided he bled them to the point of fainting (Greenstone, 2010; Rush, 1794). It would be 1836 before the French doctor, Pierre-Charles Louis (1787–1872), published the first randomized controlled trial proving that repeated bleeding had little effect on recovery from pneumonia (Louis, 1836). Unfortunately, Dr. Louis concluded that bleeding once, early in a disease, was likely to be useful.

Rush relied on personal observations, rationalizations, and his limited follow-up of patients to form his opinions. He was following contemporary standards of "science," which for centuries defined any knowledge gained by observation as scientific. The modern-day meaning of science based on hypothesis and experimentation did not overtake medical theory until the second half of the nineteenth century (Ross, 1962; Whewell, 1837). In part, the delay might be blamed on Rush's eloquent and extensive writings reinforcing the idea that bleeding could remedy a wide range of symptoms, particularly when the doctor included Rush's second favorite remedy, calomel. Calomel was a mixture of rhubarb and mercury salts that functioned as a powerful purgative, certain to rid the intestines of dreaded black poisons. Rush believed calomel was effective because it cleared poisons produced by the liver's degradation of unbalanced humor by-products. Aggressive use of both became known as Rush's heroic method (Rush, 1815).

Chapin's textbooks refined the theories of Galen and Rush somewhat by addressing a patient's energy potential (Eberle, 1831). The words used to describe patient energy sound archaic to the modern ear. "Sthenic" described a patient who appeared vigorous and active; these were people with a muscular body build. "Asthenic" people appeared frail and narrow-chested; they may also be shy, sensitive, or introverted (Ikeda et al., 2018). According to this generally accepted rationalization, some patients present in a sthenic state of plethora, excess, or irritation. Others appear in an asthenic state of deficiency, weakness, and languor. Sthenic states, marked by a bounding pulse, were to be treated heroically, bled liberally, and have their bowels purged with ipecac, jalap, or calomel. Diuretics were often added for good measure. In asthenic cases, blood was released cautiously and diuresis was avoided. Asthenic cases were treated with tonics containing spirits (alcohol), quinine, or opium, all classified as stimulants. Pale asthenic women might have iron added to their stimulant regimen (Eberle, 1831). Opium was given to patients as a liquid called laudanum that had been introduced in England in the sixteenth century. It was used for most any discomfort, particularly rheumatism, but was also prescribed for insomnia and diarrhea. Physicians made laudanum by mixing the juice of the poppy with alcohol; the extract was then mixed with brandy. Dr. Chapin followed these precepts, though some apprentices wrote that he underutilized bloodletting and intestinal purging (L. F. Allen, 1896).

During Dr. Chapin's career, hospitals in Paris, Germany, London, and Edinburgh began publishing observations based on large numbers of similar patients gathered in multi-bed wards where recordkeeping and treatment comparisons superseded rationalization. Coincidentally, the cost of printing declined and the medical literature expanded. When Dr. Chapin started practice, only six institutions offered a medical degree of reasonable quality in the United States. They were University of Pennsylvania in Philadelphia, Columbia College of Physicians in New York, the College of Physicians and Surgeons at Dartmouth, Harvard, and medical colleges in Baltimore, Maryland, and Lexington, Kentucky. About a hundred men graduated from medical colleges or apprenticeships in New York State each year, but a third or more of those practicing medicine and calling themselves doctor never completed a college term or an apprenticeship (Burnham, 2015). Nonetheless, like preachers, most doctors were literate and among the most widely read men in their villages. Literacy elevated men and was the likely reason for twenty-six doctors serving as state representatives to the Continental Congress. In the first half of the 1800s, between twelve and eighteen physicians served each session of Congress (Starr, 1982).

Rules by which to determine whether a doctor was qualified to serve society remained elusive. In 1311 AD, Philip IV decreed that only individuals who underwent an examination administered by a royally authorized source could practice medicine in Paris. It did little to improve care (Rutkow, 2022). In 1760, New York City attempted to create standards for competency by requiring anyone practicing medicine to pass an oral exam, but the law proved unenforceable as barbers, bonesetters, and sectarians demanded the right to provide patient services. In 1797, New York State offered a license to any student who could provide evidence of having studied medicine for two years, usually as an apprentice. Dr. Chapin was already established in New Amsterdam when, in 1805, three doctors from New York's Saratoga region—Drs. Fitch, Stearns, and Sheldon—convinced the New York legislature to grant county medical societies authority similar to trade guilds. Things did not change fast as many regions of upstate New York were unorganized or part of large unwieldy districts, like Western New York's Genesee County. These areas awaited being divided into manageable areas capable of being traversed by a horse in a day (L. S. King, 1982). Dr. Cyrenius Chapin would later support licensing measures (covered in chapter 17), but in 1805 he assumed he should be the judge of who was qualified to practice in New Amsterdam. He was decidedly unfriendly to the first couple of doctors, Dr. Dan Chapin and Dr. Ebenezer Johnson, upon their arrival. But as Buffalo grew and his business interests expanded, Chapin changed his mind and became supportive and helpful to new doctors, particularly those who had trained with him (Samo, 1884).

~

Infectious disease accounted for about 40 percent of deaths in Chapin's day, though physicians at the time agreed that only three diseases were definitely contagious (Kennedy, 2023). These were smallpox, measles, and syphilis, which were thought to be passed from person to person by contact. When physicians called an illness contagious, they meant it acted like smallpox, as depicted in the Bible's Book of Leviticus, where garments are shown to spread disease. In 1763, during the French and Indian War, blankets and handkerchiefs used by victims of smallpox were distributed to Native Americans who were laying siege to Fort Pitt (Pittsburgh, Pennsylvania). As expected, the blankets spread smallpox through Pontiac's warriors, resulting in the British gaining uncontested control of the Monongahela and Allegheny Rivers (Jennings, 1988; Knollenberg, 1954).

Early nineteenth-century physicians were still debating the nature of the vital element responsible for the contagious nature of some illnesses. Some argued that it was a chemical; traditionalists stuck with the idea that a bad air miasma carried disease; and a few postulated that invisible "insects" might spread illness such as plague, yellow fever, smallpox, and other "contagious bilious complaints." Only a few postulated these "insects" might be the microscopic animalcules (called bacteria today) described by Antonie van Leeuwenhoek in letters he sent to the Royal Society of London in 1673 (Riedel, 2005).

For millennia, societies in the Middle East had observed that, once afflicted, patients never suffered smallpox again. They practiced a technique called inoculation or variolation in which a small amount of pus from an active case of smallpox is applied to the scratched skin of a healthy person to produce the same lifetime protection. It was dangerous, carrying a fatality rate of 2%, but much safer than the 14% fatality for naturally acquired smallpox. Also, inoculated patients had to be isolated until fully healed because of the risk that they could spread smallpox. George Washington required his revolutionary army to be inoculated and claimed it contributed to America's ultimate victory. Nonetheless, hellfire and damnation preachers challenged the idea, claiming disease was a punishment for sin and inoculation obstructed God's will (Duffy, 1993).

Then, in 1798, Edward Jenner introduced a procedure very similar to inoculation, but using the pus from cowpox lesions. He called his innovation "vaccination" (*vacca*, Italian for cow) to distinguish it from inoculation.

He got the idea by watching village doctors in England who, sometime in unwritten history, discovered that cowpox pus worked as well as smallpox pus but was safer. Jenner tested the technique on several patients, kept detailed notes, and proved the village doctors correct (Jenner, 1802).

Edward Jenner's account of cowpox vaccination made it to Boston in 1799, where Benjamin Waterhouse used the technique to protect his family and his slaves and convinced his friend Thomas Jefferson to endorse the new vaccine (Abrams, 2013). Soon doctors like Chapin were ordering their own cowpox and encouraging their patients to be vaccinated. Chapin championed vaccination and spent considerable energies convincing his colleagues to adopt countywide programs to vaccinate everyone on the Niagara Frontier. To ward off ill effects of vaccination, Chapin would have also prescribed Warner's pills, a combination of ipecac, horse radish, and blue flag root boiled with aloe and myrrh (Rochester, 1861; P. Smith, 1812).

∼

A few prescriptions written by Dr. Chapin have survived (Atkins, 1898). They confirm that he followed the dominant medical theories of his day as described by Dr. Peter Smith, a physician/author of that period. Dr. Smith also describes one management strategy we would recognize today:

> When the accident of a bruise, a cut, a broken bone, takes place, immerse the part in cold water as quick as possible, and then use a large, soft linen cloth dipped into cold water and applied to the injury to keep out the air. This cloth should be kept close; aid this by dropping cold water upon it for fifteen minutes, and continue it close for twelve hours. The inflammation by this means will be kept back, and the cure by anything else will be almost forestalled; and then a bruise, a strain or broken bone, will scarcely swell at all; and a like application to a burn will have a similar effect. In about fifteen minutes, the first pain will be over, and the future ease will be steadfast. (P. Smith, 1812)

Many families owned three books: a Bible, a hymnal, and a home medical book that was often passed down through generations. Usually, they sent for a doctor only after every remedy in their home medical book had been exhausted. The smart doctor inquired about remedies already attempted before implementing his own remedies because families were much more willing to pay for a treatment if it was different and perceived as special.

Dr. Chapin thrived in this environment. He had an insatiable taste for relieving the afflicted, and he relished being a hero. While riding from house call to house call, he would survey passing meadows for plants and herbs that might add to his arsenal. He also employed a Seneca medicine man to help find desirable plants that might expand his resources (G. F. Pratt, 1869; Welch, 1891).

Dr. Gorham F. Pratt, an apprentice and later a partner of Dr. Chapin's, documents Chapin's conservative use of strong purgatives. When a purgative was needed, which was often, Chapin resorted to roots and herbs to clear the bowels rather than mercury containing calomel. One emetic he liked was ipecacuanha or Indian physic. Even in low-energy asthenic patients, ipecacuanha was considered safe but still capable of discharging bile from the liver through an intestinal purge, while making the stomach ready to accept curative tonics after an initial episode of vomiting. Ipecacuanha is a bitter root that grows throughout the United States and can be cultivated in gardens. One sprout of the perennial plant produced half a pound of dried root within three years. Chapin dissolved one pugil (what could be grasped between thumb and forefinger) of the dried powdered root in four ounces of cider or brandy and dosed it at one half ounce every ten minutes until the patient vomited. Eating gruel or drinking cool water facilitated the action. An excessive response was reversed with a little laudanum (G. F. Pratt, 1869; P. Smith, 1812).

Bilious fevers were a common diagnosis. Typically, families summoned Dr. Chapin after several days of persistent vomiting and failed home remedies. He took a history and conducted an examination, then pulled a vial of powdered Indian physic out of his bag and mixed it with cider or brandy. The patient was instructed to drink the mix, and generally within twenty minutes the patient retched. If satisfied the result had cleared the offending poisons, Dr. Chapin declared the stomach empty of all things harmful. He then instructed the patient to swallow an "anodyne" pill he made from a half ounce of opium and one ounce of imported asafetida gum. (Anodyne referred to any medicine that relieved unwanted symptoms.) Soon the patient's abdominal spasms ceased, and Dr. Chapin followed up with columbo root that grew throughout southern Ontario. This too was dissolved in cider or brandy. He left the patient with several doses of columbo root to be taken three times a day for another week (Pharmacopoeia, 1830).

Waterborne dysentery, acute and chronic, was a stubborn malady in the wilderness. Chapin would try his more potent tonics that included mercury, opium, sulfates, quinine, sarsaparilla, and combinations of medical salts. All were ground into powders and dissolved in cider or brandy for administration. Most were used on the theory that poisons must be purged from the intestines. Dosing continued until symptoms improved.

Itchy skin was ubiquitous. Bathing was infrequent, and daily outdoor exposure was hard on the human hide. Chapin would have compounded special ointments that contained pulverized sulfur, salt, black pepper, gunpowder, or saltpeter, mixed with tar and lard. Ointments used for hemorrhoids contained stewed elder roots, burdock, or catnip mixed into lard. Instructions were simple: they were to be applied frequently until symptoms resolved (Pharmacopoeia, 1830).

Consumption dominated the chronic respiratory complaints Dr. Chapin faced. Besides asthma, bronchitis, and lingering effects of pneumonia, consumption (called phthisis when severe) was implicated in the death of nearly 25 percent of people (Landis, 1901, 1912). Until Robert Koch's 1882 isolation of the bacteria causing tuberculosis, consumption was considered an inherited disease because it often struck multiple members of a family. For millennia, the term "consumption" described a progression of cough, weakness, and weight loss that slowly "consumed" its victims. Chapin treated these patients with stimulants such as teas made from blueberry root or black snakeroot (black cohosh). Both grew plentifully in the northeast. The roots were believed to reverse lung inflammation and relieve cough. Their use extended to colic, epilepsy, hysterics, and ague. Women in premature labor were given these same roots to reduce cramping. If the labor progressed, the teas were believed to ease the difficulties of confinement. Another root, that of the North American trumpetweed (Abela), promoted a patient's energy and caused a gentle diuresis. Like so many medicines of the day, its popularity with patients may have been enhanced by the pint of brandy into which two drachms of the dried root were dissolved (Mohr, Redwood, & Procter, 1849; Pharmacopoeia, 1830; P. Smith, 1812).

Patients with eye problems received "eye-water" that the doctor made by heating equal quantities of potassium sulfate with calcine (common salt). The resulting gray powder was mixed in three gills (1 gill = 4 ounces) of rainwater, then strained through a fine rag. Two tablespoons of white sugar and a lump of sandstone the size of a large grain of Indian corn were added to the filtrate. One or two drops of this eye-water were placed in the eye as often as needed until the condition resolved (P. Smith, 1812).

Chapin would have spent countless hours in his office compounding medicines. Though most documents have focused on Chapin's activities in the community and at war, his contemporaries describe a man attentive to his medical practice. Young men from across New York and New England sought him out for their apprenticeships. Patients on both sides of the Niagara River sought his care, as did chiefs of local Native American tribes. With no promise of payment, he or an experienced apprentice journeyed out day or night, rain or shine, often following Aboriginal trails through dense forests for great distances to visit a patient (G. F. Pratt, 1869). Those doctors who sought partnerships with Dr. Chapin found that after a few years they were exhausted by Chapin's energy and capacity for work. A major portion of any apprentice's education would be the tedious and demanding focus on compounding medicine. It was also the part of the experience most likely to convince young trainees to pursue other fields.

Several apprentices confirm that Chapin charged much more than most physicians. He assumed that those able to pay would willingly subsidize those unable to pay. It was a way for Chapin to support his family while continuing to care for less-fortunate families. Partners marveled at Dr. Chapin's matter-of-fact explanation for his fee, and the success he had in convincing patients to accept the higher charges (G. F. Pratt, 1869). Besides admiring Dr. Chapin's currency with the medical literature, physicians who worked with him appreciated his willingness to provide them with financial aid when they left to start their own practices. When some apprentices (like Orlando Allen, Hiram Pratt, and others) found their initial enthusiasm for medicine misplaced, their change of heart posed little problem for Chapin. He seamlessly redirected them into other areas of business, often with one of his own expanding business enterprises.

In the social order of American villages, physicians ranked with schoolmasters, ministers, and judges. As we've seen, physician education varied, but doctors were one of the few literate men on the frontier who had regular contact with common folk. Besides being called upon to help make laws and take part in court proceedings, physicians often read letters to families and encouraged children to pay attention to their schooling. One of Dr. Chapin's favorite requests was reading a story to children before he departed a home visit, and his apprentices took note (G. F. Pratt, 1869).

Besides the sectarian Thomsonians and homeopaths, two other theories of illness and disease emerged in the late eighteenth and early nineteenth centuries. First was a concept pioneered by Franz Anton Mesmer that became known as mesmerism. Today mesmerism might be considered a form of hypnosis, though at the time many of Chapin's contemporaries considered Mesmer a faith healer. The German Mesmer and his followers built a depth of pseudoscientific doctrine based on Mesmer's theory that a universal animal magnetic "fluid" could be altered by hand-waving and suggestion (Rutkow, 2022).

The other theory, phrenology, imagined the brain to be like a muscle that could create impressions on the skull, like biceps do on the upper arm. The bumps and ridges of the skull therefore reflected areas of special talent, personality, and usage. German physician Franz Joseph Gall first wrote of the theory in 1796 and Johann Gaspar Spurzheim, a European advocate for phrenology, toured America teaching the methods. By 1810, its popularity extended worldwide and was endorsed by the Boston Medical Society. Harvard Medical College included phrenology in their curriculum (Davies, 1955). But controversy over the theory was intense—so much so that the first chapter in one American textbook on phrenology titled "Opposition to Discoveries" went to great lengths to defend the "science" behind Gall's theory (Combe, 1851; Editor, 1832).

The practice of phrenology required the examiner to touch the patient's head in a massaging motion while assessing thirty-seven different faculties, propensities, and sentiments the skull's bumps and valleys revealed. While Dr. Chapin left no record of his thoughts about phrenology, he understood the power of touch and the influence it could have on patient behaviors. It would be several years after Chapin's death before Oliver Wendell Holmes forcefully debunked the entire field of phrenology (Finger, 2020)

∼

In Chapin's day, the power of the physician lay in the bond of trust he formed with patients in his service community.[1] More than most, Chapin's demeanor was persuasive, and his ceaseless activity was powered by great

---

1. All physicians were male. Elizabeth Blackwell (1821–1910) was the first woman to earn a medical degree in the United States. She entered Geneva Medical College in Geneva, New York, in 1847.

personal energies. By today's standards, several of his remedies were unsafe, some were harmless, and a few were useful. He succeeded by being conservative in the application of "heroic" remedies popular in his day. Those apprentices who left a record of their experience with Dr. Chapin say he possessed a personality that inspired new habits and motivated patients to rise from their sickbed (Bryant, 1877; G. F. Pratt, 1869).

Chapter 6

Contemporaries, Competition, and Sectarian Chaos

A Quack's Success Lies in the Ability to Please the Patient's Fantasies

The United States conducted its first census in 1790 and found fewer than two people per square mile in Western New York. The 1800 census still showed no hint of the growth that was to occur over the next decade. An article in the *Medical Repository* analyzing the census data observed for the first time that more male children than female children were being born. The birth ratio was seventeen to sixteen, and by age twenty-six, the gender ratio equalized (Cassedy, 1986).

Because of Joseph Ellicott's survey of the Holland Land Company's holdings in Western New York, the company began offering clear title to well-defined parcels of land ready for sale. Elsewhere in the northeast, many farmers found themselves victims of inadequate or lost records, inconsistent ownership titles, and legal disputes that subsistence farmers usually lost. The family of future president Millard Fillmore moved to Western New York because his father's title to land in Cayuga County, New York, proved fictitious (Rayback, 2017). The Holland Company's guarantee of a clear title at a fair price proved attractive to families and medical men alike.

There were also jobs. New Amsterdam entrepreneurs realized there was money to be made transferring goods from Lake Ontario boats to wagons for portage around Niagara Falls to New Amsterdam and Black Rock. Goods were then transferred to Lake Erie boats heading out to emerging markets in the Midwest. Within a few years of Dr. Chapin's arrival, new immigrants and more doctors made their way to New York's western wilderness.

≈

The first physician to follow Cyrenius Chapin was another Dr. Chapin. Daniel Chapin MD (1761–1821) came to New Amsterdam from East Bloomfield, a village south of Rochester, New York. He established himself in a log house on a farm located a little over a mile northeast of the village in 1807. According to a Chapin family genealogy published in the early twentieth century, the two Chapins were unrelated, but each had a grandfather named Caleb, and many assumed the two physicians were second or third cousins (G. W. Chapin, 1924). It did not take long for Dr. Daniel Chapin's practice to rival Dr. Cyrenius Chapin's in size and territory. Both men were forceful characters and highly respected, but Daniel was a Yale Medical College graduate with significantly more formal education. Cousins or not, the two Chapins bickered frequently and took pleasure in finding fault with each other's remedies (Goldman, 1983). Their wordy rivalry occasionally spilled over into newspaper stories that patients found amusing, though of little serious consequence. One exchange in the *Buffalo Patriot* confirms both men were covetous of their preferences, strong in their dislikes, and proficient at "cussin'" ("Viewed in scrapbook at Buffalo and Erie County Library without further citation," 1909). Yet both contributed materially to put medical practice in Buffalo on a sound track. Daniel's advanced education challenged Cyrenius to keep his science fresh, likely cultivating good reading habits in both men (G. W. Chapin, 1924). In 1811, the two men would openly quarrel over starting a Niagara County Medical Society (see chapter 17).

Dr. Daniel Chapin preferred walking over riding horseback. He hiked to house calls on foot from Niagara Falls to Hamburg with a pipe clenched firmly in his teeth. Patients recalled seeing their doctor arrive with a rifle resting on his shoulder, a dog trotting along at his feet, and a plume of smoke circling his cap. In the winter of 1821, at the age of sixty, the wind, rain, and snow got the best of him. Daniel Chapin died of exposure on his way home from a late-night house call (White, 1898).

≈

The man who would become the first mayor of the city of Buffalo, Dr. Ebenezer Johnson (1786–1849), moved from Cherry Valley near Cooperstown, New York, to Buffalo in 1809. He trained as an apprentice with Cherry Valley's Dr. Joseph White, then applied for a startup business loan from Joseph Ellicott. When he was turned down for the loan, it was rumored that Cyrenius Chapin had hoped to keep Johnson from setting up another competing practice in Buffalo (Goldman, 1983). Nonetheless, Dr. Johnson opened a practice near Black Rock and established a drugstore, borrowing on the arrangement that Cyrenius Chapin had made profitable. When the War of 1812 began, he entered the United States Army as a surgeon. When Buffalo was burned by the British in 1813, military records indicate that Dr. Johnson was faithfully attending to wounded soldiers several miles away (Rizzo, 2010).

Dr. Johnson was described as a bulky but handsome man. He quickly gained a considerable reputation as a talented physician. By 1821, he was doing very little doctoring. His business and political pursuits monopolized his time. He joined Judge Samuel Wilkeson in several businesses and cofounded the Banking House of Johnson, Hodge & Co. His enterprises contributed to the building of the Erie Canal and the locks through Tonawanda in the 1820s (Rizzo, 2010).

Johnson's political life started with his election as surrogate of Erie County in 1815, an office he was reelected to in 1828. In 1832, the year Buffalo was incorporated as a city, he was elected the city's first mayor and led the region's response during America's first cholera epidemic. The cause of cholera was unknown, but Mayor Dr. Johnson pushed his city to commission a Board of Health that cleaned up streets and likely saved hundreds of lives with quarantine measures (see chapter 19). Johnson went on to establish the first water district, using hollowed logs as pipes in several sections of Buffalo. While mayor, Dr. Johnson also served as the president of the Buffalo Literary and Scientific Academy (Rizzo, 2010).

The Johnson family lived in a handsome house on Delaware avenue that later became a woman's academy. Dr. Johnson owned a yellow buggy that Buffalo's elite considered old-fashioned. His buggy and the white horse he used to pull it were quite distinctive and readily marked his travels. His perpetual urgency meant he often neglected to hitch the horse, leaving it to wander off to any nearby tree-covered shady spot, buggy in tow (Welch, 1891).

Figure 6.1. Dr. Ebenezer Johnson, the first mayor of the city of Buffalo, circa 1832. *Source:* Devoy, 1896. Public domain.

In the financial downturn of 1837, several of Dr. Johnson's businesses failed, and he joined his brother in Tennessee to look after their interests in an iron mine. He died in Tellico Plains, Tennessee, February 8, 1849, aged sixty-three (Rizzo, 2010; White, 1898).

Dr. Josiah Trowbridge (1785–1862) arrived in Buffalo on horseback from Vermont in the spring of 1811. Born in Massachusetts, he had tried farming, ran a general store, taught school, and sailed with the merchant marine before apprenticing in medicine with a Dr. Willard. A bachelor on his arrival, he first rented rooms in Fort Erie, Canada, but permanently moved to Buffalo with the start of hostilities in 1812. During the war, he volunteered as a surgeon in the local militia.

Trowbridge was noted to be brusque and even crotchety at times. Still, he enjoyed friends and relished playing whist, a card game, while sipping from a snifter of sherry. He projected a dignified deportment despite being somewhat ungainly and not exceptionally handsome (Welch, 1891). Upon arrival in Buffalo, Dr. Trowbridge joined Dr. Cyrenius Chapin's practice before striking out on his own. Though the partnership did not last, the two doctors maintained a loose association and consulted each other over many years (Rizzo, 2010).

Dr. Trowbridge is remembered for a hero's act of chivalry. During the War of 1812, he was arrested and released by the British army for duck hunting on swampy Strawberry Island in the middle of the Niagara River. Yet, at the peak of hostilities in the war, and a few months after his duck-hunting arrest, Dr. Trowbridge completed a daring capture of one Canadian citizen. Enlisting "Cupid" as his only assistant, the ardent doctor rowed a dingy across the Niagara River to Fort Erie, proposed marriage to Margaret Wintermute, and whisked her back to Buffalo. Upon reaching the American shore, Margaret was taken by coach to a friend's home and on September 22, 1813, the couple married. They would have eleven children over a long marriage (Trowbridge, 1869).

According to family records, Dr. Trowbridge was one of the last men to leave Buffalo when it was burned by the British. After the war, he continued an active practice while serving as village treasurer, vestryman for the Episcopal Society of St. Paul's Church, librarian of the Erie County Medical Society, president of the Buffalo Lyceum, and village supervisor (three times). The Trowbridges built a hotel they called the United States Hotel on Buffalo's Terrace Street specifically designed to provide for newly arriving families. It offered flexible rooms that could be connected to form lodgings of two to six rooms (Rizzo, 2010).

Dr. Trowbridge became the second physician to be elected mayor, but the year was 1837 and the country was suffering a severe economic recession. Though he had accumulated a respectable amount of property, like so many, he lost much of it. He had been a dedicated Federalist but ran for mayor as a Whig and later became a Republican. As mayor, Trowbridge convinced the Common Council to raise taxes to support public schools. By 1856, poor health caused him to cease his medical practice. He died on September 18, 1862, at age seventy-seven (Trowbridge, 1869).

≈

Dr. John E. Marshall (1785–1838) was born in Norwich, Connecticut, on March 18, 1785, and was licensed to practice medicine on August 3, 1808, by the Connecticut State Medical Society. He practiced for six years in Mayville, New York, where he married Ruth Holmes in 1810. His sense of civic duty got him elected as the clerk for Chautauqua County in 1811. As the War of 1812 began, Dr. Marshall volunteered for the Second Regiment of the New York State militia and was appointed surgeon for a unit assigned to Buffalo.

During the war, Dr. Marshall contracted a camp fever, possibly northern malaria or typhus, that would trouble him for the rest of his life. But the bustle of Buffalo appealed to him. Following the war, he and Ruth relocated, becoming permanent Buffalo residents in 1815. In 1818, he was appointed the clerk for the still-undivided Niagara County. From 1826 to 1829, he was the treasurer of the County Medical Society, becoming its president in 1830. During the cholera epidemic of 1832, Dr. Marshall was appointed Buffalo's first health commissioner by Mayor/Doctor Johnson (see chapter 19). Like his contemporaries, Dr. Marshall also gained respect as both physician and citizen. He died on December 27, 1838, of pneumonia after a brief illness (Hill, 1923).

These five physicians—the two Doctors Chapin, Johnson, Trowbridge and Marshall—constituted a phalanx of unusually skilled, strong-willed individuals who laid the foundation for medicine in Buffalo. Many lesser-trained and sectarian practitioners, attracted to booming Buffalo after completion of the Erie Canal in 1825, would challenge their work. But these original five men also encouraged well-trained and capable men to settle in Buffalo. Their contribution was crucial in establishing the medical organizations and traditions that enticed nationally recognized physicians to join as founding faculty for the University of Buffalo medical college in 1846. During their lifetime, they bullied each other, and pushed each other, to consider scientific advances. Ultimately, they set the stage that made Buffalo the logical site for the 1878 American Medical Association national meeting, where heated debates promoted a new theory for contagious disease: the germ theory (T. C. Rosenthal, 2020; Toner, 1878).

~

These pioneer Buffalo medical men would have been incensed by the introduction Samuel Stearns wrote for his 1801 textbook. In it, he described the American medical profession as the "laughingstock of society" (S. Stearns, 1801). Across America, only a third of practicing doctors would have met the standard set by the Holy Roman Empire in the twelfth century, when Emperor Barbarossa Frederick decreed that all Roman doctors must possess a working understanding of human anatomy (Willius & Dry, 1948).

In practical terms, making a living as a doctor was difficult with cash-poor frontier families seeking cures from home medical books, which, like family Bibles, were passed down through generations. One popular book was Dr. William Buchan's *Domestic Medicine*, first published in London in 1769 with many subsequent revisions and editions later published in America. A highly regarded physician, Buchan, offered practical advice and instructions for the treatment of a variety of diseases and their symptoms written in a clear, commonsense style (Buchan, 1826). When one or more of the remedies in their book failed, their next step was to seek a cure from a neighborhood healer who had some knowledge of natural herbs (Tannenbaum, 2002; Watson, 1992). Community midwives, already familiar to the family, often branched out into recommending remedies according to traditions passed down in their own family. Another class of community healers followed more dogmatic protocols, like followers of Samuel Thomson and Samuel Hahnemann. They were classified as sectarian healers and formed two domains of medical practice that competed directly with regular physicians.

One popular sectarian domain, homeopathic practitioners, followed the principles of the German physician Samuel Hahnemann (1755–1843). They administered dilutions of substances associated with illness-like symptoms. Hahnemann's own dilutions were usually one part per thirty, but some followers carried out dilutions that were equivalent to a cup of tea in Lake Erie (King, 1905).

Samuel Hahnemann was a traditionally trained German physician who conceived the three main tenants of homeopathy. First, remedies should assist nature in healing; therefore, a patient with a fever should be warmed. Second, effective pharmaceuticals, undiluted, caused symptoms similar to the patient's symptoms. Third, these pharmaceuticals became safe and useful when they were diluted. Water being the major ingredient made homeopathic medications easy on the patient and so inexpensive that practitioners often provided their homeopathic potions to patients at no additional charge. Through the first half of the nineteenth century, about 10 percent of the traditional physicians in America bought into Hahnemann's theory and newspapers trumpeted homeopathy as low risk and well tolerated (Jobst, 2005; L.S. King, 1982).

Botanical practitioners were the second-most popular domain of medical practice. The most active and widely known were the Thomsonians. These followers of Samuel Thomson built an entire scheme of remedies based on the hallucinogenic properties of lobelia. Like most sectarian practitioners, Thomsonians vigorously embraced their methods and insisted they be recognized as equals with traditional physicians (King, 1905).

Samuel Thomson had no formal education, learned about plants and herbs from a neighborhood healer, and wrote a book describing his beliefs. Those who read his book were instructed to remove the last page, write in their name, and frame it as evidence of their being a "Thomsonian Doctor." One foundation of Thomsonian theory was the lobelia plant, which grew throughout much of America. After a brief episode of vomiting, lobelia could produce several hours of euphoric ambition (S. Thomson, 1835).

Traditional doctors, like New Amsterdam's five original, formed the third domain of health care. Because of their higher fees, they were often the last to be consulted and their remedies involved pain and discomfort. In 1800, these traditional physicians called themselves "regular" doctors. Most clung to the practice of rebalancing the four humors of Hippocrates and Galen through bloodletting, intestinal purging, sweating, and urination, as faithfully as the sectarians clung to their theories. Because regular doctors compounded their own medicines, the mortar and pestle or the bloodletting lancet became their iconic symbols, much like the stethoscope is associated with doctors today. Practicing medicine meant being able to read, and literacy alone made doctors important in the community. It explains why clergy, also a mostly literate profession, were drawn to medical practice (Murphy, 1991).

When the first American *Pharmacopoeia* was published in 1820, it had the unintended effect of revealing the limited scope of regular medical practice. The *Pharmacopoeia* listed about 100 mostly herbal medicines. There were a few inorganic compounds like the very popular purgative known as calomel (mercury and rhubarb). Most practicing physicians used fewer than thirty different compounds to treat a vast array of conditions. That many regular doctors used fewer than ten compounds explains the relative success of their sectarian competition (Haller, 1982; Pharmacopoeia, 1830). Today's *Physician Desk Reference* lists 24,000 prescription drugs and over-the-counter medicines.

~

By the 1820s and 1830s, many Americans were losing their respect for the regular medical profession (Warner, 1987). Early efforts by professional groups or government to define minimum education standards met with dissension and contempt. Midwives delivered most of the babies, barbers performed surgery, bonesetters set fractures, Thomsonians prescribed botanicals, and homeopaths distributed dilutions. Meanwhile, Indian medicine men held a status that rivaled them all (see chapter 7). Each group interpreted standardizing requirements for practicing medicine, using regular medicine as the model, as an effort by the government to cut them out of an income stream. They all suspected regular doctors were bribing legislators. At the dawn of the nineteenth century, few counties had medical societies, and regular doctors lacked the organizational infrastructure of an established guild common to other trades (Warner, 1987; Wood, 1875).

The entrance criteria for most medical colleges required only that the candidate be male and able to pay for lectures. The more prestigious schools required knowledge of Latin and Greek. Within the practice community, doctors hid behind "geographic specificity" to explain their choice of remedies, implying that the local physicians knew their patients and their community better than any outsider. Therefore, their remedies were beyond reproach.

The availability of many sectarian practitioners meant a low return on an educational investment, except for those few physicians who achieved some celebrity (Starr, 1982). The general population and state legislators were easily convinced that licensing was a brazen attempt to raise patient fees.

New York State passed its first licensing law in 1804, the Medical Practices Act. It empowered county-level medical societies to license practitioners who might call themselves a physician after the candidate completed an oral exam given by the medical society's Board of Censors (Potter, 1898, 1899). Exceptions crept in from the beginning. First, graduates of medical colleges located in New York were to be granted a license without examination. Then, sectarians and others mounted unrelenting challenges to the New York law, including a petition signed by 50,000 Thomsonian supporters. Their provocations resulted in several amendments until 1806, when the only advantage of holding a license was being allowed access to the courts to sue patients for nonpayment. Once again, nearly anyone who wanted to call themselves a doctor could do so (L. S. King, 1982).

Only a few New York counties were organized enough to form medical societies in the first few years of the nineteenth century. They joined in the statewide medical society to improve medical practice by adapting a code of ethics derived from a pamphlet published by British physician Dr. Thomas Percival in 1794 (Percival, 1803). These early codes directed physicians to wear a clean shirt and collar, wash their hands, keep their boots clean and polished, and wear fashionable clothing to give the impression of gentility. Some county societies adopted rules that discouraged physicians from indiscriminately spitting tobacco juice, frequenting pool parlors, or forming business partnerships with other doctors. Members were instructed to have a third party present whenever examining a female patient and to read polite literature to enhance conversation with the cultured classes. Some counties declared it was the doctor's right to shoot a dog if he proved to be a threat (Cathell, 1882).

Specialist physicians were rare, forcing village doctors to do the best they could without the support of anyone who might have extensive experience with the problem at hand. Many physicians consulted with other physicians in their village, but they relied on medical textbooks and journals containing opinions. The vast majority of published suggestions were based on an author's personal experience with a limited number of patients, and many articles described the management of just one patient (J. B. Brown, 1812).

In his memoir, William Hodge (1781–1848), the settler who had brought his family from Albany in 1805, recalled the care Dr. Chapin provided his daughter. She was a toddler who, while playing on the lawn one afternoon, was attacked by a large bird. The incident occurred during a moment of distraction, but the child's cry drew attention as the vicious bird attempted to lift her. The bird's effort failed, but as Mr. Hodge embraced his little girl, it was obvious a claw had pierced the child's skull (Hodge, 1885).

Dr. Cyrenius Chapin was first consulted and immediately recognized the serious threat to the child's survival. For centuries, physicians had been trained to feel for the pulsations of exposed brain when examining a fractured skull. The brain was said to throb and flutter under their fingers like the soft spot of the crown of an infant, and clearly the Hodge child's injury was beyond the skill of any physician at the time (Rutkow, 2022). He called on Drs. Daniel Chapin, Ebenezer Johnson, and Josiah Trowbridge to examine the child. The four doctors agreed the injury was sure to develop inflammation, but there was debate whether pus would help or hinder the child's recovery. They concluded that the child's only hope was to encourage a free flow of the inflammatory products. So, using a trepan, they drilled a three-quarter-inch circular piece of bone from the Hodge child's skull. Despite their efforts, the child died and was buried in the Franklin Square Cemetery (Hodge, 1885).

The Hodge case reveals that, though the strong-willed and self-confident pioneer doctors of Buffalo argued frequently, they were willing to consult and do anything they thought might help a patient requesting their advice. It also reveals the limited understanding of infection and the paucity of remedies available in the first decades of the nineteenth century.

Chapter 7

Native Americans and Medicine

Stay True to the Spirit and Storms Will Carry Little Cargo

There was a domain of frontier medicine that does not fit neatly into a sectarian category. Native American medicine men held great respect among their people and practiced medicine that was remarkably aligned with early nineteenth-century European theories. Long before the French or the British arrived, Native Americans had been skilled at intestinal purging, sweating, and the use of plants, all applied according to spiritual principles that enhanced their ministrations. As the cultures mixed, it was common for white settlers to seek care from Indian medicine men as an alternative to the methods of regular doctors. Similarly, Dr. Chapin offered an alternate choice to Native Americans. Frontier life for both groups proffered many infirmities for which neither had the answer. Chapin made himself available to his Indigenous neighbors and, as was common in his day, incorporated remedies from both cultures into his routines. As Chapin's reputation grew, many prominent Senecas with names like Farmer's Brother, Young King, Corn-planter, Red Jacket, Conjockity, and Jack Berry (known for always wearing flowers in his hat) sought his attention (C. Smith, 2017; Welch, 1891).

It was much more difficult, and perilous, to become a Seneca medicine man than a white man's doctor. A young brave soul wishing to become a medicine man had to become "immortal." After an unspecified number of years of assisting a medicine man, the candidate would be declared ready for the passage. First, the candidate fasted for four days during which he prayed and received lessons revealing the heretofore secret and mysterious rituals of a senior medicine man. Then, the candidate entered the medicine lodge, where hot skewers were passed through his skin over both pectoralis muscles and several other parts of the body. Ropes attached to these skewers were used to lift and suspend the candidate off the ground until he became unconscious. The resulting scars proved the candidate's passage to the world of knowledge and wisdom offered by the Great Spirit (Kennard, 1858). It was the Great Spirit that gifted health and the medicine man who advised his people in their continual maintenance of mental, physical, and spiritual strength (Parker, 1923).

～

Before frame houses became the norm after the War of 1812, many Senecas lived much like early white settlers did. Whites occupied log cabins scattered throughout the Niagara Frontier and Senecas occupied cabins concentrated along the course of Buffalo Creek. Cash payments to the Senecas from the federal government and the Holland Land Company had been established by treaty and made the Native American community an attractive market for white merchants and doctors. Both cultures crossed easily into the other's community, generating daily interactions and exchanges.

After decades of removal and eradication tactics, official Federal policy at the turn of the nineteenth century temporarily took a passive, measured approach toward Indigenous Americans. George Washington, always resolute about European rights to expand westward, encouraged a methodical extension of white settlements to avoid further bloodshed on both sides. Washington assumed, or hoped, that Indians would voluntarily retreat westward in the wake of European civilization. His dubious analogy was that of wild wolves that seemed to disappear into the wilderness as civilization expanded. Indians choosing not to retreat were expected to comply with treaties or integrate with white settlement, become Christians, settle down in nuclear families, and take up farming. While land was plentiful, this scheme seemed to work on the Niagara Frontier. It would be 1837 before white entrepreneurs forced division among the Senecas and conned a willing few Native Americans into selling the tribal rights to Buffalo Creek (H. S. Manley, 1947).

Confounding the seemingly tranquil dream of George Washington was the value both British and American armies placed on Native American warriors (see chapter 9). Both sides had provided arms and encouraged tribes to take sides in their battles during the French and Indian War and the

Revolutionary War. Few white settlers bothered to distinguish one tribe from another, and few sought to understand or appreciate shifting tribal alliances. Broad assumptions led segments of whites and Native American populations to bigoted opinions of the other, with many whites deciding all Indians were savages and ripe for removal. Meanwhile, few Native Americans grasped the concept of personal property ownership dear to white landholders.

Chapin treaded a middle ground. He made an effort to learn the Seneca language, but unlike some of his apprentices, he never became fluent. Still, as he administered to the medical needs of more and more Native Americans, he gained an appreciation for their brand of civilized behavior, and he thought that efforts to expel them exposed a European deceit (Welch, 1891).

The Buffalo Creek Senecas were proud of their community, carried themselves erect, and presented a dignified, sober composure. The men had an easy, good-natured manner; had a casual approach to their women; and were always ready to tease any woman who scolded them. White children were delighted beneficiaries of Native American gifts that included miniature bark canoes, snowshoes, wooden snow snakes, and bows and arrows. Older men enjoyed lingering on the grass of the terraced hill in front of Dr. Chapin's office on warm afternoons. They spent hours telling stories about their early lives and wanderings, always welcoming the doctor's participation. They referred to English-speaking white settlers as "Yengeese" to distinguish them from the French in what may have been the origin of the "Yankee" nickname (Welch, 1891).

One Chapin contemporary, Samuel Welch (the boy with the Sunday-morning toothache whose memoir provides much background for this book), fondly recalled the Seneca women as "pretty." They wore their thick, shiny black hair and rich copper complexions handsomely and blushed easily. Always neat, clean, and picturesque in their Native dress, they eschewed the pads, stays, and bustles commonly worn by white women. At market, Native women were often seen carrying a basket on their back held by a band, usually red, around their forehead (Sleeper-Smith, 2018). If not carrying an infant, these baskets held items for barter or sale, including fresh berries, herbs, flowers, leeks, horseradish, sassafras root, or anything sellable (Kane, 2022). A popular item was "Seneca Oil," known to ooze from the banks of the streams in French Creek. It was used to anoint the skin and as a cure-all for cuts, bruises, aches, pains, and rheumatism (Ayers, 2023; Welch, 1891).

Figure 7.1. A diagram of downtown Buffalo showing the lots laid out by Joseph Ellicott of the Holland Land Company. Chapin owned Lot 41. *Source:* White, 1898. Public domain.

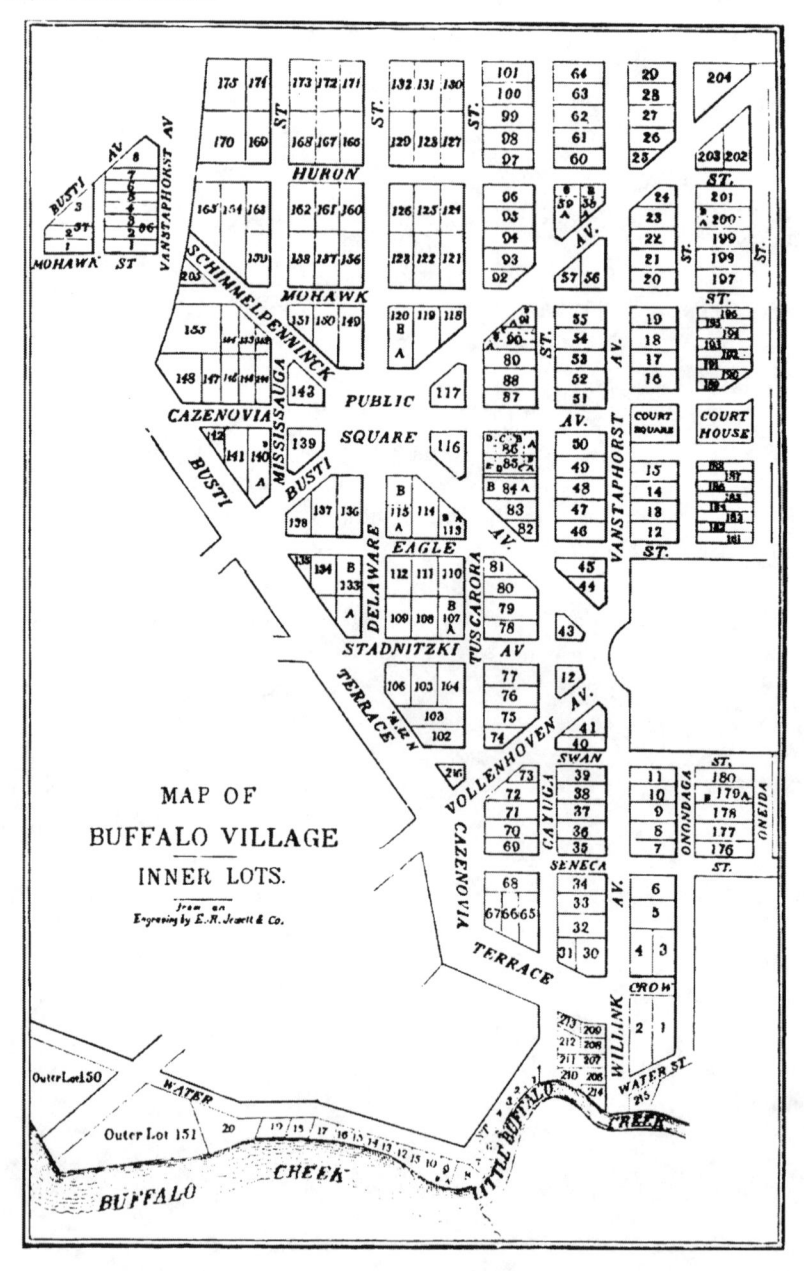

Figure 7.2. Drawing of Seneca man and woman, circa 1824. *Source:* Smith, 1884. Public domain.

Though he struggled to speak it, Doc Chapin thought the Seneca language was quite musical, particularly when listening to a gathering of women outside his drugstore. Ripples of laughter punctuated their conversations. Most white folk picked up a fair quantity of the Iroquoian language, and most Senecas learned a great deal of English, though neither group paid much respect to syntax. Daily interaction with Senecas meant anyone applying for a job in a store was advantaged if he could speak the Native tongue. Stores commonly extended credit to Native Americans they knew, confident that when tribes received their annual government annuities, they would be the first to be paid (Mt. Pleasant, 2016; Welch, 1891).

Whites and Native Americans shared a common desire for commercial gain and bargained with considerable shrewdness, though both cultures had their areas of vulnerability. Native American women liked to adorn themselves with colorful ornaments and placed high value on such items. Shopkeepers placed great value on the original designs and artistic embroidery patterns on buckskin made by Native women, eagerly buying moccasins, satchels, bags, wallets, purses, belts, leggings, and mittens for resale in their stores (Welch, 1891).

The papers of Erastus Granger, the federal agent for Indian affairs and postmaster, document the charges Dr. Chapin submitted to the government after the doctor had been called in to attend to an ailing Chief Red Jacket (1750–1830). Dated November and December 1806, the original bill and the paid-in-full receipt still exist (Atkins, 1898). Chapin's bill lists Croton oil pills, tartar emetic, opium plaster, Glauber's Salts, and powdered ipecac in quantities far exceeding doses prescribed for one individual, suggesting Chapin was collaborating with Red Jacket to provide medicine for his clan (Hollister, 1913).

Dr. Chapin's embarrassing struggle to master the Iroquois language met with good-natured teasing. But he was so well respected that the Senecas gifted him an Indigenous name: *Ah-ta-gis*, or great doctor. When his only son died in 1811 at age six, a delegation of Senecas, including Chief Red Jacket, attended the funeral.

Senecas enjoyed wearing silver trinkets and feathers in ear piercings. They symbolized status, celebration, or simply decoration, but they often ripped the skin, making torn ear lobes quite common. Dr. Chapin did a substantial business using a surgical technique he invented for cutting and stitching the dangling ends of pierced ear lobes. The "great doctor" admired the way Indian men tolerated his repair without flinching or complaint. Senecas under his care delighted in being bled, seeing it as the remedy for bad blood they too believed caused illness (Bryant, 1877). Chapin's growing relationship with the Senecas would save lives when Buffalo citizens were forced to flee directly through the Buffalo Creek reservation as the British burned Buffalo during the War of 1812.

∼

Seneca Chief Red Jacket and Dr. Chapin became good friends and frequent associates. Red Jacket (Aboriginal name: *Sagoyewatha*, or Keeper Awake, because of his oratory skill) became adept at speaking and understanding English, though he often pretended otherwise. He championed the traditional spiritual beliefs of his people, held misgivings regarding Christianity, and worried that formal education interfered with a child's understanding of the natural world—topics that filled many hours of conversation with

Dr. Chapin. Chapin enjoyed retelling one of Red Jacket's apocryphal stories. It was a response to missionaries attempting to convert Red Jacket to Christianity. Red Jacket turned the issue on the missionary, saying, "Go, preach to the people of Buffalo. If you can make them decent and sober, and learn them not to cheat the Indians and each other, we will believe in your religion." Red Jacket added, "When Jesus Christ was among you doing good . . . white people did not pay attention to him, and believe him, . . . [they] put him to death. We Indians did not do this. The Great Spirit has given white people their ways to serve him and to get your living, and he has given Indians their ways to serve him and to get their living by hunting the game he gives to us" (Atkins, 1898; Goldman, 1983; Parker, 1909, 1923).

During the American Revolution, Red Jacket's sympathies had supported the British, who gave him an embroidered British red coat for his efforts. He wore this jacket to remind American leaders that his allegiance depended on fair play. Red Jacket's stories did more than entertain—they skillfully communicated complex and often competing ideas about progress, society, and change.

In one meeting with the Holland Land agent, Joseph Ellicott, Red Jacket told a story about a negotiation he had with a white man in Tonawanda. The two men were resting on a swamp log when their discussion became deadlocked. Red Jacket demanded the white man move farther along the log. Moments later, still deadlocked, Red Jacket moved alongside the white man and again demanded, "Move along, Joe." Again, the white man complied and again the chief moved alongside him. A third time, the chief repeated his request and the white man complied. But when asked yet again to "move along," the white man said, "Why, I can't move any farther without falling off the log into the mud." "Ugh!" replied Red Jacket; "just so, white man wants Indian to move along, move along. Can't go no further, but still he say, 'move along'" (H. S. Manley, 1950).

∼

Frontier doctors borrowed many Seneca remedies, in part because they involved materials that were readily available in the fields and streams of western New York. Anecdotal accounts of Indigenous cures appeared regularly in nineteenth-century medical journals, many of which intrigued village doctors and were thought to be worth a try. Indian medicine men were also quite willing to sell their remedies to white folks and white doctors.

Common Iroquois remedies came from the roots, leaves, or bark of black cohosh, mandrake, apocynum, and spigelia. They also shared castor oil, foxglove (digitalis), guaiacum (antitussive), salicin (salicylic acid in today's aspirin), and sassafras (anthelmintic, antidiarrheal). Many of these Native American remedies came into common use in American medicine. Like white doctors, Indian medicine men also extracted teeth, set broken bones, lanced swellings, and bled patients (Kennard, 1858; Rush, 1774).

Nathaniel T. Strong was one young Native American who impressed Dr. Chapin. The boy was a hereditary chieftain, a quick read, and eager to learn English and English ways. Nat had a talent for attracting the attention of influential whites, eventually studying law at Yale University and apprenticing in the Buffalo law offices of a future president, Millard Fillmore. Despite Nat's success, many whites, particularly newcomers with no history of the integrated tolerance common to early Buffalo, questioned any attempt to civilize Indians. By the 1830s, bigotry combined with the avarice of white greed pushed the ancient Seneca culture and its people into ever smaller, more remote reservations. It was not unlike the fate of the wolf (Welch, 1891).

Chapter 8

Family, Village, and Community in Buffalo's First Decade

Villages Thrive on People Who Are Invaluable in a Calamity and Acceptable at a Dance

On March 14, 1808, the New York State Legislature started carving upstate's sprawling Genesee County into smaller counties. The first version of Niagara County included the northwest corner of New York and all the future Erie County. It stretched from Lake Ontario, along the Niagara River and Lake Erie to Cattaraugus Creek in the south. The village of "Buffaloe" was designated Niagara's county seat and the New Amsterdam name began its final fade into history. By the end of 1808, a courthouse and jail were completed on land chosen by Joseph Ellicott and the Holland Land Company. It was a substantial structure, located on Washington street, fronting today's Lafayette square. Augustus Porter of Niagara Falls became the county's first judge. He and his brother Peter were businessmen and transporters of goods who later played a major role in supplying American troops in 1812. Ebenezer Walden was the only licensed attorney west of Batavia; he would soon become Judge Walden (Devoy, 1896). Asa Ransom was appointed the first sheriff. It would be thirteen more years, 1821, before Erie and Niagara Counties were split at Tonawanda Creek. At that point, Buffalo would become the county seat of Erie County while the canal town of Lockport would be designated the new county seat for Niagara County (White, 1898).

As 1810 approached, Chapin's practice was immense and the constant motion he thrived on was now an essential force in his life. With a growing family and increasing expenses, he not only kept busy with patients, but also chased several opportunities to improve his finances. Though he allowed little time for contemplation, friends and patients recall that he frequently bragged about his wife, Sylvia. She, too, possessed an energy level that created impressions. According to Chapin, Sylvia was always spinning, knitting, darning, or attending to one of the children. Sylvia's church friends noted with envy that Cyrenius was generous in his expressions of pride about his family and his gratitude for Sylvia's exertions. On house calls, he often boasted about his family and illustrated actions he wanted the patient to duplicate with revealing family stories. Very few stories about Chapin's home life have survived, but comments are numerous enough to conclude that he enjoyed being a husband, father, and provider. In one breath, he might complain about parenting being a taxing responsibility. In the next, he would beam about the joy of watching his children mature. The value he placed on family encouraged patients to accept his idiosyncrasies and furthered his reputation as a trustworthy physician (C. W. Evans, 1903).

A tribute given to Dr. Chapin by a former apprentice who became his longest tenured practice partner adds a few detailed snippets about the Chapin family. The aforementioned Gorham F. Pratt, like most apprentices, lived with the Chapin family during his training. Gorham Pratt was born in New Hampshire and came to Buffalo in 1830 to work with Dr. Chapin. Apprentices paid room and board and, by their second year, helped their supervisor expand patient services. Pratt became a member of the Erie County Medical Society in 1833, and Dr. Chapin nominated him to be secretary the next year. He continued as secretary from 1834 to 1840, becoming the society's president in 1841. He partnered with Chapin until Chapin's death in 1838, when he assumed the care of many first families in Buffalo (G. F. Pratt, 1869).

Pratt delivered his very personal tribute to the Erie County Medical Society in 1868 with Chapin family recollections that are corroborated by the historical record of Buffalo's St. Paul's Episcopal Church (C. W. Evans, 1903). Sylvia Burnham Chapin is described as a woman with an independent mind who enthusiastically supported her husband, but she did not share his desire for the spotlight. Her birth date is uncertain, but their relationship started early in life in the Massachusetts hometown they shared. They were married for forty-five years, and she outlived Cyrenius by another twenty-five years. Sylvia endured Chapin's long workdays and several long absences, the longest being the nine months Cyrenius was a British prisoner of war during the War of 1812. With Cyrenius making house calls on horseback over a wide area of the Niagara Frontier and taking part in both local and statewide Federalist politics, Sylvia had to take charge of their household. Later, with financial success, the family employed a free Black man named James who served as a footman. James and Cyrenius behaved like pipe-smoking, drinking buddies, so it was up to Sylvia to make work assignments for James. In her own areas of responsibility, Sylvia was Cyrenius's equal. We see her courage and strength when, in 1813, she organizes the family's escape the night the British burn Buffalo. During the nine months her husband was in a British prisoner-of-war camp, Sylvia was a homeless single parent who moved the family to Canandaigua to live with friends until hostilities ceased (Council, 2017).

Very little has been written about the Chapin children. The couple's third child, Louise Maria, born March 19, 1803, is the only child to survive a long life. Louise provides a window to her parents' philosophy about female potential. Louise was encouraged to read and do well in school. She married the up-and-coming Thaddeus Weed and, in her obituary, is described as a critically useful confidant to her husband's business. Men in those days got all the credit, but Thaddeus Weed became a wealthy hardware and tool merchant while Louise apparently kept tabs on the accounts (C. W. Evans, 1903; G. F. Pratt, 1869).[1]

It was difficult for women to excel outside of the home early in the nineteenth century. Prevailing medical theory blamed this on a woman's uterus, thought to be the source of the emotions expressed by the more "sensitive" gender. The theory claimed that a woman's naturally keen response to passion was influenced by nerves emanating from the uterus. Hysteria, derived from the Latin word for womb, became the diagnosis whenever a woman showed distress. Having a uterus became a rationale for providing girls with an education focused on domestic skills that prepared them for a life devoted to family. Leading physicians like Benjamin Rush wrote that the sensitivity of the uterine-brain connection demanded women be sheltered from the external stresses of modern life. He would have found the degree to which life with Cyrenius Chapin stressed Sylvia to be unwise (Rush, 1812).

As the first teacher of young children, it can be assumed that Sylvia was as well read as her family. It is likely that Sylvia Chapin was aware of writings of two contemporaries, Mary Wollstonecraft and Margaret Fuller. Widely published in periodicals and books, these two women started the intellectual crusade to challenge the limits society placed on women.

---

1. More on the Chapin children in chapter 21.

First to begin the discourse, Wollstonecraft wrote in 1792 that cultural structures teach women that they must focus on beauty as their strength. Therefore, from early childhood, young women are taught to emphasize being pretty and talented regarding household work. They are instructed to make themselves a "rational companion" for husbands (Wollstonecraft, 1792). This cultural norm restricted a woman's role in the health professions to midwifery or nursing. It would be 1848, ten years after Dr. Chapin's death, before the first woman, Elizabeth Blackwell, was admitted to an American medical college (Nimura, 2021). Even then, Blackwell had to conceal her gender to gain admission to Geneva Medical College in Geneva, New York. (Geneva Medical College was later absorbed into Syracuse University.)

Wollstonecraft was one of the first to argue that women must be educated, or educate themselves, to fulfill an essential role that society overlooked: that of a child's first teacher. She asserted that education made wives more effective partners to their husbands, and she redefined female sensitivity as a strength. Wollstonecraft observed that an educated and sensitive woman enhanced her role as companion and partner. Gender equality, she declared, was a natural and inalienable right given by God. Treating women as ornaments or property and denying them equal rights was, therefore, a sin. In fact, Wollstonecraft wrote, the only reason women seemed inferior to men was their limited access to education (Wollstonecraft, 1792). Tragically, Wollstonecraft would die of childbed fever following the birth of her second daughter.

While romance has always been the subject of novels, in the nineteenth century, most couples found each other as a matter of convenience. Rigidly imposed courtship formalities were intended to allow couples time to negotiate a relationship and determine its potential for lifelong collaboration. The rules emphasized negotiation over infatuation (Bogue, 1852). Working as a teacher in the 1820s, Margaret Fuller became a confidant of Ralph Waldo Emerson. She identified four types of marriage, finding the household partnership to be the most common. These partnerships were built on a shared commitment to mutual dependence, with the man providing a house and the woman tending to it. Her second type was mutual idolatry, in which both husband and wife find the other more near perfection than all others in the world. Fuller's third type was the intellectual companionship, where the man and woman are confidants in thought, feeling, and trusting friendship. Her fourth type was a religious union encompassing the best of the first three, but advanced to mutual dependence and respect (Fuller, 1845). The Chapins enjoyed each other's company, spent many evenings reading to each other, and worked as partners toward a common goal of keeping a respectable home that supported child-rearing as well as Dr. Chapin's professional and community work.

Though there is no evidence that Sylvia or Cyrenius dwelled on the existential meaning of their relationship, it appears that they would have subscribed to Wollstonecraft's contention that educated women make better mothers and raise better children. The doctor's long hours placed a heavy burden on Sylvia, quite unlike the frivolous upper-class communions depicted in nineteenth-century novels. Fuller wrote that husbands and wives must each assume aspects of masculine and feminine behavior to achieve a lifelong marriage. Dr. Chapin presented a domineering presence, and outwardly Sylvia and Cyrenius fulfilled traditionally defined roles. But those who knew them well described them as self-dependent individuals who relied on each other to raise talented and well-educated children and to achieve economic success. Cyrenius, or his apprentices, may have chopped most of the firewood, but we can imagine that Sylvia found it necessary to split and replenish wood stores on many a wintry day.

~

Having staked his reputation on being a skillful practitioner, Cyrenius Chapin soon became known for his actions as a public-spirited citizen. From 1803 to 1813, his first decade in Buffalo, no person exercised greater influence in the expanding village. His strong will, self-confidence, energy, and ability to goad others into action attracted many friends and a fair share of enemies. The self-effacing bedside doctor, confident about his remedies, cultivated a political persona that some put down to arrogance. Nonetheless, there was hardly a project that did not include Dr. Chapin (H. P. Smith, 1884).

One early project was the Franklin Square Cemetery. In early 1805, months before Chapin's campaign for the New York Assembly, Dr. Chapin and Captain Samuel Pratt (the former fur trader nursed back to health by Native Americans and now a New Amsterdam resident) made a trip to Batavia. Their objective was to convince the Holland Land Company that New Amsterdam needed a cemetery and that the company should provide the land. Pratt described the roles they played in their negotiations with Joseph Ellicott. First Dr. Chapin opened by demanding a cemetery within the village with easy access to families. Pratt played a conciliatory and friendlier role, encouraging Ellicott to present his interests and concerns. Pratt and Chapin left quite pleased with their success. Ellicott granted the village title to property at the village's northern border on Terrace Street near the main road to Black Rock and Niagara Falls. It is likely that surveyor Ellicott knew what Pratt and Chapin did not. Bedrock underlying the new cemetery made the land difficult for digging graves and useful for little else. Buffalo's City Hall stands on the site today (Devoy, 1896).

The first person interred in the new cemetery was a traveling stranger from Connecticut by the name of John Cochrane. Digging his grave revealed the parsimony in Ellicott's gift. Several axes and picks were dulled cutting away the roots of scrub oak and reaching a depth adequate for Cochrane's grave. The next person interred in Franklin Square Cemetery may have been a very tall Indian nicknamed "The Infant." That both Native Americans and whites were buried in Franklin Square Cemetery adds evidence of the integrated society white settlers and Native Americans enjoyed in those early years. After the War of 1812, the distinguished Seneca war chief, Farmer's Brother, received military honors when buried at Franklin Square. Later, Samuel Pratt and Dr. Chapin, and their families, would be buried there (Atkins, 1898; Letchworth, 1874). Finally, in 1850, bodies from this and other small cemeteries were moved to the eighty-acre "City of the Dead," today known as Forest Lawn, on Delaware Avenue (Devoy, 1896).

~

By 1809, the United States government determined that the Niagara Frontier needed a Custom House. Both Black Rock and Buffalo vied to be the host site in a rivalry that foretold their later competition for the western terminus of the Erie Canal. The Black Rock harbor accommodated vessels of much greater tonnage than the harbor at Buffalo Creek, the latter being blocked by a sand bar most of the year. The sand bar made row boats the largest vessel able to cross over into Lake Erie. But Black Rock's Niagara River harbor had its own problems. Dangerous rapids guarded it and boats returning to Lake Erie had to be pulled against the strong Niagara River current by teams of horses walking a towpath. Many captains preferred to load and unload their ships using small boats that could safely reach docks on Buffalo Creek. Eventually, President Madison compromised by establishing a Custom House shared by the two communities and housed in two buildings, one in Black Rock and another in Buffalo. In 1810, a year later, regular ferry service crossed the Niagara River between Black Rock and Fort Erie, Canada. That year also saw the Black Rock firm of Porter, Barton &

Co. organize a commercial portage service to move goods around Niagara Falls linking Lake Erie and Lake Ontario (Devoy, 1896).

By the 1810 census, the population of the area known today as Erie County was about 4,000 and everyone, with the possible exception of Joseph Ellicott, was calling the burgeoning New Amsterdam village Buffaloe, with an e. A society organized by uniting Congregationalists and Presbyterians under the direction of Rev. Thaddeus Osgood began planning the first major church project (Devoy, 1896).

Also in 1810, Joseph Ellicott decided it was time to shed the frontier ambience of Buffaloe. He contracted to have the tree stumps, still haphazardly obstructing Main Street, removed. After this, one could ride down Buffalo's primary avenue "transfixed by a grand view of Lake Erie." The next year Buffalo got its first newspaper. The Buffalo "*Gazette*" was established by the Salisbury brothers as the only newspaper published west of Canandaigua. It was a small sheet, originally being 20 by 24 inches in size. The first issue was printed on October 3, 1811. Two years into publication, it was considerably enlarged and later changed its name to the *Buffalo Patriot*. It was the *Gazette* that standardized the spelling of Buffalo without the e (Devoy, 1896; White, 1898).

Chapter 9

Native Americans and the Prelude to War, 1810–1812

Bearing Gifts That Destroy a Nation

Shadowing the developments on the Niagara Frontier was the protracted march to the War of 1812 that defined the first decade of the nineteenth century. It had been nearly three decades since the Revolutionary War, fewer than twenty years since the United States' new Constitution, and only a decade since *Jay's Treaty* tried to reconcile lingering animosities with Britain. Most Americans were preoccupied with clearing land, planting crops, and making a living while a cautious but ill-tempered mood shadowed the political relations between Britain and the United States. Federalists, like Dr. Chapin, continued to believe that a strong federal government was essential to confront Britian's antagonism while nurturing trade. King George III was still on the throne, and he and his parliament were angry about being cut out of the Louisiana Purchase and annoyed by American leaders who promoted the idea that the Canadian provinces should join the United States. No less than the former emissary to Britain, Benjamin Franklin (1706–1790), had called for including language that prequalified Canadian provinces as future states in the Articles of Confederation. After the United States Constitution replaced the Articles in 1789, the southern states openly supported Canadian annexation if the northern states would support their desire to annex Spanish Florida (J. W. Pratt, 1925).

Fearful of losing their hold on North America, pressed by continued wars with France, and desperate for soldiers and sailors, the British sought to maintain influence and weaken the United States by effecting their own undeclared blockade of American shipping along the Atlantic coast. The blockade aligned with the need for sailors as British ships—navy and pirate—began boarding American merchant ships, kidnapping sailors, and even confiscating goods and material they claimed were intended to aid a British enemy. These seizures mocked American sovereignty and the intent of *Jay's Treaty*.

Canadian provinces openly placed advertisements in American newspapers offering free land to any American willing to make Canada their home and pledge fidelity to the Crown. These advertisements played to the outrage some Americans were feeling about the tax burden the United States imposed to pay war debts, build roads, and expand postal service (Devoy, 1896; Jasanoff, 2008).

American merchants could do little more than seethe as British warships and their licensed privateers hovered off major seaports, waiting to board and inspect every passing ship for suspected English subjects and sailors. Any sailor unable to prove he was born after the Revolutionary War was defined as an English subject. With only two frigates and about sixty-eight smaller gunboats, the United States Navy was little match, and the United States Army had been reduced to a mere 3,287 men by the first decade of the 1800s (J. W. Pratt, 1925).

Though never formally declared, the British blockade had its effect. It was the tightest around New York City and Boston, and slightly more selective along southern ports to allow cotton to reach British textile manufacturers. The British navy dismissed the United States as a "Mob Government," too weak to enforce its own sovereignty (J. W. Pratt, 1925)—an impression that had been magnified when President Jefferson tried to frustrate the British blockade by imposing a cessation of shipping out of American ports.

As the Jefferson administration entered its last year in office in 1808, the prospect of war festered in Congress. On the other side of the Atlantic, King George believed the Louisiana purchase proved that the United States was aligned with France, and if left unchallenged, the purchase threatened British hopes for their own westward development. The British calculated that nearly half of the land now claimed by the United States lay under the control of Native Americans. Once the American experiment met its inevitable demise, a brief war would return North America's dominion to the British. To prepare, the Canada-based British army stepped up its program of generous gifts of food, guns, and ammunition to Native American tribes in America from New York to the Midwest.

However, Britain's most immediate threat was its war with Napoleon, making it impossible to move significant numbers of troops to protect British/Canadian and North American interests. Add to this, threats by the majority French population of the Lower Province, and most of the troops assigned to Canada had to be garrisoned near Quebec to assure English control of the St. Lawrence River. The governor-in-chief of British North America, Sir James Craig, agreed that defending British interests across the Great Lakes and Upper Canada depended on loyal Indian allies, and he encouraged the lieutenant-governor of Upper Canada, Francis Gore, to do everything necessary to secure Native American loyalty (J. W. Pratt, 1925).

Native Americans on the Niagara Frontier listened to British entreaties, but member tribes of the Haudenosaunee could not reach a consensus about whom to support. Officially, the Haudenosaunee confederation chose neutrality, but individual tribes were allowed to seek their own alliances (Benn, 1998; C. Johnson, 1876). By the first decade of the nineteenth century, enough of the Haudenosaunee tribal units had found profit in their own farm economy and wished it not to be disrupted. Had the Haudenosaunee aligned with the British, the basic elements leading up to the War of 1812 would have changed significantly. The envoys sent by Lieutenant-Governor Gore met greater success with Native Americans in the Midwest and later with Haudenosaunee-affiliated tribes based in Canada. With both the Americans and the British placing great value on Native American warriors throughout the War of 1812, it would be the high point of Native American power in the nineteenth century (Benn, 1998; Kane, 2022).

The wild card was Shawnee Chief Tecumseh (1768–1813). Tecumseh lost his father and a brother in battles when expanding white settlement pushed the Shawnee out of Ohio in the 1790s. In 1806, Tecumseh and another brother, Tenskwatawa (a Shawnee spiritual leader), began organizing a new confederacy of diverse Native American tribes in the Midwest. Their goal was to prevent further intrusions on their Aboriginal way of life. In 1808, they established the village of Prophetstown in the Indiana territory between the Wabash and Tippecanoe Rivers. It soon contained 6,000 Native Americans of mixed tribal origins, making it larger than Cincinnati or Pittsburgh. Tecumseh and his brother preached Native American rights, communal ownership of land, and rejection of any treaty that ceded more territory to white settlement. Any expansion-minded American was an enemy to Tecumseh (Ayers, 2023; Sugden, 1985).

Lieutenant-Governor Gore's Indian Department began providing food and guns directly to Tecumseh's community in 1809. British/Canadian support freed Tecumseh to travel the Midwest, recruiting more tribes to join his vision for Native American sovereignty. Gore also established an Indian council house along the Niagara River, adjacent to Fort George, to strategize with all Indian tribes willing to support Britain in a war against the colonies (Sugden, 1985).

In the winter of 1811 and 1812, American agents were likewise attempting to influence Native American fidelity. White settlers were horror-struck by the Indian's reputation for violent scalping and terror, a reputation Indian warriors cultivated to intimidate their enemies. White fear was so intense that rather than simply arming more Indian braves, gifts of tools and seed were tied to offerings of guns and ammunition, with the hopes that more Indian families would become farmers. President Madison invited regional chiefs to Washington, DC, for "pow wows" meant to discourage affiliations with the British. These American initiatives further agitated the British army, which cared less about North American settlement than access to furs and territorial control. Ultimately, they wanted to take back the colonies (Sugden, 1985).

～

When Peter Buell Porter and his brother Augustus arrived in Black Rock in 1795, they were preloaded with ambition. Their Porter ancestors came to America in 1637 and settled in Connecticut. Peter Porter graduated from Yale and studied law with Judge Reeves in Litchfield, Connecticut, before relocating to Western New York's Black Rock village. Together, the brothers developed a large mercantile and shipping business on the eastern Great Lakes. Under the name Porter, Barton & Company, their enterprise became the principal transporter of goods from east to west. They blazed a shipping route from central New York to Buffalo that began with a road they cleared from Oneida Lake to Oswego, where goods were transferred to Lake Ontario boats for shipment to Lewiston. From Lewiston, goods were transferred to wagons for portage past the swift currents of the Niagara River and the Falls. In Black Rock, they reloaded the merchandise on boats for Lake Erie and the far western reaches of American expansion. Of the American sailing vessels on Lake Erie, more than half were owned by Porter, Barton & Co. It was this path that the Hodge family had taken on their trip to Buffalo in 1805 (Illustrated, 1906–1908).

Peter built a mansion in Black Rock near the wharves and warehouses he and his brother owned. In 1808, at the age of thirty-five, he won the election to the United States Congress, an office he won again in 1810. He also served on the New York State commission charged with planning the canal to cross upstate New York.

Peter Porter was hard-drinking, amiable, and gregarious. Contemporaries described him as old school, portly, but handsome. He had a dignified demeanor that amplified his talent for fluent speeches. Initially a Federalist, he converted in 1801 as the Jefferson Democrat-Republicans came to power. He remained a close confidant of the influential Whig, Henry Clay, even after his party conversion, and became one of the great military leaders of the War of 1812 (Brands, 2018; Clay, 1959; Illustrated, 1906–1908).

Cyrenius Chapin and Peter Porter became close friends and forceful advocates for Western New York. They both argued a vigorous defense of their respective villages of Buffalo and Black Rock, though by midcentury (1853) the two municipalities would merge. With the growing concern about British intentions in the region, they shared in denouncing Britain's disregard for America's rights on the high seas and echoed the increasingly bitter arguments by legislators in Congress and state houses. America's newspapers further fueled debates heard at public meetings throughout the country. The majority Democrat-Republican party agitated for war. Federalists demanded forceful, more effective negotiations. To Porter and Chapin, Britain was the enemy of progress in North America (Taylor, 2010).

∼

By 1811, Tecumseh's efforts in the Midwest reached the level of alarm. American leaders and Native Americans who preferred accommodation with the United States feared Tecumseh's rising strength in the Indiana territory. In November 1811, the governor of Indiana and the future United States president, William Henry Harrison, received word that Tecumseh was out of Prophetstown recruiting tribes to join his confederacy. Tenskwatawa, more religious leader than warrior, was left in charge. Seeing an opportunity, Harrison led a militia to attack Prophetstown, easily defeating Tenskwatawa in what became known as the Battle of Tippecanoe. Harrison's militia destroyed Prophetstown and Tecumseh's confederacy was dispersed (Sugden, 1985).

For a few months, fears regarding an organized Native American confederacy lessened, but by the spring of 1812, Tecumseh reemerged, leading a Native American army supported by the British of Upper Canada. With regular British troops still preoccupied with European battles, Britain's efforts to supply Native Americans with weapons had intensified. Regular British forces in Upper Canada, now withered to 1,450 troops, were responsible for defending a thousand miles of frontier that included French-leaning Lower Canada (White, 1898). The essential nature of the Indian collaboration is summarized by a letter circulated to British commanders: "[It] appears that, dreadful as the effects of his [Native American] treacherous courage undoubtedly are, it is perfectly justifiable against an enemy [the former colonies] who seeks the occasion to embarrass its parent." British communications discounted the American militia as defiant children whose men were "half-horse, half-alligator" and "unskilled in the amenities of civilized life." The memo described unsophisticated American soldiers as "fitted well to cope with the original owners of the soil" (Bonnycastle, 1852).

British Major General Sir Isaac Brock (1769–1812) understood the terror that Indian fighting tactics generated in American settlers and believed a large army of Indian allies would daunt both American invaders and its citizens. In the Michigan Territory, it was common knowledge that Native Americans outnumbered white settlers 10,000 to 4,700, with white settlers occupying only a narrow band along the Detroit River. A mere 100 American troops were garrisoned in the fort near Detroit.

In February 1812, Congress passed a law authorizing an army of 25,000 men, and in New York, Democrat-Republican governor Daniel D. Tompkins (1774–1825) pushed the New York legislature to prepare for war (Taylor, 2010). Unfortunately, both federal and state legislators found agreeing to authorize new armies easier than agreeing to appropriate the funds needed to purchase supplies and pay the wages soldiers needed to assemble and fight.

Laying the groundwork for war renewed heated debates between the majority Democrat-Republicans and the Federalists. In the end, Congress favored raising an army but narrowly defeated authorization to build warships for the navy. By default, the lack of a navy meant the Democrat-Republican majority had chosen a land war with the British. Federalists considered this an incoherent folly (Taylor, 2010).

Rumors spread about an army of British and Native Americans being assembled at Newark (Niagara-on-the-Lake), across the Niagara River from Fort Niagara. Anticipation of a British invasion led to a public meeting at Buffalo's Cook tavern to discuss raising a militia. Anxiety among Western New York citizens was palpable as stories of Indian outrages circulated almost daily. The United States Army announced that any man willing to enlist for five years would receive 160 acres of land, three months' extra pay, and a bounty of $16 (D. S. Brown, 2022; Taylor, 2010).

Figure 9.1. Painting of Fort Niagara, circa 1810. *Source:* Devoy, 1896. Public domain.

In February 1812, the *Buffalo Gazette* published a note about a civil trial in which Dr. Chapin, a passionate advocate for liberating Canada from British control, was accused of slandering the County sheriff in an apparent argument over war. The newspaper article does not describe specifics of the complaint, but at the time Chapin was eagerly encouraging Buffalonians to prepare for war and was critical of anyone who did not share his resolve. The verdict favored Dr. Chapin. The sheriff, Asa Ransom, appealed the verdict, but the court ruled that an appeal was unwarranted (*Buffalo Gazette*, February 5, 1812).

~

In 1812, it generally took news from outside of Buffalo an average of six weeks to appear in the *Buffalo Gazette*, though truly urgent news from Washington, DC, sometimes made it to Buffalo in as little as a week. On June 27, 1812, a bulletin in the *Gazette* reported that earlier that day, Buffalo residents watched a commercial vessel leave Black Rock and enter Lake Erie, loaded with salt for the western territories. Minutes after it entered the lake, an armed British frigate left Fort Erie, Canada, came alongside the American boat, boarded it, and towed it to Fort Erie. That evening, well after press time, a special express rider delivered news from Washington, DC, that nine days earlier, June 18, 1812, President Madison had signed the bill passed by Congress declaring war on Britain. A similar announcement had reached the British army at Fort Erie earlier in the day (H. P. Smith, 1884; Wilner, 1931).

The War of 1812 had begun.

Chapter 10

How to Start a War: 1812

No War Is Begun Without Exaggerated
Faith in How It Will End

As 1812 wore on, Britain's harassment of shipping, indifference to borders, and arming of disaffected Native American tribes had intensified. War hawks in the United States took Britain's actions as an affront to American sovereignty. Merchants and exporters took the actions as a menace to their livelihood. Settlers in the Great Lakes regions took Indian armament as a threat to their lives.

Born in 1738, Britain's King George III reigned from 1760 to 1820. His reign had never been more complicated than when Britain and France reignited their on-again-off-again war in the first decade of the 1800s, this time against Napoleon. America's declaration of war in 1812 made fulfilling the empire's obligations perilous. The overextended British navy became even more anxious for able-body sailors and the war declaration provided a convenient excuse to step up their boarding of American merchant ships, abducting seamen and confiscating cargo. Congressional belligerents in President Madison's Democrat-Republican party pressured the administration for definitive action but fumbled their responsibility for providing appropriations (D. S. Brown, 2022).

~

The global empire under Great Britain's control had grown immensely during the sixty-year reign of King George III, but wars in the early nineteenth century placed heavy demands on his subjects to support the empire's soldiers and sailors. The drain on the British navy was so great that the Crown authorized independent privateers to challenge international trade thought to assist any of the empire's various enemies. Privateers did little to increase the import of raw materials to London, and with Jefferson's self-imposed United States embargo, English manufacturers suffered scarcities of cotton, indigo, and tobacco. Nonetheless, King George viewed Jefferson's self-imposed embargo as evidence of America's weakness.

The War of 1812 started slowly, and the management of Fort Niagara illustrates the disconnect between the United States' intentions and actions that constrained early military actions. Fort Niagara, because of its commanding view of the Niagara River's release into Lake Ontario, had been a focus of international interest since it was built by the French in 1725. After capturing the fort in 1759, the British had reinforced the stone strong house as well as the extensive earthworks and stockades that sheltered powerful cannons overlooking the river. The signing of *Jay's Treaty* in 1795 meant that the British army finally abandoned the old fort and relocated across the river, where they reinforced a much newer Fort George. But full possession of Fort Niagara did not bring American investment. Declaration of war did little to change the underfunded United States Army's failure to maintain soldiers and materiel at the strategic outpost (Taylor, 2010).

Though the United States had contemplated war with Britain for several years, but little had been done to develop the military anywhere. Before turning over the presidency to Madison, Jefferson had naively encouraged congressional war hawks in an 1807 conversation with the French Ambassador, saying, "If the English do not give me the satisfaction we demand, we will take Canada, which wants to enter the Union. With Canada, we shall have Florida and no longer have any difficulties with our neighbors" (Cruikshank, 1912). According to Jefferson's calculations, an army of 5,000 American soldiers could cross into Upper Canada and liberate the province from British control because a great mass of Canadians would immediately side with the American troops.

American leadership might have understood the people of Canada better had they followed an itinerant American Baptist preacher, Michael Smith, as he wandered through the Upper Province of Canada over several years around 1810. Collected into a book, not published until 1813, Smith noted that one out of every sixth inhabitant of Upper Canada was a new immigrant or the child of immigrants from England, Ireland, or Scotland. He estimated that nearly two-thirds of the population had roots in the United

States, but they, or their parents, had supported the British King during the Revolution. Approximately one in six inhabitants were Native Americans (Cruikshank, 1910). Smith also noted that the citizens of New York and Upper Canada paid little attention to the unguarded border, moving back and forth for friendships, family, and commerce.

James Madison became president in 1809. By 1812, he joined with the war hawks in judging England's vulnerability. The Napoleonic Wars and limited access to raw materials were causing banks to fail as the London economy stagnated. Over 100,000 soldiers and sailors were dying in the empire's battles. Napoleon's hectic march into Russia intimidated Europe, but Britain feared that should he retreat from Moscow, Napoleon would concentrate his attention on striking the English shore. If the United States believed that a North American war was necessary, it was a good time to declare it (Wilner, 1931).

By a margin of nearly two to one, the House and Senate voted for war on June 5, 1812. Then, on June 18, Democrat-Republican President James Madison signed the declaration of war (Wilner, 1931).

Before the declaration, trepidation about the killing and destruction fundamental to war overshadowed Dr. Chapin's long-held conviction that Canada would benefit by being part of the United States. He feared for friends and patients on both sides of the Niagara River and joined his fellow Federalists in the belief that wars were an unwise use of resources (Strum, 1980).

However, once the British seized that Lake Erie merchant boat carrying salt, Chapin reconsidered. His Canadian patients told him of being forced to enlist in provincial militias and to train with the British army. Clearly, the British were preparing to bring the fight to America. Then the British regiment at Fort Erie started drilling in full view of Buffalo in an obvious attempt to intimidate Western New Yorkers. By early September 1812, Britain had reassigned 600 regular troops to the Niagara Peninsula and supported untold numbers of militia and Native allies who were ready to fight (Wilner, 1931). It was time, Chapin believed, for America to take the fight to the British and complete the North American revolution his father had fought in.

∼

Congress continued to be more eager to declare war than fund the military needed for war. They encouraged battle plans that were disconnected from appropriations and offered conflicting directives to an army that was unorganized and undermanned. Congress wanted a quick and decisive three-pronged attack that called for the army to: (a) advance up Lake Champlain to take Montreal; (b) Invade Canada from Detroit, and (c) from Buffalo, take control of the Great Lakes. To the few experienced military strategists in the United States Army, the naivety of the plan was baffling (Wilner, 1931).

In New York State, the militia was largely voluntary and organized according to a state legislative act passed in 1793. Its intent was defense, not offense, and it was definitely not organized to invade Canada. New York's militia had four divisions, each one further divided into brigades and regiments. All were under the command of the governor. Regiments with 60 to 100 men each were required to drill twice a year. Regiment leaders met with other regional leaders only once a year. The United States secretary of war supplied state militias with arms based on the number of enrolled soldiers but otherwise had limited authority. Though all able-bodied, free, white men between the ages of eighteen and forty-five were expected to serve, there was little enforcement. Regiments chose their officers by election, making leadership a popularity contest influenced by social status, wealth, participation, or financial support of the regiment. Military experience was a secondary consideration, and Dr. Chapin took part when he could (Hickey, 2012).

The United States regular army had been advertising for new recruits since May 1812, but because white settlers feared Native American warriors so intently, recruiting Indian fighters was discouraged. Stories about Indian atrocities had reached mythical proportions. Most whites believed that, from a young age, Native Americans were trained to be highly skilled hunters and learned to handle muskets better than white folks. It was rumored that they could reload a musket in half the time it took a white man. Dime novels depicted Native Americans being able to approach their targets in total silence before suddenly erupting in furious war whoops and piercing screams capable of sapping the spirit of all but the most hardened foes. In hand-to-hand combat, a warrior's skilled use of knives and tomahawks made quick work of enemies who might be scalped before they were dead. Providing Indians with weapons was more than many settlers could accept. Instead, the aim of the United States Indian Service in negotiations with Chief Red Jacket was to keep the 700 Seneca soldiers in Western New York neutral and on the sidelines (Benn, 1998).

When early battles were engaged, they confirmed how unprepared the United States was for war. Compared to the British fighting machine, the United States was bootless, figuratively and literally. The fledgling US Military Academy at West Point, established in 1802, graduated officers after a haphazard curriculum and with little or no battlefield experience (White, 1898). Because America had behaved as if the revolutionary war would be its only war, it was difficult to identify effective and determined officers able to train and lead a disciplined army.

Though neither Dr. Chapin nor his friend, Congressman Peter B. Porter, had welcomed war, once declared, they both joined the ranks of war hawks. Porter was the better informed and experienced of the two men regarding war. While in congress, Porter chaired the House Foreign Relations Committee, and as a resident of Black Rock, he not only saw British troops training across the Niagara River, but his shipping enterprise depended on peace. Like so many others, Porter believed the war would be brief because most Canadians wanted to be part of the United States. Stories in the *Buffalo Gazette* seemed to support this idea; it reported that four Canadians "escaped" to Buffalo from Long Point on the Canadian side of Lake Erie in a skiff on July 14, 1812. On July 21, three more "escapees" arrived on American shores, and eleven more "refugees" arrived on August 11 (Cruikshank, 1912). These stories and others feed into the misperception that many Canadians would gladly defect.

The generation of Porter and Chapin really only knew those Americans who had recently moved to Canada to take advantage of the generous British land grants. They were less aware of the scores of British loyalists Reverend Smith described who had fled to the security of British Canada. The heavily advertised Canadian land-grant program did, in fact, have its greatest impact in the years following 1791 when liberal land policies tripled the number of former Americans living in Canada. Chapin and Porter believed these emigrants sought land rather than the yoke of the British Crown.

The British were concerned about the fidelity of recent land-grant immigrants. A few months after the war began, the governor of Upper Canada announced that every former citizen of the United States living in Canada was required to sign a new document of allegiance to the Crown. Those not signing were considered American sympathizers and could be subjected to imprisonment (Cruikshank, 1912).

～

Once mobilized, armies need supplies and paychecks. Congress continued to dither about allocating money for food, tents, shoes, clothing, firearms, ammunition, artillery, horses, draft animals, and medicine. To fight a war involving the Great Lakes, American soldiers also needed boats. As in most wars, local residents were willing to accept a limited degree of sacrifice, but they also expected to be paid if they provided support.

The Porter brothers, Peter and Augustus, may have moved a large share of Great Lakes shipping, but it was the British navy that controlled the Great Lakes. With no protection, the declaration of war forced the Porter brothers and the United States Armed Forces to rely on land-based transport across roads through New England, New York, Ohio, and points west to Detroit. The roads were rugged at best. Heavily traveled roads, like the one between Batavia and Buffalo, were "corduroy" with side-to-side logs in wet spots. But gaps between logs were often large enough to swallow a wagon wheel in mud. A military supply wagon carrying a day's worth of food was so heavy it got stuck several times a day (J. W. Pratt, 1925).

Both the British and American armies were forced to rely heavily on civilians to meet supply needs, causing major disruption to local economies wherever they went. Prices rose with demand, and soldiers on both sides used coercion, force, or outright theft to gain essentials. The first battle had yet to be fought when New York militia Brigadier General William Wadsworth wrote to Governor Tompkins complaining that his troops had no tents or camp kettles. The few regiments with flour had no way to bake it and entire units lacked uniforms, firearms, cartridge boxes, and the tools needed to clean muskets. One regiment was without coats and many lacked shoes or stockings. Soldiers became desperate. Fences got torn down for firewood and foodstuffs disappeared from fields and barns. As the war raged on, battle lines shifted, and sometimes property was destroyed simply to prevent the enemy from using it. For the soldiers, days of inaction were nearly as demoralizing as battle, and lack of pay sent many recruits back home at the first opportunity.

∼

Chapin's support for the war opened fractures within the New York Federalist party, which officially denounced the hostilities at their September 1812 convention in Albany. Democratic-Republican Daniel Tompkins defeated the Federalist candidate in the November 1812 election for New York governor, and Chapin's New York Federalists took a trouncing. With that, Dr. Chapin turned his attention to executing a role of his own design (Chazanof, 1970).

By October 1812, the disorganization of the war effort could not be ignored. Dr. Chapin and Peter Porter decided they needed to assume higher-profile roles, knowing that without proper defense, Buffalo, Black Rock, and Western New York would suffer badly. Joseph Ellicott, though a faithful Democrat-Republican and a personal acquaintance of Thomas Jefferson, remained on the sideline. His focus was land sales and for now, he would hedge his bets (Wilner, 1931).

Once Dr. Chapin's mind was made up, fervency propelled him to action. At his own expense, he posted notices in newspapers and on street corners to recruit a Buffalo-based militia regiment. The posters called for all Buffalonians who were friends of "Peace, Liberty and Commerce" to join him at Pomeroy's Tavern for enlistment. Volunteers were to bring "all the pistols, swords and sabers you can borrow at the risk of the lender." His "lender's risk" comment acknowledged the reality that not all recruits, nor their weapons, would return (Wilner, 1931). Ultimately, 136 men responded to Dr. Chapin's call for action and signed onto his Buffalo militia, a force that would add to a complex web of militias who would take up arms to support the United States regular army. To no one's surprise, Dr. Chapin was elected the regiment's leader (C. Johnson, 1876).

Figure 10.1. Peter Buell Porter as Major-General, New York State militia, in the War of 1812. *Source:* Wikimedia Commons/US Army Center of Military History. Public domain.

When fighting actually began, between fifty and sixty men would consistently serve in Chapin's unit. Though they were responsible to both New York State and the United States government, their first allegiance was to Chapin. The group functioned as nearly independent rangers, allowing for activities that may not have been condoned by a formal military structure. Nonetheless, they became a force to be reckoned with, and much like Chapin's personality, they alternatively agitated the British army and frustrated American army commanders. They became known as Chapin's "*Forty Thieves.*"

~

As the summer of 1812 closed, the Senecas, led by Red Jacket, stuck to their decision to remain neutral and held the Haudenosaunee Nations in New York to their declaration of nonalignment. When some affiliated tribes, mostly Mohawks residing in Canada, sided with the British, the Iroquois Nation cast them out of the Haudenosaunee Confederacy. There were a few minor capitulations by individuals or tribal units, but they were mostly ignored by the Confederacy.

As autumn progressed, Joseph Ellicott also decided that annexation of Upper Canada would improve prospects for land sales in the long run. Ellicott feared the disruptions of war, but with the high crop prices for the 1812 harvest, more farm families made good on their mortgage payments, and some even expanded their landholdings. Later, as the war raged on, land sales did slump, but Ellicott turned his frustrations on President Madison for the incompetency of the army's launch. He also leveled criticism at the United States regular army's commanding officer in Western New York, General Stephen Van Rensselaer, calling him ineffective and unable to prosecute a war. In a letter to his superiors at the Holland Land Company, Ellicott wrote, "Had our Executive pursued war with energy, all Upper Canada might have been annexed to the United States in two weeks" (Chazanof, 1970).

One apocryphal story describes the frustrations war leveled on the average Canadian and American farmer. In the summer of 1812, a Queenston farmer is said to have sold a cow to a man in Lewiston, New York. He delivered the cow via the Queenston ferry. However, the cow, apparently a British loyalist, broke out of her Lewiston barnyard and swam the turbulent waters of the Niagara River back to Canada. Appreciating the bovine's dilemma, her original owner sheltered the cow for the duration of the war.

Once hostilities ended, the Queenston farmer forcefully returned the cow to Lewiston (McKenzie, 1971).

As troops of the regular army and the local militia gathered for war, the fall of 1812 became prime for the spread of disease among volunteers and citizens alike. Joseph Ellicott deemed it as "the most sickly" time he could remember, saying, "the sickness [is] the most mortal we have experienced since I have been in this country." The illness became known as "The Buffalo Fever" and reached as far east as Albany, where thirty-three members of the state assembly became ill and three died. By February 1813, the *Buffalo Gazette* ran a story about doctors fiercely debating the best remedy. Some claimed copious bleeding was essential, and others recommended large doses of laudanum, alcohol, and laxatives (Chazanof, 1970). The agent causing Buffalo fever may have been a novel strain of influenza.

Chapter 11

Chapin Enters the Fight

I May Bleed, but I'll Fight

As autumn 1812 approached, Congressman Peter B. Porter resigned from the House of Representatives and was appointed brigadier general and quartermaster for the New York militia by Governor Tompkins. Porter's struggle to fix supply lines proved difficult, but he had success organizing an entire militia brigade composed of regiments and new recruits from New York and Pennsylvania. Governor Tompkins acknowledged Porter's enlistment success by promoting him to major-general. Porter also reopened discussions with the Senecas based on his extensive commercial experience and interactions. The Senecas remained officially neutral, but they gifted Major-General Peter Porter the Native American name *Conashtustah* and promised, "Where *Conashtustah* leads, we follow." As quartermaster, Peter Porter played a key role in securing a federal contract for his brother Augustus, whose company became the major freight conveyance for army provisions serving troops from Fort Niagara to Detroit (Wilner, 1931).

Chapin's Buffalo militia was a unit within, and responsible to, the New York militia. However, as the war played out, Chapin's unit remained marginally distinct and allegiant to the doctor's command. The situation strained the Porter and Chapin relationship but never broke it. Chapin's Buffalo unit would prove useful, flexible, daring, and undisciplined.

∾

Porter's first concern was the vulnerability of Black Rock, Buffalo, and Western New York. Almost nothing had been done to fortify the American side of the border in decades. From the windows of his warehouse, Porter could look across the Niagara River and see the British were constructing new batteries, arms depots, guardhouses, and a relay of signal stations to convey warnings. On the American side, Fort Niagara was nearly thirty miles north of Buffalo and Black Rock, and it was still the only formal American military base in Western New York. In the summer of 1812, it garrisoned only eighty troops and had been allowed to deteriorate into a ruinous condition. It was grossly outmatched by the 600 British regulars rumored to have turned up at the newly fortified Fort George (Wilner, 1931).

United States strategy through 1812 continued to focus on the three-pronged approach that supposed quick control of Great Lakes shipping. But simultaneous invasions emanating from Detroit, Buffalo, and Lake Champlain relied on makeshift armies of regular soldiers, militia, and informal volunteers. Success would require a large number of Canadians joining the American fight against English troops.

The enormity of the challenge should have been understood after one of the early battles of the war. In August 1812, General William Hull, governor of the Michigan territory and a veteran of the American Revolution, warned President Madison that an invasion into Canada from Detroit would expose Michigan to destruction by Indigenous tribes. Hull recommended a delay. He wanted time to recruit and train a military force robust enough to defend the Michigan frontier. Hull also recommended building a fleet of vessels that might take control of the western shores of Lake Erie. Without boats, he believed it would be impossible to secure any American victory. No one in Washington was listening, and Hull was ordered to invade Upper Canada from Detroit with the 2,000 troops (mostly volunteers) he had at hand (Quaife, 1913).

Hull's invasion failed. On August 16, 1812, Hull was obliged to surrender his entire garrison at Fort Detroit to the British. It was Tecumseh, now leading a multi-tribe army of over 500 Indians allied with the British, who sealed the victory. Afterward, the British commanding officer, Sir Isaac Brock, pressed Tecumseh and his tribal mercenaries to ransack Michigan, just as Hull had predicted. Within days, Tecumseh and his warriors reached Chicago, where a massacre unequaled in the history of American–Indian relations was carried out. It has since been known as the Fort Dearborn massacre. The United States court-martialed Hull for cowardice and his once-exemplary military career was destroyed (Hannings, 2012; Quaife, 1913).

The next month, September 1812, Tecumseh attacked Fort Harrison on the Wabash River in Indiana. Zachary Taylor, then a junior captain in the United States Army, and his garrison successfully defended the fort in what was the first American victory of the war. Later, the Mexican War would make Zachary Taylor, a Louisiana plantation owner, a hero of great fame. It would get him elected president of the United States in 1848. Also in September 1812, future president General William Henry Harrison of Tippecanoe fame initiated another campaign to subdue belligerent Native American forces in territories of Indiana, Illinois, and Michigan (Eisenhower, 2008). Elected president in 1841, William Henry Harrison, would serve only thirty-one days.

Meanwhile, summer 1812 saw General Stephen Van Rensselaer commissioned to lead the Western New York war strategy and start a navy yard. Like Dr. Chapin, Van Rensselaer was among the few Federalists who supported the war early on. He was a wealthy, Harvard-educated, upstate landlord, having inherited thousands of acres worked by hundreds of tenant farmers in eastern New York State. Van Rensselaer possessed gracious manners and popularity derived from his reluctance to press his tenants to pay their rent when times were hard. He had been a New York legislator and served as the lieutenant governor under Governor John Jay. Statewide, Van Rensselaer was an early advocate for building a canal across New York and had been the Federalist candidate for governor in 1801. Joseph Ellicott disdained Van Rensselaer's lack of battle experience, but in the traditions of the New York militia, he had served as a financially supportive volunteer officer since 1786 (Strum, 1980; Taylor, 2010).

~

In early October 1812, Van Rensselaer learned that two British warships, the *Detroit* and the *Caledonia*, had dropped anchor off Fort Erie. The *Caledonia* had been a United States navy boat, then named the *Adams,* that the British captured as part of Hull's Detroit surrender. The British navy refitted the boat, and it now was loaded with valuable furs in transit to Montreal's North West Fur Company. On October 8, 1812, Van Rensselaer ordered then Lieutenant Winfield Scott, with a force of 124 men, to leave Black Rock at midnight in three boats. Dr. Cyrenius Chapin had just been promoted to a captain's rank and was given command of the smallest boat in Winfield's flotilla, a rowboat carrying six men. While Fort Erie and its guns slept, the Winfield's little navy quietly crossed the river, and by 3:00 in the morning, both British ships were seized and their crews taken prisoner (H. P. Smith, 1884; White, 1898). The heavier *Detroit* was scuttled off Black

Rock on the shore of Squaw Island. The lighter *Caledonia* made it to Black Rock, where her cargo of furs was sold for $200,000.

As dawn broke, the mortified British command responded to the raid with a daylong cannon barrage striking homes and buildings in Black Rock, Buffalo, and Fort Niagara. Under cover of this cannon barrage, Dr. Chapin and his men returned to the *Detroit* and removed a canon for use by his Buffalo militia unit. It was the first of many daring, and unauthorized, exploits by Chapin's *Forty Thieves* (Ketchum, 1865). Chapin's efforts were dismissed by Van Rensselaer as foolhardy, but Chapin's heroism attracted the attention of New York Governor Tomkins, who soon promoted Chapin to lieutenant-colonel (G. F. Pratt, 1869).

Five days later, on October 13, 1812, Van Rensselaer ordered the start of the first major American offensive, later known as the Battle of Queenston. Under the cover of darkness, 1,000 American troops (regulars and state militia) crossed the Niagara River from Lewiston onto the Canadian shore near the village of Queenston. There, they ascended a steep hill to occupy the bluff overlooking Queenston. Plans had called for a combined force of 2,500 US Army troops and New York militia, but only 13 small boats had been readied for the invasion. Even worse, the oars for all thirteen boats had been stored in the first boat to cross, a situation not immediately obvious to the men in the first boat. In the chaos, several of the boats were lost to the stiff Niagara current, further slowing the shuttling of troops into Canada. Confusion ignited fear, which overtook many of the troops still on the New York side. As a result, nearly 1,200 men refused to continue the invasion (C. K. Adams & Trent, 1909; Glenn, 2013).

Despite the confusion, the first wave of American invaders continued to push gallantly up the Queenston hill, gaining control of the Queenston Heights plateau. The advancing Americans then pursued the few defending British troops to the very edge of the village of Queenston. British General Sir Isaac Brock, now stationed at Fort George seven miles downriver, immediately hurried reinforcements to Queenston. By a quirk of fate, one British regiment was led by Captain Thomas Manners, the son-in-law of famed American patriot Dr. Benjamin Rush (Fried, 2018).

The American invasion force was still struggling to cross the Niagara River when Brock's forces reinforced the village defense. Through much of the morning, each army exchanged temporary advantage. But with only a few reinforcements reaching the lead force, the Americans tired and the superior numbers of British regulars prevailed. In all, 900 Americans were taken prisoner, and another 190 were killed or wounded. Among the British, approximately 130 were killed or wounded. The Battle of Queenston Heights proved a disastrous performance for the mismatched, hodgepodge American troops. The goal had been achievable, but profound incompetence in planning, staging, and implementation was unmasked. And Colonel Stephen Van Rensselaer was wounded (Glenn, 2013).

As the war stalled and winter 1812 to 1813 approached, the shortage of food and supplies that the British forces and American forces confronted became critical. Maintaining discipline is difficult among hungry troops and hired mercenaries in any army, and nearly impossible if rations must be cut to feed prisoners. Soon, the British army freed all American prisoners who were enlisted as volunteer militia and sent the regular army American soldiers to Quebec for long-term imprisonment (Greenhous, 1970).

As the militia returned to their homes, they faced hunger and the raging Buffalo Fever. As many as 10 percent of victims died from this influenza-like illness, while many others faced long bouts of dysentery. To make matters worse, an outbreak of measles soon followed. Dr. Chapin called a meeting of local physicians to organize a response to the contagion, but their interventions did little good. It would be the end of January 1813 before the illness abated (Glenn, 2013).

Coming on the heels of Hull's surrender at Detroit, the defeat at Queenston further dampened morale as the soldiers set about enduring the cold winter months. The injured Colonel Van Rensselaer resigned his command three days after the Queenston battle. It would take four weeks of rest at Buffalo's Landon Hotel until he could return to his Albany home (Assembly, 1812).

The still-zealous Dr. Chapin gathered his militia to present a gunner's salute in honor of Stephen Van Rensselaer at his departure. Chapin also selected a name for his unit, the *Independent Buffalo Matross*. Matross is a Dutch word for a sailor of low rank, but it may also be used to identify soldiers assigned to artillery. Its selection by Dr. Chapin is unexplained, and it made little difference. Chapin's preferred monicker never supplanted everyone else's favorite, Chapin's *Forty Thieves* (Taylor, 2010).

Chapter 12

The Realities of Making War

Decision-Making and Making Sense Require Different Skills

General Alexander Smyth replaced the wounded Stephan Van Rensselaer as the commander of American forces on the Niagara Frontier. Smyth had a reputation for elevating disagreements into treasonous offenses and castigating anyone who disagreed with him. Ominously prophetic, Smyth had been the officer of the regiment that refused to follow as Van Rensselaer's vanguard crossed the river to Queenston. Not inclined to take responsibility for failure, Smyth shifted all blame for the failed Queenston invasion onto Peter Porter. According to Smyth, it was impossible for his troops to cross the river that day because military quartermaster Porter failed to provide adequate supplies (Graves, 2024).

Smyth so riled up the animosity between his regular army troops and local militia after the Queenston debacle that a group of fifty regular soldiers under his command looted and burned the Pomeroy Tavern in Buffalo. The tavern was a popular gathering site for local militia supporters of Porter and Chapin. Though he had been warned about the raid, Smyth did nothing to discourage his soldiers from their foray (Ketchum, 1854; White, 1898).

A month later, in November 1812, Smyth's regular army and militia forces stood at 4,000 men and he announced plans for a repeat invasion of Canada. This time, the American forces would cross the river near Fort Erie where troops could land on terrain much gentler than Queenston. Smyth wanted an overwhelming force and made several very public appeals for more volunteers from Buffalo. Proud of his "infallible" invasion plans, Smyth provided detailed descriptions of his plan in several public speeches.

Of course, British ears populating his audiences relayed the details of the invasion to the British army.

At 3:00 a.m. on November 27, 1812, the first American soldiers landed on the Canadian shore. Though they immediately met resistance, one band of Americans captured several British artilleries. As with Queenston, Smyth was almost immediately overcome by indecision. Despite having an overwhelming force compared to the 500 British soldiers defending Fort Erie, he dithered. First, he held half his force back on the American shore. Then, he suddenly postponed the invasion and, in the process, abandoned sixty of his bravest men on the Canadian shore.

Smyth procrastinated for four days, allowing time for the British to realign their forces. Finally, on the morning of December 1, 1812, Smyth ordered his men to reenter boats for a second attempt. Porter and Chapin were there with their militias, ready to follow Smyth's orders. But before any soldier could set a paddle in the water, Smyth ordered another withdrawal, suddenly deciding against any further invasion of Canada for the winter season (White, 1898).

Both the assembled troops and the public were disgusted (C. Johnson, 1876). Dr. Chapin and Peter Porter openly accused Smyth of cowardice. Newspapers reprinted angry statements made by many of the assembled soldiers (H. P. Smith, 1884). Smyth admitted to vacillating, but again he blamed every unfavorable conclusion on the inability of Peter Porter to guarantee adequate provisions.

Peter Porter published a notice formally charging Smyth with cowardice in the December 8 *Buffalo Gazette*. Smyth responded with a challenge for a duel. On the afternoon of December 14, 1812, the two men, with their seconds, faced each other on Grand Island. One shot was fired by each, with neither bullet meeting its mark. The duelists then agreed to withdraw all previous uncomplimentary statements (H. P. Smith, 1884). Dr. Chapin followed their apologies with his own accusatory statement. Published in the *Buffalo Gazette*, Dr. Chapin leveled all culpability for the failed invasions on the cowardice of Smyth and denounced him as entirely unfit to lead brave American soldiers into battle. This time, Smyth resigned his commission and scampered off to his home in Virginia (Graves, 2024).

∼

Despite efforts by Peter's brother and shipping partner, Augustus Porter, the supply problems were real and persistent. Troy, New York, was designated as the major transit point for food and munitions for American military on the Canadian front. However, with the British patrolling Lake Ontario, all attempts to use lake transport resulted in British capture and diversion of supplies to the Crown's army. The overland route from Troy to Buffalo was arduous and slow.

To assure accountability and hence quality, Porter and the United States Army in Troy required suppliers to label their produce with the supplier's name and content. One supplier was a beef packer named Samuel Wilson. Wilson's barrels were marked with his name and the initials U.S. Before long, teamsters and soldiers alike referred to Sam Wilson's barrels as supplies from "Uncle Sam" (Matthews, 1909).

By winter of 1812, the need for a Great Lakes navy finally caught the attention of Washington. Plans were initiated to build war boats at three American naval bases: Sackets Harbor at the eastern end of Lake Ontario, and Black Rock and Erie, Pennsylvania, for operations on Lake Erie.

~

In November 1812, James Madison was reelected president over the New York Federalist De Witt Clinton. Once elected to his second term, Madison sought to improve his administration's management of the war by appointing John Armstrong as the secretary of war. Armstrong knew the Great Lakes, having resided in both New York and Pennsylvania. American forces led by William Henry Harrison gained control of Lake Erie's southern shoreline and Andrew Jackson was given command of regiments in the southern United States (Cozzens, 2024). In March 1813, Commodore Oliver Hazard Perry (1785–1819) was appointed to organize the Great Lakes naval efforts.

Somehow, despite the ongoing war, Buffalo became incorporated as a village on April 2, 1813. Cyrenius Chapin joined with Eli Hart, Zenas W. Barker, Ebenezer Walden, and Oliver Forward to form the first board of trustees, each elected to one-year terms. Their priority list included: a survey to clarify village boundaries, writing policies for licensing inns and taverns, and constructing new streets. The village board also claimed authority over all land under the water at the eastern end of Lake Erie and Buffalo Creek, granting itself the power to commission building wharves and piers to support Great Lakes shipping. Buffalo officially remained a village until it was incorporated as a city in 1832 (H. P. Smith, 1884).

Dr. Chapin was still practicing medicine, but ever eager to take action, he now added to his obligations as a New York militia lieutenant-colonel and village trustee by officially accepting the position of interim sheriff for the Buffalo village. He held the title for most of the spring in 1813 (C. Johnson, 1876).

∽

Through the early spring of 1813, both armies remained underfunded and undermanned, leaving battle action to haphazard mutual harassment. In April, Dr. Chapin's partner, Dr. Josiah Trowbridge, went out for an afternoon of duck hunting on a marshy spit of land in the Niagara River called Strawberry Island. He was accompanied by Lieutenant Dudley, an officer from Commodore Perry's fleet. Gunshots from their duck blind drew British attention, and both men were taken prisoner. Though Dr. Trowbridge was soon released, the episode further cemented Dr. Chapin's antipathy of all things related to the British Crown (Trowbridge, 1869).

∽

Later, in April 1813, Commadore Perry sent Captain Isaac Chauncy and fourteen American warships carrying 1,700 soldiers from Sackets Harbor, New York, onto a stormy Lake Ontario. Their target was the village of York, the provincial capital of Upper Canada, where the British were building warships. (The village of York would be renamed Toronto in 1834.) American troops fought well and, within five days, took control of the village. During the battle, American soldiers set fire to the parliament buildings and destroyed much of the garrison. Chauncy accepted York's surrender in exchange for guaranteeing the Americans would not loot or destroy private property. He also agreed to parole the Canadian militia who had attempted to defend the village (Auchinleck, 1972).

The occupation of York temporarily disrupted British supply routes, but the Americans stayed less than a month. In May 1813, York was returned to British control as Chauncy's troops were ordered to join an American attack on Fort George. The American commander for northeast operations, Major General Henry Dearborn (1751–1829), had assembled 4,500 troops at Fort Niagara to invade Canada and seize Fort George along with the neighboring village of Newark. At the time, the British had only 1,000 regulars, 300 militia, and 100 Indians defending Fort George (Taylor, 2010).

Outgunned and outnumbered, the British destroyed large quantities of weapons and ammunition stored in Fort George and fled. British General

John Vincent retreated to Burlington Heights (today's Hamilton, Ontario), sixty miles to the west, leaving much of the Canadian Niagara River shoreline in full possession of the Americans (White, 1898). According to the *Buffalo Gazette*, "Dr. C. Chapin was in the vanguard." Chapin's militia was described as "showing up where they were least expected, always ready, and effective whenever engaged in their unique style of hit and run warfare."

Over the next few months, American troops, including Dr. Chapin's *Forty Thieves*, burned Canadian government buildings and plundered anything they deemed official Canadian property (Glenn, 2013). The only resistance they encountered came from Indian mercenaries under British employ who were assigned to lie in wait in the woods around Fort George. With only a few war whoops and musket shots, the warriors could panic conventional American platoons into a quick return to the safety of the American-occupied Fort George. The *Forty Thieves* countered by adopting a similar strategy, hiding behind trees and ambushing the ambushers.

Soldiers in both armies found plundering essential, as supply problems remained paramount. Raiding and looting of Canadian citizens was necessary to sustain the American occupation of Fort George as the Niagara Peninsula turned into a no-man's-land, stripped of food and materiel. Any perceived act by a Canadian citizen that might appear disloyal to whichever army was close by made for a ready excuse to plunder, and any animal, wild or domestic, found wandering about became fair game. One Canadian farmer reported, "They killed about 50 or 60 of my hogs, 3 heifers, dug all the potatoes, took a great deal of my meat and 5 or 6 tons of hay." But he was unsure which army was responsible (Taylor, 2010).

For the Americans, Chapin's *Forty Thieves* were unquestionably successful at procuring food and supplies for the troops stationed at Fort George. Fifty-five-year-old James Wilkinson (1757–1825), now the commanding officer in charge of America's occupation of Fort George, applauded "the patriotism and enterprise of Major Chapin" and declared that "all [the] enemy's property should be good prize for any of our citizens who may take it." Wilkinson, himself suspected of foul play, chose to discount any criticism of Chapin's methods (Taylor, 1866; White, 1898).

Chapter 13

Forty Thieves at War

In War, All Rules Are Imperfect and Often Disregarded

As spring became summer in 1813, Major-General Wilkinson's support emboldened Dr. Cyrenius Chapin and his militia as his disdain for British forces grew. Chapin's *Forty Thieves* lived up to their nickname with procurement methods that became notorious throughout Canada's Niagara peninsula (White, 1898). Now forty-four years old, Dr. Chapin was in his element. Chapin alleged that he only confiscated property that was public or held by British supporters. The latter group included all magistrates, militia officers, or anyone who defended British rule. Looting by his band of *Forty Thieves* grew so rampant that Chapin accumulated enemies and confounded any support the occupying American forces might have enjoyed. Many Canadians leaned apolitical but began viewing Chapin as a brigand (Cruikshank, 1912; James, 1818; Thompson, 1897).

One British officer, the thirty-two-year-old Lieutenant James FitzGibbon (1780–1863), was determined to stop Chapin's raiding parties and, in the process, secure his own reputation. Lieutenant FitzGibbon was an Irishman who lacked the wealth and social connections usually associated with military officers. But he was endowed with ambition that equaled that of Dr. Chapin. After beginning his career fighting Napolean, FitzGibbon was transferred to Upper Canada, where he was assigned to training Native American mercenaries. In so doing, he had become a specialist in nonconventional warfare (McKenzie, 1971).

FitzGibbon moved his unit of fifty regular soldiers to within sixteen miles of Fort George, taking possession of a house at Beaver Dams owned by John DeCou. DeCou's home would serve as the base for FitzGibbon's own brand of scouting and guerilla actions (McKenzie, 1971). FitzGibbon's regulars were mostly Irishmen who dressed in distinctive green uniforms and shared their commanding officer's desire to prove their worth to the British army. They were reinforced with several hundred Algonquin warriors. The Algonquins were deployed to intercept American patrols and foragers like Dr. Chapin, earning themselves the nickname "Bloody Boys." Their success stifled much of the free rein Chapin's *Forty Thieves* had enjoyed (Barbuto, 2014; Berton, 1981).

So it was that in June 1813, Dr. Chapin proposed a plan he felt certain would clear the Niagara peninsula of British supporters. His rationale included a liberation of Canadians the British had jailed under suspicion of supporting independence. Of course, Chapin's real obsession was capturing FitzGibbon and DeCou's farmhouse. He convinced his commander, General Henry Dearborn, that his plan would work. Dearborn, however, was not convinced that Chapin was the man to lead a large military operation.

On the morning of June 24, 1813, Lieutenant-Colonel Charles G. Boerstler, a thirty-five-year-old United States regular from Maryland, was ordered by General Dearborn to lead the attack on Beaver Dams and Dr. Chapin's unit was placed under Boerstler's command. Boerstler was old school. He believed that war should be fought in open fields by advancing troops and considered Chapin's methods of having soldiers hide behind trees to be uncivilized. He viewed Chapin as a self-aggrandizing civilian rabble. The two men despised each other, though Boerstler had to concede that Chapin knew the terrain well. As they marched to Beaver Dams, Boerstler placed Chapin and his *Forty Thieves* in front of the 570 troops, artillerymen, and two cannons assigned to the operation (Berton, 1981).

～

Two days before the planned assault on FitzGibbon, Chapin and several officers had dinner at a tavern near Queenston. The tavern was owned by Laura and James Secord, who, typical of many living on Canada's Niagara Peninsula, had friends on both sides. They knew Dr. Chapin well and Chapin viewed the Secords as friendly to the American cause. Laura Secord had been born in Massachusetts, where her father served as a captain in the Massachusetts militia during the Revolutionary War. Her family moved to the Niagara Peninsula in 1793 when her father received a Canadian land grant for a farm outside of Queenston. Her husband, James Secord, was a second-generation Canadian of French Huguenot descent. Politics had not been a major interest of the Secords; that is, until the October 1812 Battle of Queenston. James had been a soldier in the Canadian militia when General Stephan Van Rensselaer attacked Queenston. During that battle, not only had American bullets injured James Secord, but American soldiers looted their food stores (Berton, 1981). After the Battle of Queenston, Laura Secord nursed her husband back to health, managed the farm, and discovered an abiding appreciation for the protections promised by the British army.

The evening of Chapin's dinner, thirty-seven-year-old Laura Secord proved a generous hostess. She was attentive to every need of Chapin's guests, pouring wine and refilling dishes. All the while, she carefully absorbed the details of their conversation. By all accounts, it was a pleasant evening loosened by considerable drink and heated by tactical debates about the imminent attack on FitzGibbon.

At 4:30 the next morning, the petite but durable Laura Secord downed a bonnet and began a twenty-mile hike to Beaver Dams. According to legend, she drove a cow part of the way so no one would suspect the true nature of her mission. It was dusk when Laura reached the DeCou farm, but Mrs. Secord had stamina enough to provide FitzGibbon with all she heard the night before. Then, having set the stage for battle, she walked back to her Queenston farm (McKenzie, 1971).

Laura Secord lived a long life, but she never discussed her role in the battle and never confirmed that it was her friend, Dr. Chapin, who had divulged the American plans. Nonetheless, her efforts likely altered the outcome of what became known as the Battle at Beaver Dam (McKenzie, 1971). It is possible that Dr. Chapin's scouts got their numbers wrong, or perhaps Laura Secord's warning brought 500 more Algonquins to join FitzGibbon at Beaver Dam (Thompson, 1897).

～

As the lead regiment approaching Beaver Dams, Dr. Chapin's scouts observed several of FitzGibbon's warriors sprinting across an open field to take up positions for an ambush. Chapin and his men gave chase, initially causing those lying in ambush to retreat. He then rushed to inform Boerstler of the encounter, but Boerstler dismissed Chapin as a coward. For Boerstler, Chapin's warning became an excuse to send the *Forty Thieves* to the rear, a demotion that would assure that the glory of the expected victory would be all Boerstler's.

The American troops continued their advance. Two miles short of DeCou's farm, precisely as Dr. Chapin had warned, Native American warriors sprang from trees in a sudden assault. Boerstler ordered his regulars to charge into the trees with bayonets drawn, but the warriors came from all directions, dodging from tree to tree, reloading their muskets under cover and resuming their assault. For three hours, fierce combat continued on a blistering-hot June day. Thirty Americans lay dead with only five Indians killed when FitzGibbon sent a white flag to Boerstler demanding he surrender or face a general massacre by the Indians. FitzGibbon's message claimed that, should any more of their braves be murdered, the Indians could not be restrained. He also reported that another 700 fresh British regulars would soon join the battle.

The claim of impending reinforcements was a bluff, but Boerstler capitulated. He allowed FitzGibbon and his Algonquin braves to take 462 men prisoner, including Dr. Chapin and his men. The Americans were immediately removed of boots, swords, and uniforms, while the Algonquins removed scalps from the American dead (McKenzie, 1971).

~

The terms negotiated between Boerstler and FitzGibbon stipulated that the American officers would be paroled. However, when FitzGibbon realized that his nemesis, Cyrenius Chapin, was among the captives, he reneged. By late afternoon, Chapin and his men were loaded on two large rowboats for transport along Lake Ontario to the British prisoner-of-war camp in Kingston, Ontario. What followed is best described in one of the few surviving documents written by Dr. Chapin himself (C. Chapin, 1836). Chapin's version of the battle is corroborated by several participants in the battle at Beaver Dams and was published in an 1836 pamphlet titled *Chapin's Review of Armstrong's Notices of the War of 1812.*

Chapin states he was placed in one rowboat and Captain Sackrider, his second in command, was placed in another boat for the Lake Ontario passage to Kingston. Sixteen British soldiers were assigned to guard twenty-eight captives in the two boats. A greater portion of men were in Sackrider's boat, and the rowing of both boats was delegated to the American captives (C. Chapin, 1836).

Once out on the open waters of Lake Ontario, Chapin distracted the British guards by telling lewd and boisterous stories. Curious about the laughter in the other boat, guards in Sackrider's boat ordered their boat maneuver alongside the first. Suddenly, Chapin shouted an order to seize upon the British guards. The British guard closest to Chapin knocked the doctor to the bottom of the boat, threatening to kill him with the point of his bayonet. But chaos had its effect, and the British guards were quickly overpowered. Chapin's prisoner revolt started at 4:30 p.m. and by 2:30 a.m., he, his two captured boats, twenty-eight soldiers, and sixteen British prisoners arrived at Fort Niagara. By early morning they were on their way to Fort George (C. Chapin, 1836; J. L. Thomson, 1818).

~

The capture of Boerstler's command and the debacle at Beaver Dam eroded confidence in General Dearborn's leadership in the regular army. At age sixty-two, Dearborn had served in George Washington's army and invaded Quebec under Benedict Arnold. He had been the secretary of war under Jefferson and now, in 1813, had been pressed into service as the commanding officer of the army for the northeast sector from Lake Erie to New England. But with age, Dearborn had become grossly overweight, slow, and insecure. He was unpopular with the Federalists and seemed to have no strategy to stop repeated British raids on New York villages for food and valuable supplies. A month after the Beaver Dams failure, another embarrassing skirmish near Fort George resulted in the capture of ten American soldiers. Most exasperating was the inaction in July 1813 as the mostly idle American troops suffered from mosquitos, dysentery and northern malaria more than battle (Elting, 1991).

It was time for a change. General Dearborn was recalled to Washington in July 1813 and the man in charge of America's occupation of Fort George, James Wilkinson, received a promotion to major-general, replacing Dearborn. Wilkinson immediately accepted Peter Porter's newly negotiated deal with Western New York's Senecas and secured a commitment for 400 warriors (White, 1898). Within a few days, the reorganization paid off.

~

Late in July 1813, the British took action. Well before sunrise, the sound of gunfire woke Peter Porter as British/Canadian troops came ashore at Black Rock. Quartermaster-General Porter rushed to Buffalo, alerted the regular army, and gathered 300 local militia supported by Seneca Chief Farmer's Brother and his newly allied warriors. Chief Farmer's Brother was well known and respected by Native Americans and Buffalonians alike. Before noon, Porter led his army back to Black Rock and engaged the raiding British in a firefight. The British troops quickly returned to their boats and crossed back to the Canadian shore, but only after setting fire to military buildings and several homes. They had what they were after: several barrels of United States Army whiskey, flour, salt, and pork. A few days later, on August 3, General Peter Porter retaliated by leading 400 men, half of whom were Senecas, across the Niagara in a predawn raid of Fort Erie. The Americans seized seventy horses and cattle and took twenty prisoners. Contrary to Porter's orders, a few renegade soldiers plundered private homes, hauling off furniture and clothing (White, 1898).

After the Beaver Dams humiliation, Dr. Chapin spent most of August 1813 in Fort George, where accounts describe him as "very impatient to engage the enemy." At least once, on August 17, he was given orders to venture out of Fort George into the Canadian countryside with about 300 volunteers, including militia, Indians, and 200 regular soldiers. Heavy rain snarled the operation, but British troops were engaged and sixteen prisoners were taken. Frustrated by lack of follow-up, on September 7, Chapin, his volunteers, and most of the Senecas returned to Buffalo.

∼

As autumn 1813 approached, war on the Niagara Frontier entered its most destructive phase. Oliver Hazard Perry's efforts to build ships and recruit a navy bore resulted when, on September 10, his sailors defeated a British flotilla at the Thames River near Detroit. Flying the flag "Don't Give Up the Ship," Perry's squadron comprised nine vessels carrying fifteen long cannons. They were up against fewer boats, but the British ships were heavily armed with thirty-five cannons. Perry's strategy proved one of the most remarkable in naval warfare. Perry exposed his flagship, the *Lawrence*, to a storm of shots, soon rendering her a battered hulk. Of the 103 officers and crew, 22 died and 61 were wounded. The situation seemed critical as Perry was rowed to the American ship *Niagara* in an open dinghy amid a shower of bullets. Taking command of his second ship, Perry sailed the *Niagara* and his seven other remaining vessels straight into the British fleet, engaging the British in close quarters. By 3:00, the British vessels had been boarded, and they soon surrendered. On the back of an old letter, Perry wrote a brief note to his commanding officer, General William Henry Harrison, stating, "We have met the enemy and they are ours" (White, 1898).

Lake Erie was now controlled by the American Fleet. However, Tecumseh, who had encouraged British General Proctor to hold and defend the Michigan territory gained in their earlier victory over Hull, resumed his nettlesome skirmishes at the western end of Lake Erie. After one successful raid, a group of his warriors began executing their American prisoners.

Tecumseh scolded his warriors and stopped the slaughter, then formally rebuked British General Procter for failing to protect the prisoners (Sugden, 1985). It was the move that secured the legend of Tecumseh.

As battle lines shifted, Proctor chose a position along the Thames River to make a stand against an attacking American land force under the command of William Henry Harrison. Hesitant to expose his own regular army, Proctor placed Tecumseh and his braves in position to withstand the full onslaught of Harrison's army. Outnumbered three to one, Tecumseh was killed on October 5, 1813. His warriors fell to defeat, and Harrison added another decisive victory to his growing reputation (Sugden, 1985).

As winter 1813 approached, American optimism was excited. Over several days, the *Buffalo Gazette* reported on a grand celebration held in honor of Commodore Perry's victories on the Great Lakes. It was capped by a multi-gun salute arranged by Dr. Chapin and his militia. Chapin then led a large procession of musicians through the streets. Later, William Henry Harrison also visited Buffalo and Chapin organized another parade and dinner reception at the newly refurbished Eagle Tavern, this time for both Commodore Perry and General Harrison (White, 1898).

∾

Figure 13.1. Drawing of the Eagle Tavern, 1812. *Source:* Devoy, 1896.

As early winter snows fell across the Great Lakes, both Lake Erie and Lake Ontario were under American control, making it easier for Harrison's troops to protect the farms along the American shore from Buffalo to Detroit. Good weather in 1813 had produced an abundant farm harvest, and American patriotism peaked. Dr. Chapin, fueled by his hatred of the British, remained confident that democracy and the American experiment could succeed against a powerful foe.

Paradoxically, news of Perry's success and persistent supply problems convinced General Wilkinson to withdraw most of his regular army American troops from Fort George. Satisfied that the Niagara Peninsula was substantially cleared of the enemy, Wilkinson convinced his superiors that it was time to redirect his troops.[1]

Wilkinson's withdrawal infuriated Dr. Chapin, who, in October 1813, independently gathered a mixed group of volunteers to search the Niagara Peninsula and rouse remaining British posts near Fort George. Chapin's excursion paid a heavy price to prove that the British were lurking. Within days, three of Chapin's men were killed and eighteen British soldiers died in several skirmishes within a few miles of the fort (White, 1898).

But, based on Wilkinson's reassurances, the war office in Washington had made their decision. The US Army was to shift its full attention on attacking the British along the St. Lawrence River and march on to Montreal and Quebec. Like before, poor planning, inconsistent leadership, and winter weather would mount unexpected barriers.

---

1. Sixty-five years later, James Wilkinson would be found to have been a double agent and a traitor throughout much of his career (Broadwater, 2012).

Chapter 14

Civilians, Fodder, and War

The Damage We See Is Not Always the Damage That Kills

In October 1813, all war calculations changed. Britain's defeat of Napoleon at the Battle of Leipzig forced President Madison and Secretary of War John Armstrong to consider the likelihood that King George would soon shift his trained armies and powerful navy to the war with the United States. If seizing Canada was the linchpin in winning, the United States had to act quickly and decisively. Full-scale invasion of Canada was one method, but gaining control of the St. Lawrence River would mean dominating all of Canada. Major General James Wilkinson's knowledge of the battlefront at Fort George and his reputation as a general, though clouded, easily overcame any reservations held by the politicians. Only years later would Wilkinson's motives be questioned.

∾

By December 1813, back at Fort George, Brigadier-General George McClure (1771–1851) of the New York State militia was named to replace Major-General Wilkinson as commander of the few remaining American forces. McClure was a politician whose background included carpentry, milling, land speculation, and self-promotion. Most of the regular army left for Sackett's Harbor and eastern Lake Ontario with Major-General Wilkinson to join the campaign down the Saint Lawrence River to capture Quebec and Montreal. It was mostly militia left at Fort George, and many were nearing the end of their term of service

Figure 14.1. War of 1812 battles along the Niagara River. *Source:* Adams & Trent, 1909. Public domain.

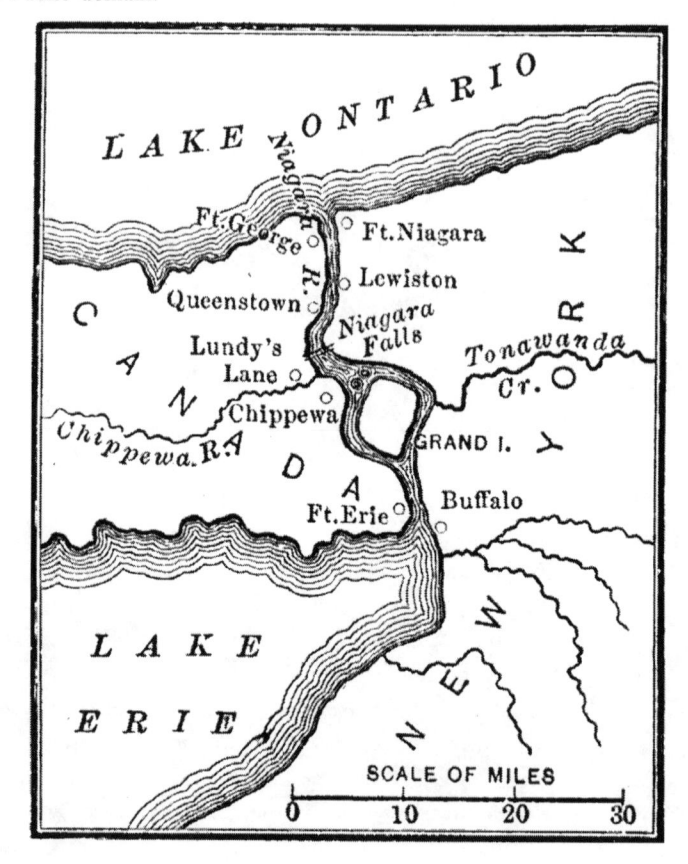

and eager to return home for winter. In a letter cosigned by Peter Porter and Dr. Chapin, General McClure requested that General Wilkinson reinforce Fort George with regular troops, but his request was denied and Wilkinson recommended the fort be abandoned. McClure concurred and requested authorization from Secretary of War Armstrong to destroy Fort George and vacate the Canadian shore. McClure also advised that the adjacent town of Newark be burned to thwart any potential that its residents could offer refuge for British troops (Ketchum, 1854; White, 1898).

On December 10, 1813, McClure ordered a group of Canadian defectors under his command to commence burning Newark. They knocked on doors, giving residents one hour's notice before torching eighty houses and sending mostly women, children, and the aged into a Niagara Frontier winter.

Incensed by the needless destruction and threat to civilian life, Dr. Chapin made a last-ditch appeal to prevent Newark's burning. Finding General McClure at a store owned by Joseph McCarthy on Queen Street in the village, he openly confronted McClure, his superior officer. Egos and tempers at a flash point, Chapin and McClure engaged in a passionate argument easily heard above the chaos. Chapin stood fast to his belief that it was enough to destroy the barrack buildings at Fort George and the 1,500 tents that lie in storage. In a thundering tirade, he called McClure callous and spiteful. Burning Newark, he said, would accomplish nothing short of satisfying a wish to visit undeserved misery on noncombatants. McClure's return volley accused Chapin of being an unpatriotic partisan who typified Federalists from the uncivilized backwoods of New York (Berton, 1981). Holding the upper hand, McClure charged Chapin with mutiny, ordered him arrested for treason, and had him escorted to jail at gunpoint. McClure's report on the incident reads: "There is not a greater rascal [who] exists than Chapin, and he is supported by a pack of Tories and enemies to our government" (Ketchum, 1865). Within hours, a few of Chapin's supporters confronted the jail's guards, liberating him without a fight.

This was not the first quarrel between Dr. Chapin and McClure. The two men had rekindled a disagreement Chapin started before Wilkinson's departure. Chapin disagreed with abandoning Fort George and felt he had proven that British forces were still a threat on the Niagara Peninsula. Only days before their argument, he had again defied orders and ventured into the countryside where his men soon encountered the enemy hiding in the thickets. At the time, McClure refused to send troops to support Chapin's rangers and told his officers that he hoped the British would capture Chapin.

The morning after Newark was destroyed, Chapin resigned his militia appointment. In part, his letter read: "The ill-fated town of Newark was burnt, under his [McClure's] orders, the night of the 10th of December, 1813. Here was exhibited a scene of distress which language would be inadequate to describe. Women and children were turned out of doors in a cold and stormy night; the cries of infants, the decrepitude of age, and the debility of sickness, had no impression upon this monster in human shape; they were consigned to that house whose canopy was the heavens, and whose walls were as boundless as the wide world" (Ketchum, 1865).

The *Buffalo Gazette* sided with Chapin and excoriated McClure for the burning of Newark, sparking a widespread condemnation of McClure's command. Other newspapers, including the *Pittsburgh Gazette*, called McClure's order a "wanton and abominable act" (Berton, 1981).

Angry over the humiliation he encountered, McClure ordered his entire army, totaling 2,000 militia and a few regular soldiers, to retreat 30 miles inland to Batavia. Buffalonians protested, and several witnesses signed affidavits claiming McClure's decision to abandon Buffalo centered on his loathing for Dr. Chapin. A fuming McClure responded by declaring that if the citizens of Buffalo would arrest "that damned rascal Chapin [he would] keep his troops in Buffalo and defend the city." Several militia volunteers refused McClure's orders to join the move to Batavia, preferring to defend Black Rock and Buffalo from British attack under Chapin's command. McClure denounced Chapin for fomenting disorder and desertion and again ordered Chapin arrested on charges of treason and mutiny. As before, men of the Buffalo militia freed Chapin from jail (Taylor, 2010). To the satisfaction of everyone, when McClure reached Batavia, he surrendered his command to Major General Amos Hall.

～

Meanwhile, despite having reassigned thousands of troops to the St. Lawrence River campaign, American efforts to control the gateway to Upper Canada faltered within weeks. Control of the St. Lawrence would have secured the northeastern border of New York State and New England by safeguarding Lake Champlain and its outlet, the Richelieu River, where it empties into the St. Lawrence River between Montreal and Quebec. It was a major commercial route and had proved an important military route through three wars. Upon his reassignment to Sackets Harbor on the eastern end of Lake Ontario, Major-General Wilkinson assembled an army of 7,000 men. But before they could encounter the British, the Americans confronted bitter winter winds and rough seas that thrashed boats, supplies, munitions, and men. Like many of his troops, Wilkinson became seriously ill with dysentery and was forced to relinquish command to his subordinates. Resulting delays advantaged the British, who reassigned their own army of regulars to defend a position at the first set of rapids constricting the St. Lawrence flow. The American forces were repelled. Major General George Izard replaced Wilkinson, but he could not dislodge the defending British army.

Once again, the three-pronged American war strategy to conquer Canada was faltering just as the shortest days of winter were bringing increasing cold in 1813. And though Napoleon would not abdicate until April 1814, his defeat at Leipzig was about to release the British navy to tighten its blockade of United States seaports on the Atlantic.

$\sim$

The torching of Newark had a stinging effect on British and Canadian troops on the Niagara Frontier. Already short of winter supplies, now they were desperate to feed themselves and Newark's refugees. On December 18, 1813, British/Canadian troops crossed the Niagara River and seized Fort Niagara. It was not much of a battle, as only a few militiamen remained at the fort and most of them deserted as the British force approached. British bayonets quickly eliminated the few soldiers who remained. The British removed 27 cannons, 3,000 stands of arms, and massive quantities of ammunition and provisions to their barracks in Canada. The stolen supplies comprised nearly all the American military stores along the Niagara River and postponed starvation of the British troops and their dependents (Taylor, 2010).

The British returned to Canada as suddenly as they had arrived, but before leaving, they and their Native American mercenaries burned every house in the nearby village of Lewiston. After a few Tuscarora men saved one family in the village, a nearby Tuscarora village was also burned. When American troops returned to the fort, they found mutilated bodies, many torn open, hearts removed, and decapitated. Some were scalped. Newspapers describing the barbarism claimed the British were paying Indian mercenaries to heighten the alarm (White, 1898).

The meager response to the British raid on Fort Niagara confirmed what British spies had reported: McClure's withdrawal had left the area undefended. Within days, Canadian spies told American authorities that a major collection of British troops was staging for an invasion of western New York. By Christmas, General Hall, still in Batavia, made contact with Dr. Chapin to coordinate several hit-and-run raids on British positions in Canada, hoping to delay or at least confuse the British while acquiring more detailed intelligence. General Hall also hoped that Chapin's action would buy a few days to prepare the 2,000 troops McClure had marched to Batavia for their march back to Buffalo. Losing supplies from Fort Niagara added to General Hall's predicament.

Loose lips and spies on both sides of the Niagara River realized the obvious: a British invasion was probable. Near midnight on December 29, 1813, nineteen days after the burning of Newark, British soldiers with their Indian mercenaries, under the command of British General Phineas Riall

(1775–1850), landed a detachment near Fort Niagara. The sparse American military crew who had returned to Fort Niagara after the previous British raid was actually a hurried assemblage of independently lead militia units responsible to General Hall. They decided that repelling the invasion was impossible, and once again Fort Niagara was abandoned to the British. Upon learning of their retreat, Dr. Chapin dashed into the deserters' makeshift encampment with his mounted militia. One American soldier from Fort Niagara described Chapin's arrival that night: "The irascible doctor furiously damned the two colonels and their men for not having driven away the British, and delivered General Hall's order that they should immediately make an attack." But the British had already begun their destructive march south along the Niagara River to Black Rock and Buffalo. They were burning everything in their path and were being reinforced by more British/Canadian troops crossing the Niagara River along the way (H. P. Smith, 1884).

Residents of towns along the New York side of the Niagara River fled eastward to Batavia and Williamsville and southward to Hamburg and Aurora, while Dr. Chapin's small militia harassed the advancing British troops in a series of hit-and-run attacks. Near Lewiston, his paramilitary encountered the Reverend Elkanah Holmes and his wife. The attack on their home had been so sudden that the Holmes family fled without any of their belongings. One soldier agreed to accept a one-dollar fee to retrieve a trunk the family had packed, but the reverend had no money. A frustrated Reverend Holmes spiked his cane on the ground, hitting something hard that, with a little digging, revealed a silver dollar. Considering the discovery an act of Providence, the reverend promptly gave it to the volunteer. Chapin sent the Holmes family to Buffalo in hopes they could join in with the caravan of fleeing families. Reverend Holmes and his family survived. Over the years, the reverend delivered many apocryphal sermons based on versions of the story and God's deliverance (Letchworth, 1874).

With a shrinking group of men, Dr. Chapin continued his cut-and-run strikes on the marauding British forces, but he accomplished little. When he encountered fresh British reinforcements who had just landed at Scajaquada Creek, Chapin's men were showered by a crushing volley of musketry. Mostly untrained and inexperienced, Chapin's makeshift force withered under the attack. Musket shots seemed to arise from everywhere in the nighttime darkness, and Chapin's militia broke ranks. Mounted soldiers galloped through men on foot, creating even more chaos as the militia scattered into the woods. Most retreated toward Buffalo to look after their families (Hill, 1923).

British General Riall continued his march toward Buffalo as reinforcements continued to join his men at several points along the New York shore. Riall's attack now included 50 Canadian militiamen, 400 Indians, and 1,000 British regulars. They burned six villages and every home they encountered along the way, paying little heed to Chapin's assaults or those of other impromptu groups of defenders. The British regulars marched in formation along the portage route that paralleled the Niagara River while their Algonquin mercenaries cleared their advance, spooking everyone within earshot with war screams. Like a swarm of armed bandits, they laid the whole countryside to waste.

Chapin knew the few men remaining at his side personally. They were farmers fighting to protect their families, and it was apparent that getting their families to safety had replaced all other priorities. With the British regulars approaching the northern limits of the Buffalo village, Chapin gave the order to release all those still fighting (White, 1898).

Chapter 15

Buffalo Burns

All That Man Builds Can Be Destroyed

As the British advanced, a hurried mass of citizens, ox sleds, wagons, carts, women, children, and dogs clogged every path heading south and east from Buffalo. They were interspersed with fleeing militia men supporting their families. Some soldiers were resigned to the inevitability of defeat; others had reached the limit of their courage. The exodus was energized by terror, with families searching desperately for shelter as far as possible from Buffalo and Black Rock (White, 1898).

As he hurried into the Buffalo village, Dr. Chapin passed neighbors who, for nearly a decade, had been his friends and patients. His first stop was the Pratt home. Dr. Chapin's close friend, Captain Samuel Pratt, had died just four months earlier. Anxious and harried himself, Chapin burst into the Pratt home shouting that the Pratt family must leave immediately. More emphatic than pious, Mrs. Pratt later recalled that Chapin's alarm was awash with expletives (Letchworth, 1874).

Dr. Chapin's next harried stop was his own home, where he instructed his wife Sylvia and his three daughters—nineteen-year-old Sylvia, twelve-year-old Amelia, and nine-year-old Louise—to walk to the Chapin farm in Hamburg. It was one of the season's first bitterly cold days and now snow was falling on not-yet-frozen ground, meaning that wagon wheels would soon churn roads into mud. Chapin advised his family to use the footpaths that cut through the Buffalo Creek reservation. He directed his apprentice, Samuel Pratt's thirteen-year-old son Hiram, to serve as escort. Hiram's eleven-year-old sister, Mary, joined the Chapin family as they struck out for Hamburg on foot. They had barely left the village when several fainthearted American soldiers passed them on horseback (Letchworth, 1874). Mrs. Pratt joined other neighbors traveling by wagon and, after several delays, caught up with her son and the Chapins at Smoke's Creek. Sylvia climbed aboard the Pratt wagon, but nothing could induce Hiram or the Chapin girls to accept a ride for fear of overburdening the horses and dooming the wagon wheels to the moiled mud (C. Johnson, 1876).

As they neared the Hamburg farm, now having returned to the roads, the fleeing Chapins passed piles of discarded possessions. The mud and the strain on their animals had pressed families to cast off furniture, kettles, and heirlooms they had so optimistically loaded on their Buffalo wagons. Horses were driven to gallops, and oxen felt the persistent application of the whip to keep pace with the panicked flight (C. Johnson, 1876). The extended Chapin family arrived at the Hamburg farmstead just after dawn, their fourteen-mile hike taking most of the night. It was an amazing feat and proved them as tenacious as their father.

~

Back in Buffalo, one man, Job Hoysington, took a position on the corner of Main and Utica Streets to give his family and neighbors several more precious minutes to flee their homes. Carrying two small children with little more than the clothes on her back, his wife fled on foot. Exhaustion quickly overtook Mrs. Hoysington just as two fleeing cavalrymen offered to transport the children on their horses. In the reigning chaos, the planned rendezvous was missed.

It would be spring's thaw before the extent of Job's heroism was revealed. His gun powder and pellet pouch were empty and his well-used musket lay by his side. Job had saved his family, stopped only by the bullet that pierced his brain. He was scalped for good measure. Fretful and alone, it would also be spring before the widow Hoysington found her children. A family in Clarence had taken in one child, and the other was under the care of a family near Batavia (C. Johnson, 1876).

~

Earlier that morning, December 29, 1813, General Hall had officially promoted Dr. Cyrenius Chapin to lieutenant-colonel. The promotion was little noticed as the social and military structure dissolved. Chapin's disposition was to assume responsibility anyway, particularly now, with an imminent threat to his home and his adopted village. He had done what he could for his family. Now he returned to fighting the British. Somehow, he found a handful of men and boys willing to make another stand. One report claims his brave little squad numbered only five. Defending his village was beyond possible, but slowing the British advance might save more lives (White, 1898). Chapin retrieved an old 9-pounder cannon, perhaps the one he had removed from the *Detroit*. He and his "boys" set the cannon on a makeshift roadblock near the corner of Main and Niagara Streets, referred to as Black Rock Road, in some accounts. The position was next to the cemetery he and Samuel Pratt had wrangled from Joseph Ellicott.

It was a hastily drawn line of defense and, as expected, the British soon emerged out of the forested darkness of Niagara Street. Highly disciplined, the British regulars maintained their formation, marching shoulder to shoulder just as the moon peaked out from the clouds, its light reflecting off British bayonets like torches (C. Johnson, 1876).

Chapin lit the fuse and fired his cannon into the British troops. His aim was good and true. The ball opened a sizable hole in the advancing British column. His boys immediately reloaded and fired again, but this time, the cannon flew off its makeshift carriage.

Chapin tore off his white shirt, though some say it was his handkerchief, and tied it to the point of his sword. Mounting a horse, he shouted to his men, "Every man for himself and the Devil for us all." According to one member of Chapin's squad, twelve-year-old James Aigin, the doctor rode toward the advancing British army, alone, as his men and boys raced into the village, shouting a final, urgent message to leave (Aigin, 1814).

Chapin later wrote, "A large body of British troops were now within thirty rods of us, and the Indians had nearly surrounded the town. [Some] were in full pursuit of the distressed inhabitants, who had no means of making a rapid retreat, or [offering] the least resistance. In this situation, I conceived it my duty to resort to some stratagem to save the people from inevitable destruction" (Ketchum, 1865).

Chapin's best hope was further delay. He parleyed with British General Riall out in the open at the Franklin Square Cemetery. The doctor and newly minted lieutenant-colonel offered total surrender of Buffalo and all public property in exchange for protection of private property and an agreement that women and children would not be hurt or molested. Riall's stipulation was that Chapin have all intoxicating liquors destroyed to prevent

Figure 15.1. Painting by Raymond Massy (circa 1975) depicting Dr. Chapin lighting the cannon aimed at British forces marching toward Buffalo on Black Rock Road. Eyewitness accounts describe a barrier across the road that is not seen in the painting. *Source:* Courtesy of the Buffalo History Museum.

his soldiers and the Indians from getting access (Turner, 1849). Dr. Chapin offered himself as a prisoner of war.

There was still one American unit approaching Buffalo. General Hall, still in Batavia, sent a unit from nearby Williamsville led by Lieutenant John Riddle to reinforce Dr. Chapin's forces. Riddle was known for being independent and was determined to be the hero who saved Buffalo, a determination that ignored reality. He had only forty troops under his command, most of whom had been discharged from a temporary military hospital in Williamsville. Riddle arrived just as Chapin surrendered to the British, but in the chaos, he was unaware of Chapin's capitulation. Buffalo's Judge Walden, himself just informed of the surrender, made a wild dash to intercept Riddle and convince him to abandon his advance. Riddle argued that Chapin had no proper authority to capitulate. To Riddle, Chapin's admission of defeat was not only invalid, but cowardly. Riddle and Walden exchanged angry words until finally Riddle agreed to stand down, but he was not finished. As he prepared to retreat, Riddle ordered his one and only cannon to be fired at the British redcoats. His act ended any hope of preventing the burning, pillaging, and raping of Buffalo (Turner, 1849).

Isolated individuals in the village continued to defend their homes, either unaware of or opposed to Chapin's capitulation. Riall had all the excuses he needed to claim he had been double-crossed. Difficult communications and chaos made it unlikely that General Riall could have done anything to stop the destruction of Buffalo anyway. His diverse army was intent on plunder and revenge, especially when excited by the smoke starting to blanket the village.

～

In the early hours of the morning, December 30, 1813, British troops followed their Indian mercenaries into Buffalo village proper. The British paid tribes to fight, not individual Indians. The only reward for the individuals who had risked their lives was plunder. But Riall's regulars joined in the looting. Every home was entered, then torched with few prisoners taken and fewer left alive. Dr. Ebenezer Johnson's elegant home was one of the first to burn. The houses owned by Mrs. St. John, Mrs. Lovejoy, Dr. Chapin, and Judge Walden, and the village blacksmith shop, were the last to be torched. Mrs. Lovejoy stood in defiant confrontation as Indian troops broke into her house. They stabbed her and threw her body into the street. Judge Walden carried her body back into the house, and hours later, it too was burned (Turner, 1849). Porter's warehouse was plundered and left empty. Initially left standing, Dr. Chapin's home was burned on the second day, New Year's Eve.

In Black Rock and Buffalo, fires destroyed 104 homes, 43 barns, and 18 stores. The British also burned four schooners trapped by ice in Black Rock harbor. They blew up Peter B. Porter's stone mansion and stone storehouse. Joseph Palmer's schoolhouse, built in 1808, was also demolished. One eyewitness reported that by 3:00 p.m. on New Year's Eve, the British began loading their boats to return across the river to Canada. They carried with them the belongings of most every citizen on the Niagara Frontier (St. John Skinner, 1870).

New Year's Day 1814 began quietly. Only a few looters roamed the streets. Unworthy to be called Americans, these thieves materialized at a scene of near-total desolation to steal and carry off what little the enemy left behind (Turner, 1849).

A couple of days later, several citizens returned to gather the dead. Theirs was a ghastly sight. Most of the bodies were stripped, tomahawked, and scalped. Bodies not claimed by friends or family were placed on the frozen ground in the Franklin Square Cemetery and covered with boards for later identification by relatives and friends. Only the walls of two stone buildings broke Buffalo's landscape: the Seneca Street blacksmith shop and the jail on Washington Street near Eagle (St. John Skinner, 1870).

~

The British invasion dispossessed 12,000 inhabitants and depopulated a tract of 160 square miles of Western New York, from the Niagara River eastward. Terror and confusion scrambled families. Some mothers searched for months to reunite their children. In the process, they frequently took charge of another mother's orphaned children whom they found wandering the scornful scene. The villages of Buffalo, Black Rock, Niagara Falls, Lewiston, and Youngstown, and every farmhouse along the way, formed a panorama of ruin and devastation. Batavia became the rallying point for scattered remnants of an army. Joseph Ellicott's home became the officer's quarters and the Holland Company's office became a hospital. Previously abandoned log cabins, barns, and sheds became homes for many desperate families. More fortunate refugees moved in with relatives (Turner, 1849).

The British took 130 prisoners, including Dr. Chapin. General Riall proudly sent the notorious Dr. Cyrenius Chapin under heavy guard to the British prisoner-of-war camp in Montreal. The British held him for nine months before his parole in September 1814 (C. Chapin, 1836; Turner, 1849).

~

Throughout the early winter weeks of 1814, there were rumors of another British attack. General Hall assigned soldiers to guard Buffalo's ashes, and twice they repelled a British squad crossing the river. The boredom of frigid winter days was occasionally broken by army buglers from rival camps on both sides of the Niagara River, exchanging volleys of bugle calls to cheer the shivering troops. A few residents returned to Buffalo, but they were desperate for food and the army shared what they could from the already stretched army commissary. The *Buffalo Gazette* set up publication in a Williamsville print shop, issuing its first postburn edition on January 18, 1814.

Warmer spring weather eased the desperation somewhat. A traveler passing through Buffalo in May 1814 reported that three taverns, sixteen stores, and over fifty assorted dwellings had risen from the ashes (Turner, 1849).

~

The undermanned United States Army simply could not conduct simultaneous offensive actions from Detroit to the St. Laurence River and defend the long Atlantic coastline. The army of 35,000 men authorized when they declared war in June 1812 never grew beyond 18,500, and those who enlisted were often late in receiving their pay. In July 1814, Peter Porter, seeing little encouragement from the federal government, stepped up recruitment efforts in New York and did what he could to encourage the retention of as many militia volunteers as possible.

Winfred Scott and Commodore Perry continued their heroics on Lake Erie and made it possible for the Americans to once again consider invading Canada (Glenn, 2013). Late in July 1814, Porter's newly reinforced troops successfully laid siege to Fort Erie and finally occupied that Canadian fort with its commanding view of the Lake Erie entrance to the Niagara River. Before August, the Americans attempted to retake Fort George. That effort failed in what many believe to be the most decisive engagement in the war. Known as the Battle at Lundy's Lane, it was the bloodiest battle ever fought in the province of Upper Canada. Meanwhile, at the eastern end of Lake Ontario, the Americans continued to meet insurmountable resistance, and neither the British nor the Americans gained a decisive advantage (Hickey, 2012). The St. Lawrence River remained firmly under British control.

Dr. Chapin was still in a British prisoner-of-war camp in Montreal when, in August 1814, the British conducted a major Chesapeake intrusion, humbling the United States by burning the Capital and the White House (D. S. Brown, 2022). The British then turned their attention to Baltimore, where a well-organized American defensive stand defeated them. It was during the battle for Baltimore that a young Maryland lawyer, Francis Scott Key, wrote "The Star-Spangled Banner." Key had been sent to negotiate a prisoner exchange and found himself observing the American flag waving over Fort McHenry from the deck of a British ship, the *HMS Tonnant* (D. S. Brown, 2022).

Sylvia and her daughters moved in with friends in Canandaigua, where, after his September release, Dr. Chapin spent a couple of weeks regaining his health. To support his family, he took an appointment as the surgeon at a temporary military hospital in Buffalo. He would later write, "Although I failed in saving the town, still I succeeded in securing the retreat of many inhabitants who would have otherwise fallen victims to savage vengeance" (Assembly, 1812; Turner, 1849).

Meanwhile, back in England, the population was growing tired of continuous wars and the taxes needed to fund them. Parliament pressured the king to seek a treaty and end the war, known today as the War of 1812. Finally, on Christmas Eve, December 24, 1814, the *Treaty of Ghent* ended the hostilities.

As the treaty was being finalized, a British force of hardened veterans from the Napoleonic wars sailed into New Orleans. Their assignment was to move up the Mississippi and take control of America's western flank. One of the most remembered battles of the war, the Battle of New Orleans, began on January 8, 1815, before either army had received news of the Ghent treaty. Led by Andrew Jackson (1767–1845), the victorious Americans secured New Orleans and handed the proud British navy a major defeat. The *Buffalo Gazette* published the New Orleans story on January 15 with a special edition, and the Battle of New Orleans joined a list of battles that launched the political career of a future United States president.

$$\sim$$

The War of 1812 accomplished little strategically, but it matured America's view of the federal government and established the need for the nation to maintain a professional and permanent military organization. It also convinced Americans that they possessed the grit and stubbornness needed to outlast a distant power. Historians have been left to ponder a different outcome, had Napoleon not threatened England and ensnared both the British army and navy. The *Treaty of Ghent* essentially restored prewar boundaries (J. W. Pratt, 1925).

During the war, American General George Mathews (1739–1812) attempted an invasion of Florida. The south had pressured for the invasion because the Spanish were promising freedom for runaway slaves and the Florida Seminoles were protecting runaway slaves. In 1818, General Andrew Jackson again invaded Florida, but the Americans soon made peace with the Spanish. By 1819, the Adams-Onis Treaty was signed by President John Quincy Adams, adding Florida to the United States. It became a state in 1845 (J. W. Pratt, 1925).

Peter Porter received the Congressional gold medal for his capture of Fort Erie, and New York State presented him with a ceremonial sword. President Madison offered Porter the position of commander-in-chief of the United States Army, but Porter declined, satisfied to live out his years at his rebuilt mansion in Black Rock.

Reflecting on Dr. Chapin's war effort, Peter B. Porter said "that with the means at his command, none rendered more valuable service to the army and country" (J. W. Pratt, 1925). For his part, Dr. Chapin remained adamant that Buffalo burned because one foolish American commander ordered the unnecessary burning of the Canadian village of Newark.

Chapter 16

In the Aftermath of War,
Buffalo Comes of Age

A Successful Village Must Provide Faith in Tomorrow

War did not change Cyrenius Chapin's predisposition to chart a contrarian course shaded by contradictions. He viewed himself as a populist, cultivating the admiration of common folk, and he took pride in the trust given to him by Native Americans. He remained an active Federalist who was not particularly respectful of authority. Those in authority found Chapin an asset for many community initiatives, though they did not trust him to get the details right. Those he sided with held him in high esteem and remained loyal. Those he abused could hate him intensely.

In hearings before the United States Congress conducted after the war, Dr. Chapin found that he needed to defend his militia against his detractors who thought they had earned the nickname *Forty Thieves*. Chapin rationalized that the actions of his militia were essential "for the purpose of clearing the frontier of persons inimical to the States." Chapin's unwillingness to curtail these raids or take orders from General McClure did more than divide the two men—it confounded military policy. To Chapin, McClure had failed to do everything possible to win the war; to McClure, Chapin was not just a rival, but a traitor who did not follow orders (Ketchum, 1865).

Indeed, the *Forty Thieves* included a few unprincipled and lawless persons who used any excuse to loot Canadian homes. There is no evidence that Chapin attempted to rein in the excesses of his militia, suggesting he either endorsed their actions or could not manage his ragtag unit of volunteers. In his testimony, Dr. Chapin bemoaned that "our people [shot] cows, sheep, ducks and poultry of the Canadian farmers" (Ketchum, 1865).

As he entered the postwar years, Chapin was both a hero and a braggart. Finally, opportunity would grant him some time to mellow. It is helpful to return to Chapin's release from the British prisoner-of-war camp in Montreal in September 1814 to understand the postwar years.

∾

The ashes of Buffalo had not yet cooled when British General Riall had Chapin transported to Montreal under heavy watch. During his nine months as a prisoner of war, Chapin reported that the British treated him with the respect due to an officer, but his notoriety meant he was always well guarded. In a letter to the king's representative, British Lieutenant General Drummond explained the importance of holding Lieutenant Colonel Chapin for the war's duration: "[Col. Chapin] took command of the remaining force at Buffalo and, holding a commanding position in front of the town, annoyed our troops with cannon and grape-shot from a six [sic] pounder whilst our troops attempted an advance. It was not until he found that his exertions to arrest their progress were without effect that he came out from Buffalo as a self-constituted flag of truce." But in New York, Governor Tompkins viewed Chapin as a hero. While he was still in British confinement, Tompkins promoted Dr. Chapin to "Major of Volunteers" (Ketchum, 1865).

Upon his release in September 1814, Chapin's first task was to locate his family. Apparently, none of Sylvia's letters reached Chapin in Montreal, leaving her uncertain her husband was alive. Sylvia's letters to friends who had returned to Buffalo expressed her concern and provided the trail that guided Dr. Chapin to a reunion with his wife and daughters living with friends in Canandaigua.

Dr. Chapin's second challenge was supporting his family. All of his medical equipment had been destroyed and his patients were dispersed, so Chapin accepted a position as a surgeon at a temporary military hospital in Buffalo. When the war ended in the winter of 1814–1815, he moved his family 100 miles east of Buffalo to Geneva on the shores of Seneca Lake, where he worked in the practice of Dr. William Hortson for two to three years (Ketchum, 1854).

∾

The War of 1812 destroyed frontier Buffalo and heralded the start of a modern nineteenth-century Buffalo. The fur trade moved westward as the tributaries of Lakes Erie and Ontario played out. More critically, Native American relations in both Canada and the United States entered a new, less respectful era. Before the war, Native Americans had been treated like poker chips in the manipulations of expansionist European civilization. After the war, the distribution of gifts and rifles ceased as the Indian Departments of both Canada and the United States took on an odious paternalistic approach to Native Americans, imposing treaties that moved tribal units to smaller and more remote land areas white men called reservations (Cruikshank, 1912; Hauptmann, 1999). American expansionism turned its attention to the western territories and the citizens of Canada took on a more durable identity within the British Empire.

As Britain began recalling its Canadian-based soldiers, many decided there were greater opportunities to own land and prosper in North America. Some of these men simply disappeared from their units, making tracking difficult, but in 1815, at least 145 fled to the United States in April, another 295 in May, and 140 in June. It would be 1817 before the United States and Britain agreed on the details that created a demilitarized Great Lakes and drew a permanent western United States–Canadian boundary at the 49th parallel (Atkins, 1898).

The War of 1812 destroyed all public records and left the people along the Niagara River and in Buffalo impoverished. Joseph Ellicott personally contributed $200 for relief efforts and convinced the Holland Land Company to donate another $2,000. Dr. Chapin suffered as much as anyone, and some citizens blamed his botched surrender for the destruction of their homes. Those with money to pay doctor's fees were few and far between. Chapin stayed anchored in the practice of medicine with Dr. Hortson in Geneva, but he expanded his vision to support his family. Several other physicians found the immediate postwar years so difficult that they sought other employment entirely (Atkins, 1898).

On April 9, 1816, Cyrenius Chapin testified under oath before the United States Congress. His testimony, and that of others, resulted in reparations for Buffalo. The ruling listed several issues, including: (a) soldiers had been billeted in private homes and many of the destroyed buildings had been used for military purposes; (b) the conflagration of Newark by the United States Army provided the enemy with a powerful incentive for retaliation; and (c) repeated outrages committed by the enemy were evidence of their "barbarous design for indiscriminate destruction." The legislation concluded that it was a civil and moral obligation of a government to compensate its citizens for injuries produced by its acts, because the strength of every nation depends on the patriotic devotion of its people (Congress, 1824).

The summer of 1816 saw Mother Nature take another swipe at Buffalo and the northeastern United States. The months of June, July, and August brought a frigid, red fog that dimmed the sunlight in a sulfuric aerosol. It was the coldest summer ever in the northern hemisphere, bringing snow to upstate New York on June 6 and frosts in late June. By mid-August, frosts had returned. It became known as the year without summer and was caused by the April eruption of Mount Tambora in the Dutch East Indies (Indonesia). Crop failures caused thousands of families to suffer a hungry winter (Klingaman & Klingaman, 2013). Farms on compromised, burned-out soils of New England suffered the most, starting a new push for westward migration.

Slowly, Buffalo's business economy improved, and the agricultural potential of Western New York and Upper Canada rallied. The antagonism that separated the people across the Niagara region during the war receded, as mutual economic interests once again brought people together. Though the war had devastated both shores of the Niagara, an agreeable peace laid the foundation for a lasting friendship between nations.

In 1818, the government finally remunerated Dr. Chapin for his unpaid services during the war and awarded him a military pension of $250 annually. While it is unclear exactly when the Chapin family returned to Buffalo, the government payments allowed the Chapins to rebuild their home and office in Buffalo.

~

As the future for Dr. Chapin and Sylvia brightened, so too did Buffalo's development. As early as August 15, 1815, the *Buffalo Gazette* listed several boats arriving from Detroit loaded with fish and wool, as well as other boats heading west with salt and pork. There were still only two arduous ways to get to Buffalo from points east, including New York salt mines near Syracuse. Goods were transported in oxcarts along primitive roads, or by boats on Lake Ontario. In fact, everything came to Buffalo in one of these two ways, including whiskey, dry goods, household goods, naval stores, groceries, hardware, mill irons, farm tools, and building stone (White, 1898).

As people repopulated Buffalo, organized religion resumed its position as society's anchor. In 1817, Presbyterians and the closely aligned Congregationalists made up Buffalo's most predominant denomination. Methodist numbers began increasing because of the enthusiasm of Reverend Glezen

Fillmore, who led his church to a position of importance in both numbers and church property. Economic revival funded a religious building spree, with new churches springing up across Western New York on the lots originally set aside by the Holland Land Company. Dr. Chapin made contributions toward the building funds of several churches and was a signatory to the deed for St. Paul's Episcopal Church that was finished by 1820 (C. W. Evans, 1903).

Employment in shipping and transferring goods attracted many new immigrants. In August 1818, when the first steamboat built in Black Rock launched its maiden voyage, an immense crowd gathered to cheer its trip up the Niagara River into Lake Erie. But *Walk-in-the-Water*, as the boat was named, proved underpowered for the swift currents of the Niagara River. Twelve oxen and a long cable were rigged to pull the boat into Lake Erie. It was an experience that convinced Buffalo advocates to reexamine the potential of dredging the sandbar that obstructed the mouth of slower-moving Buffalo Creek (Hodge, 1885).

Shipping interests quickly realized that keeping the outlet of Buffalo Creek navigable required annual dredging. In 1822, Dr. Chapin invested $100 of the $1,300 collected to form a company charged with maintaining and improving navigation of the Buffalo Creek harbor (Hodge, 1885). By 1823, the first steamship built in Buffalo Creek's harbor, named the *Superior*, sailed for Detroit. A navigable Buffalo Creek increased the value of property along the creek and started development that would eventually force the Seneca reservation farther south. It also tilted the debate in favor of making Buffalo the terminus for the Erie Canal.

As Buffalo regained its footing in the decade after the war, regular mail service resumed, arriving by stagecoach on Mondays, Wednesdays, and Fridays in 1817. That same year, President Monroe, also traveling by stagecoach,

Figure 16.1. Dr. Chapin was a signatory on the deed of St. Paul's Episcopal Church. *Source:* Evans, 1903. Public domain.

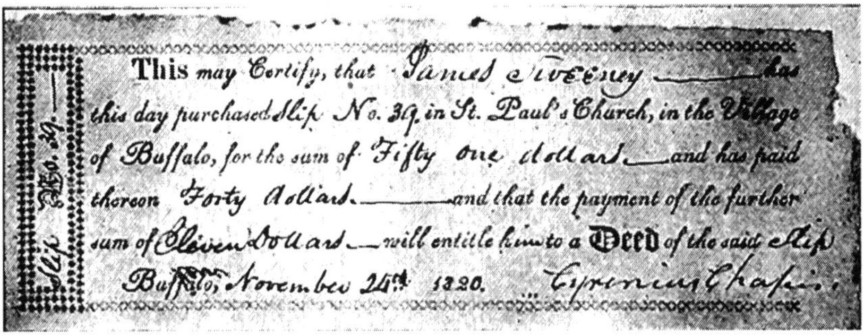

Slip No. 39.

This may Certify, that James Sweeney has this day purchased Slip No. 39. in St. Paul's Church, in the Village of Buffalo, for the sum of Fifty one dollars and has paid thereon Forty dollars and that the payment of the further sum of Eleven Dollars will entitle him to a Deed of the said Slip

Buffalo, November 24th 1820. Cyrenius Chapin

visited Niagara Falls and attended a reception held by the area's prominent citizens at Black Rock. Even for presidents, stagecoach travel was tortuous. Passengers were not just jostled incessantly, but frequently called upon to lift the stage out of muddy hollows. Regular passenger stagecoaches packed nine travelers inside and one customer outside in the lower-priced seat next to the driver. There were three rows of seats inside. The front seat and back seat had solid back rests, but the middle seat had only a broad leather strap that offered minimal support and occasionally came loose, spilling middle passengers onto the laps of those in the rear seats (Chazanof, 1970). Most coach lines stopped for a rest or a change of horses every five miles, and each stop offered travelers a beverage, usually beer, whiskey, or hard cider (Rorabaugh, 1979). A one-way ticket from Buffalo to Albany was fifteen dollars, three weeks' pay for many laborers, so most people walked or rode a horse. But for those who could afford it, stagecoach travel would remain the best mode of land transportation until replaced by railroads shortly before the Civil War.

Steamboat travel through the Great Lakes brought economic growth and people to the states of Ohio, Illinois, and Michigan and stimulated ever-greater Buffalo enterprise. Many new harbors and ports opened throughout the upper Midwest, each with their own buried rocks and choppy currents. Experience was essential for navigation, and Buffalo became the home port for captains, masters, and mates who made good incomes. They were a special breed of men, shrewd in their business transactions, eager to accumulate wealth, and bawdy about their entertainment (Welch, 1891). Their steady incomes supported the building of several grand homes on Buffalo's Delaware Avenue.

~

In 1819, Dr. Chapin became involved in another fight with Canadians over control of Grand Island. Grand Island splits the Niagara River north of Buffalo and just south of Niagara Falls. It had been the setting for the Porter-Smyth duel in 1812, but before the War of 1812, its sovereignty had been contested. After the war, Peter Porter represented the United States in negotiations that ended with Canada being paid $11,000 in exchange for a firmly defined border in the main flow of the Niagara River on the Canadian side of Grand Island. The smaller Navy Island, just north of Grand Island, was assigned to Canada ("The History of Grand Island," 2022).

But the years of hardship following the war drew squatters from Canada to Grand Island to harvest the virgin white oak trees in the island's dense forests. They milled the wood into staves that were portaged to Lake Ontario for shipment to the West Indies, where they were made into barrels used to transport molasses and rum. The squatters built themselves a log-cabin village that housed the approximately 150 Canadians making a living off the island's trees ("The History of Grand Island," 2022).

Grand Island's deforestation angered several Buffalonians. Led by Dr. Chapin, the concerned citizen's group sent a letter to Governor Dewitt Clinton, requesting that the squatters be removed. In the letter, Chapin described the squatters as "a collection of the refuse of society, constantly committing depredations on the island by destroying, cutting and carrying off the valuable timber with which it abounds." The letter complained the squatters had shattered the "peace of this vicinity." Governor Clinton instructed his attorney general, Martin Van Buren, to intervene. Van Buren drafted legislation to evict the squatters that passed both state houses on April 13, 1819. The bill empowered the sheriff of Niagara County (Erie County was not yet created) to begin the eviction by whatever means necessary.

In December 1819, Sheriff Cronk led the men of the New York militia along River Road from Buffalo to Seeley's tavern, where hired boatmen rowed them to the island. Over the next five days, December 9 through 14, 1819, the unlawful tenant in each cabin had Van Buren's act read to him. They gave each squatter a few hours to collect their possessions, then set each cabin ablaze. All the families returned to Canada save one, Pendleton Clarkes. Pendleton relocated to the mainland and founded the Niagara County village of Pendleton, New York. Sheriff Cronk sent a bill for $578.99 to the state that included expense for a raucous celebration at the completion of their project. An editorial on July 10, 1821, in the *Republican Press* reported that several of the squatters had returned to the island, but no further attempt was made to evict them ("The History of Grand Island," 2022; White, 1898).

~

Dr. Chapin's efforts to preserve Grand Island got the doctor elected village trustee for a second time, serving from 1820 to 1823.[1] It was an optimistic time for Buffalo, prime for projects that could replace the laborious transportation chain from points east. As more goods were being shipped westward, the cost of transportation was becoming prohibitive. The trip

---

1. As recorded in the Buffalo Directory of 1820.

from New York City still involved a boat up the Hudson River to Albany, then along the Mohawk to Oneida Lake and the Oswego River to Lake Ontario to Lewiston, where they were transferred to wagons for the trip to Black Rock or Buffalo and a Lake Erie boat (C. W. Evans, 1903). The only alternative was by wagon over a still-tortuous overland trip route. In 1807, a Canandaigua newspaper printed a series of articles by Jesse Hawley describing canals in Europe and prompting the New York State Legislature to authorize five million dollars to engineer a canal. Several pilot segments of a canal had been under construction when the War of 1812 interceded (White, 1898).

Dr. Chapin's time as village trustee was a burgeoning era for New York State as a whole and Buffalo in particular. State laws crafted a supportive environment for commerce and business with regulations that were accommodating yet precise enough for enforcement. The labor market continued to grow, attracting immigrants with skills and a willingness to take on any employment, and non-farm work meant a shift from a barter economy to a cash economy. Soon, New York's population was the largest in the United States. New post offices opened across New York, and on April 2, 1821, the state legislature divided Niagara County along Tonawanda Creek. To the north, Niagara County got Niagara Falls and Lockport became its new county seat. South of the creek, a new Erie County emerged, with Buffalo as its county seat (White, 1898). Buffalo now boasted regular-scheduled service of nine stagecoach lines.

Delayed by the War of 1812, segmental construction of the canal restarted on July 4, 1817. De Witt Clinton won the election for governor that fall by promising to complete the project. Chapin's investment in the Buffalo Harbor Company was beginning to pay off. Regular dredging and other improvements complemented a successful lobbying effort to get the Buffalo Creek harbor, instead of Black Rock, designated as the western terminus of the canal. When the Erie Canal was completed in 1825, harbor traffic increased from 2,700 boats in 1824 to 7,000 in 1826. Buffalo was poised for rapid change (Shaw, 2012; Vogel, Patton, Redding, & Foy, 2009).

The canal lowered shipping costs of wheat, corn, and lumber. Able-bodied immigrant workers were welcomed in Buffalo, and they preferred northern communities over competing with slave labor in the south. They were desperate for work and willing to work in exchange for food, clothing, and essentials until crops were harvested, loaded on barges, and sold in New York City or Europe. As a result, these new workers received lump-sum paychecks, like a savings program, that provided cash for investing in homes and starting their own businesses (Dunlop, 1833). Dr. Chapin saw an opportunity, bought several more farms, and not only employed skilled immigrants, but also promoted them in ways that kept them attached to his growing network.

With his additional sources of income, Dr. Chapin helped capitalize a Buffalo and Black Rock Jubilee Water Works Company that began delivering water along Delaware Avenue in 1827. The new company's initial worth exceeded $20,000, including an unspecified amount invested by Dr. Chapin. Over the next few years, wooden water conduits were laid along sections of Buffalo, taking advantage of gravity flow from the source at Jubilee springs (White, 1898).

The growth of Buffalo and Black Rock meant that not only was open land between the villages shrinking, but new projects were binding the two communities. The earliest joint project had been sharing Madison's 1809 Custom House, but by the 1820s, the two communities realized they shared another problem: nearly one in ten children were orphaned, and many of those children were forced to live on the streets. When the New York State Legislature passed a bill to fund building almshouses, Buffalo and Black Rock collaborated to build a new stone structure halfway between the two communities. The new Erie County almshouse opened in 1828 with Dr. Chapin's former partner, Dr. Josiah Trowbridge, as the superintendent and Dr. Chapin as the attending physician. Average expenditures per occupant totaled eighty-three cents per week, as the vibrant business climate attracted increased numbers of homeless and unemployable poor to the orphan class (Meeks, 2022). Also in 1828, another large stone building was erected for a high school, two new banks and two new breweries opened, and a future president, Millard Fillmore, started a mutual fire insurance company (Welch, 1891; White, 1898).

~

By the 1830s, Buffalo's population reached 8,653, having quadrupled in the five years since the Erie Canal opened. Village attorney Millard Fillmore was engaged to draw up paperwork to designate Buffalo as a city. With formal incorporation in 1832 came the election of another physician pioneer, Dr. Ebenezer Johnson, as the city's first mayor. By then, Erie County's population had grown to 35,719, a 47 percent increase since the canal opened (US Census, 1830). The growth meant Erie County gained three more seats in the New York State Assembly and elected Millard Fillmore to his first political office as an assemblyman. The city directory of residents filled thirty pages, plus a separate section for residents of color. There were forty manufacturing establishments and ten warehouses dedicated to canal business (White, 1898). A contract was let to macadamize the road from Buffalo to Williamsville based on a new process developed by John Macadam (1756–1836) of Scotland. The year 1832 also saw a charter granted to build a railroad from Buffalo to Albany and city real estate values increase so rapidly that property holders, like Dr. Chapin, prospered.

~

The lives of Dr. Chapin and his family were not all work. When Buffalo winters slowed navigation and commerce, Buffalonians turned their attention to skating and sleigh parties where warmly dressed ladies and gentlemen showed off fur coats and mittens. Snow made sleighs the preferred mode of transportation, with some families taking great pride in their fashionably upholstered and ornately decorated sleds pulled by matched horses wreathed in bells. The Firemen's Winter Ball was festooned with flags and ornaments complemented by an orchestral band boasting the county's finest musicians (Welch, 1891).

In the summer months, society welcomed a sloop-rigged yacht of about twenty tons named the *Lapwing* that transported parties of thirty with picnic baskets to the ruins of Canada's Old Fort Erie. There the men shot game in the surrounding woods while the ladies searched for old military buttons, broken sabers, and bullets from the War of 1812 (Welch, 1891).

One fall afternoon, Sylvia packed lunch for Cyrenius, his apprentice Orlando Allen, and Gorham Chapin, a nephew and apprentice, for a little hunting and apple-picking. The trio paddled across the Niagara River to Fort Erie in the only boat they had available, a primitive dugout canoe. The apples were so large, red, and ripe that the idea of hunting was abandoned while the trio loaded their canoe with apples before pushing off for their return paddle. Once afloat, the weight of their apple bounty dipped the canoe gunnels almost to the water's surface, causing both boys to suggest dumping the apples to navigate the strong Niagara current. But not the full-steam-ahead Doc Chapin. He instructed the boys to "keep still, don't stir, and I will take you safely across." They, and every large red apple, made the crossing without incident (Bryant, 1877; Burr, 1927).

On another occasion, not long after the new Chapin's home was complete, a proposal was circulated about starting a dancing school in Buffalo.

Figure 16.2. The only known image of the Chapin home appeared in a newspaper in 1927. It is the house Dr. Chapin built at 55 Swan Street in Buffalo between 1818 and 1820. Today the downtown Buffalo baseball stadium sits on this site. *Source:* Burr, 1927. Public domain.

When organizers could not find an appropriate place to hold classes, Dr. Chapin and Sylvia offered their new home parlor, becoming temporary hosts for the first dance school in Buffalo ("Viewed in scrapbook at Buffalo and Erie County Library without further citation.," 1909).

The War of 1812 had made Dr. Cyrenius Chapin a prominent Buffalo citizen. He was widely respected for his sacrifices and, as age mellowed his brusque nature, his reputation for honesty and practicality prevailed. He eventually purchased five farms, usually at bargain prices from failed homesteaders. Though his days were fully occupied, each evening Dr. Chapin returned home, brushed the stains of travel from his clothes, and filled his pipe with tobacco. He logged the charges from the day's professional calls while sharing whiskey and medical stories with his several apprentices. During this time, Dr. Chapin took on a valet who became a steady sidekick. Old Jack was a loquacious freeman Negro and capable of adding accent to any Chapin story. Both men relished embellishment but never allowed the other to speak a lie (Bryant, 1877).

Dr. Chapin's office was on the second floor of a wooden building on the northeast corner of Main and Swan. His drugstore occupied the first floor and was managed by a former apprentice, Mr. George Keese. An outdoor flight of stairs accessed the doctor's office on the south side of the building. Just behind the building was a stable for convenient access to the doctor's horse. Before building their new home, Dr. Chapin and Sylvia lived in the rear of the second floor. When George Keese's wife died, Mr. Keese moved east and Hiram Pratt, the now grown-up boy who shepherded the Chapin family to Hamburg when Buffalo burned, assumed responsibility for the drugstore, changing its name to Chapin and Pratt (Bryant, 1877).

Dr. Chapin's statewide reputation attracted a steady succession of apprentices and medical partners. Besides the earlier mentioned Josiah Trowbridge, partners included Drs. Asa Coltrin, Bryant Burwell, J. W. Clark, Orson Carey, and G. F. Pratt (G. F. Pratt, 1869). Medical partnerships were uncommon in the nineteenth century and Thomas Percival's code of ethics discouraged them, so it was not entirely surprising that after a couple of years most of Chapin's partners struck out on their own (Percival, 1803). As Percival might have foreseen, both partners and apprentices found it difficult to work day-to-day with the opinionated and inexhaustible Cyrenius Chapin. Yet, they remained friends and supporters of the man they forever considered as their mentor (G. F. Pratt, 1869).

Orlando Allen, a future mayor of Buffalo, commenced an apprenticeship with Dr. Chapin in 1819 and abandoned medicine to join Hiram Pratt in the drugstore beneath Chapin's office. But Orlando left a legacy with Dr. Chapin in the form of a skeleton. One summer day, Orlando had gone exploring along Buffalo Creek's sandy embankments and noticed that a recent storm had exposed several caskets in an old cemetery. Some had lost their lids and become filled with sand that encased skeletal remains. Returning to the office, Orlando convinced Dr. Chapin that a human skeleton would enhance his training of apprentices. The next dark, moonless night, Orlando returned to the burial ground and from one casket collected every bone, including the small bones of the hand and feet. Over the next few weeks, mentor and apprentice assembled all the bones to create a skeleton that Dr. Chapin displayed in his office for many years (Bryant, 1877).

The 1830s saw many physicians, including Chapin, change their view about the human experience with disease. The medical literature conjectured that the sthenic (an excess of heat, blood, or emotions) was giving way to the asthenic (weakness or deficiency). Society's image of the rugged American was giving way to a more gentile persona and changing the nature of disease. Dr. Chapin's use of the bloodletting lancet decreased and his use of heroic remedies lessened. The shift was gradual and implied a general attention to nascent experimental science rather than any condemnation of previous practices (G. F. Pratt, 1869). Under these new conditions, the doctor's task became one of returning the patient to a natural, balanced, and healthy state—a state considered unique to each individual. Balance no longer called for universal depletion of overexcited processes. The asthenic patient needed stimulation of functions that had become enfeebled. The natural (normal) condition was determined by ethnicity, gender, moral values, employment, and social status. Selecting the correct remedy required the physician to become acquainted with the patient on a personal level and to be knowledgeable about the peculiarities of the local environment (Burnham, 2015; Starr, 1982). Chapin thrived in the nuances of this reformation and delighted in relating his many insights about people with his apprentices.

Chapter 17

Chapin Establishes a County Medical Society, Twice

Discovering the Use of a Second, Third, and Fourth Wheel May Have Taken Greater Genius Than Inventing the First

It is necessary to return to pre–War of 1812 America to understand Dr. Chapin's role in the evolution of organized medicine in Buffalo. Most of America's early medical colleges were located in New England, New York, and Pennsylvania, supplying many costal New England and mid-Atlantic villages with adequate numbers of graduate doctors who covetously guarded their established practices regardless of wars or market economies. By the early nineteenth century, new medical college graduates were looking west for opportunity, and by the 1820s, Buffalo's rapid growth at the terminus of the Erie Canal experienced a flood of traditional medical graduates, as well as sectarians and quacks. There were two phases of medical society development in Western New York, prewar and post-canal, and Dr. Chapin played a role in both.

∼

From his arrival in New Amsterdam, and despite his many community projects, Dr. Cyrenius Chapin maintained a focus on patient care and placed great value on the large patient panel he accumulated. Throughout his career, apprentices, former partners, and competitors expressed admiration for the currency of his medical knowledge and his acquaintance with the expanding medical literature. Like his contemporaries, Chapin used about thirty remedies for a broad range of conditions. Still, his reputation attracted a steady stream of apprentices and young graduate doctors (G. F. Pratt, 1869). Many found Dr. Chapin to be cantankerous, difficult, indefatigable, and fond of hard liquor, but he was considered a consummate teacher and preceptor. They tolerated and occasionally emulated his excesses because they not only learned medicine, but also how to make a living.

Three decades after Dr. Chapin's death, Gorham F. Pratt, a former apprentice and partner, wrote a tribute to Dr. Chapin that is frequently referenced in this book. Pratt describes Chapin's skills in the sick room as displaying kindness and benevolence that patients found heartening. He made himself available day or night, rain or shine, traveling great distances through unbroken forests, often following nothing but an Indian trail — and none of these house calls came with a promise he would be paid (G. F. Pratt, 1869).

Pratt observed that to sustain his style of practice and provide for his family, Chapin charged well more than most physicians. He simply expected that those able to pay would subsidize those unable to pay. Partners marveled at Dr. Chapin's ability to explain his fees openly without disturbing the feelings of his patients (G. F. Pratt, 1869). Chapin also took advantage of his apprentices. Once they had proven themselves capable, they expanded Chapin's availability and enhanced his income. Chapin was confident about his practice model and urged apprentices to emulate it.

Apprentices paid room, board, and a small stipend that likely covered the expenses Sylvia and Dr. Chapin incurred by their presence. But Dr. Chapin was unique in that he often provided financial aid and startup loans when apprentices or partners left to start their own practices (G. F. Pratt, 1869). While there seemed to be a revolving door of apprentices and associates, each one seems to have held a lifelong respect for their mentor. Given the medical stature he felt he earned, and his community connections, it was natural for Chapin to believe he was the one doctor best positioned to start a county medical society. However, he was not the only Buffalo doctor interested in medical leadership.

≈

The inconsistencies of laws governing medical practice in the first decades of the nineteenth century have already been referenced. They had been a moving target ever since 1760 when New York City first passed a law requiring individuals to pass an oral exam if they wished to call themselves a doctor. Most people ignored the constraint.

Benjamin Franklin had been one of the first to recommend a higher standard for American medical education by founding the University of Philadelphia in 1765. New York King's College (later renamed Columbia) opened in 1768, and by 1800, Harvard and Dartmouth joined the list. These schools offered a series of lectures over several months and required students to attend two semesters of lectures. From one semester to the next, the lectures were identical in both semesters unless the professor changed. Apprenticeships, with or without college lectures, provided serious practitioners with basic clinical training, but those who were really interested in achieving upper-crust stature as a physician spent a year or two doing fellowships at large European hospitals. Training paths and curriculums were idiomatic and produced practitioners of vastly different skills and knowledge.

Dr. John J. Stearns[1] was one of the first to worry about the care delivered by poorly trained, and occasionally illiterate, frontier practitioners. A graduate of Yale College and the University of Philadelphia, Stearns practiced medicine in Saratoga, just north of Albany, New York. He described the untrained doctor as "ignorant, degraded and contemptible" (J. Stearns, 1827). Many villages had practitioners with little or no formal education who were joined by barber surgeons, bonesetters, homeopaths, and botanical healers, all fearing that licensing requirements would cut them out. Some "regular" physicians who had invested years of work to establish a community reputation thought it unfair to suggest a newcomer might be considered equally qualified simply because they passed a licensing exam (Samo, 1884).

There was also the reality that it was difficult to make a living practicing medicine. As previously described, families first consulted their home medical book and then a neighborhood healer, and only if that failed did they invest in the services of a doctor. This type of do-it-yourself medicine fed into the self-sufficient individualism characteristic of the American culture of the early nineteenth century. Regular doctors spent years establishing a reputation that could attract enough patient clients to provide financial well-being in their own families (Starr, 1982).

The domain of the neighborhood healer was huge. Most were well-meaning people who had taken an interest in folklore remedies. Some were sectarian devotees of one particular theory. It was the sectarians who mounted the most organized campaigns to prevent official recognition of "regular" medicine. The anti-scholar botanical practitioner, Samuel Thomson,

---

1. No known relation to Samuel Stearns referred to earlier as the author of the first American medical textbook.

was a prime example. Thomson preached that formal education perverted the valuable insights he offered about the use of lobelia and sweating to manage illness. His lectures and his book started by describing regular doctors as frauds (S. Thomson, 1835).

Regular medicine itself was a moving target. By the 1810s, regular physicians were losing confidence in Benjamin Rush's heroic bloodletting and purging remedies. Homeopathy was offering a highly structured and competitive theory that had the advantage of its benign dilutions (essentially water) being easy on patients. Homeopathic dilutions were so gentle that their occasional "success" forced "regular" physicians to accept a hard truth: proper nutrition could result in cures for a good number of illnesses.

Confident he possessed the knowledge, experience, and reputation to maintain his practice, Dr. Chapin felt it was in his best interest to align with Dr. Stearns's proposal for uniform training standards. A desire to eliminate quacks competing for patient fees motivated Dr. Chapin, and guidelines would define the apprentice experience he seemed to enjoy providing. Training standards, once shared across the profession, would also encourage the development of medical science that relied on clinical observation, experimental research, and dissection (Samo, 1884).

~

The first successful attempt to organize physicians to adjudicate the qualifications of their colleagues began in November 1805. Saratoga's Dr. Stearns teamed up with Dr. Asa Fitch, of New York's Washington County, and Dr. Alexander Sheldon, a member of the New York Assembly from Montgomery County. The three doctors presented the New York legislature with a proposal to formalize an infrastructure based on county medical societies. These county societies were to examine and license those wanting to be designated as a "physician." Each county society would send a delegate to sit on the Board of the Medical Society of the State of New York. That board would set statewide policy and provide oversight (Ebert, 1952). The newly organized Medical Society of the State of New York elected Dr. Alexander Coventry of Utica as its first president (J. Stearns, 1827; Zimmermann, 1995).

Stearns's initiative included the publication of a table suggesting the fees physicians might charge for services as members of the New York State Medical Society. It listed a charge of $5 for an initial consultation, with charges for subsequent visits set at $2 dollars each. The suggested charge for delivering a baby was set at $15 to $25 and bloodletting by lancet was valued at $5. The fees were high given that the average weekly wage of a laborer in 1805 was about $5. They exceeded those Dr. Chapin charged even his most well-to-do patients. But the table was likely a ploy to attract society membership (Zimmermann, 1995). The *New York Journal of Medicine* endorsed Stearns's legislation in an editorial declaring that the new regulations would achieve "the suppression of empiricism and the encouragement of regular practitioners" (L. S. King, 1982).

Stearns's law was passed by the New York legislature in 1806 and immediately opposed by sectarians, quacks, and purveyors of patent medicines. Even New York's medical colleges opposed licensing by medical societies for fear it would discourage students from enrolling in their lectures. Proposals for amendments flooded the legislature. One early amendment empowered New York–based medical colleges to grant a license to their own graduates, leaving only out-of-state graduates for examination by a county society's Board of Censors. Another amendment allowed licensed physicians to recover unpaid fees in courts and established a fine of $25 for each month an unlicensed partitioner passed themselves off as a licensed doctor (Potter, 1898, 1899).

～

Twenty counties in New York either organized or reorganized their county medical societies to comply with the new law. (There are 62 counties in New York State now.) Many areas upstate lacked an effective county organization, including the large Niagara County (still encompassing the future Erie County). Dr. Cyrenius Chapin was slow to act on the new legislation, so in 1808 it fell to Yale-trained Dr. Dan Chapin, Buffalo's second physician, to initiate organizing a Niagara County Medical Society. Dr. Dan Chapin started by inviting a group of physicians to meet several times between 1808 and 1810. However, his group never completed the paperwork necessary to receive official recognition from the Medical Society of the State of New York.

Finally ready to push ahead, or frustrated by the delay, Dr. Cyrenius Chapin began his own effort to form a Niagara County medical society on November 17, 1811. Ignoring the efforts of Dr. Dan Chapin's group, Cyrenius started by publishing an invitation to physicians of his acquaintance to organize the Niagara County medical society. The announcement for that first meeting was signed by Dr. Asa Coltrin, Cyrenius's partner at the time. Six weeks later, Dr. Dan Chapin followed with an announcement on

December 31, 1811, claiming his group was the only legitimate organizing group. Cyrenius countered with another announcement in the January 22, 1812, issue of the *Buffalo Gazette*. This time, Cyrenius accused Dr. Dan Chapin's group of improper procedures that "failed in accomplishing their object." Dr. Cyrenius referred to his new group as "the Regular Medical Society of the county" (Horton, Douglass, & Williams, 1947).

For several weeks, both men exchanged invectives, dutifully printed in the *Buffalo Gazette*, and claimed leadership of a Niagara County medical society. Dr. Daniel Chapin called Cyrenius "a mutilated, ill-starred brat scotched with the characteristic marks of its empirical accoucheur" and little more than an untrained midwife.

Figure 17.1. Chapin's medical society announcement in the *Buffalo Gazette*, January 22, 1812. *Source: Buffalo Gazette*, January 22, 1812. Public domain.

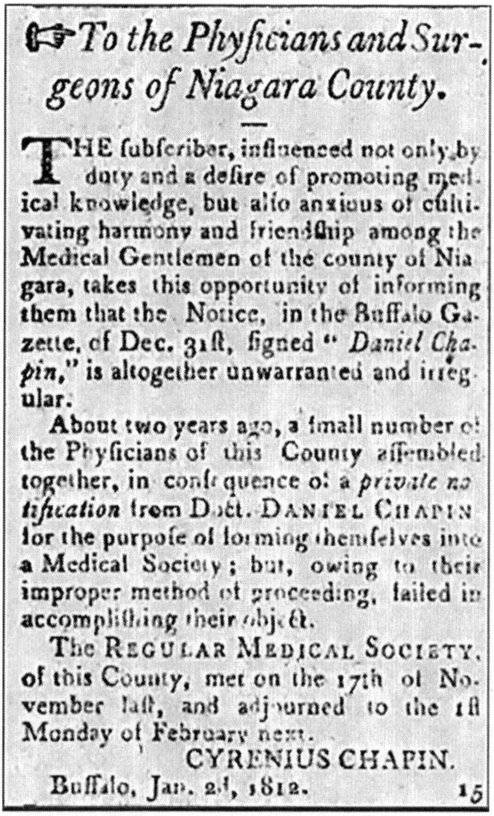

☞*To the Phyſicians and Surgeons of Niagara County.*

THE ſubſcriber, influenced not only by duty and a deſire of promoting medical knowledge, but alſo anxious of cultivating harmony and friendſhip among the Medical Gentlemen of the county of Niagara, takes this opportunity of informing them that the Notice, in the Buffalo Gazette, of Dec. 31ſt, ſigned "*Daniel Chapin*," is altogether unwarranted and irregular.

About two years ago, a ſmall number of the Phyſicians of this County aſſembled together, in conſequence of a *private notification* from Doct. DANIEL CHAPIN for the purpoſe of forming themſelves into a Medical Society; but, owing to their improper method of proceeding, failed in accompliſhing their object.

The REGULAR MEDICAL SOCIETY, of this County, met on the 17th of November laſt, and adjourned to the 1ſt Monday of February next.

CYRENIUS CHAPIN.

Buffalo, Jan. 2d, 1812. 15

Apparently uncomfortable with the public battle being played out in its pages, the *Buffalo Gazette* published its own announcement in the February 19, 1812, issue, titled "Who shall decide when doctors disagree?" The editorial states the obvious: Niagara County could recognize only one medical society under state law. Declaring impartiality, the *Gazette* stated that if the two doctors were to continue their foolhardy battle in print, they would need to purchase space. The newspaper concluded, "And while this furious warfare between brethren of the same profession exists, that confidence we have in physicians (which is half the cure) will be virtually destroyed, and a door will also be opened for impostors to introduce themselves into that society which may be most in want of recruits." The February 19 issue also contained the last published shot by Dr. Dan Chapin that objected to Cyrenius using the name "The Regular Medical Society" (Editor, 1812).

Overall, the *Gazette* offered a generous view of regular doctors, writing, "We cannot conceive of a more worthy character, of a more estimable citizen, than the physician, whose practice extends alike to the indigent as well as the opulent, and whose conduct in his profession shows that he is as much interested in the welfare of his fellow creatures, as he is attached to the fascinating pounds, shillings and pence." In this conclusion, the *Buffalo Gazette* gave recognition to the virtuous qualities it saw in both Dr. Dan and Dr. Cyrenius (Editor, 1812).

Dr. Josiah Trowbridge, the secretary to the Cyrenius faction and former partner of Cyrenius Chapin, prepared and submitted an application for a county society to the Medical Society of the State of New York. Upon its acceptance, the *Buffalo Gazette* congratulated the Cyrenius-led group for receiving formal recognition from the State Medical Society. In one last volley, Dr. Dan accused Cyrenius of stealing the letter of acceptance from the post office, claiming it had been meant for his group.

Once the Cyrenius group received its approval, Dr. Ebenezer Johnson, in Buffalo since 1809, attempted to referee the shillyshally between the Drs. Chapin, but the War of 1812 soon overshadowed his efforts at reconciliation. It would be 1816 before the Niagara County Medical Society regained a toehold adequate to send Dr. James H. Richardson to the New York State Medical Society as a delegate (Devoy, 1896; Samo, 1884; White, 1898).

~

The creation of Erie County, carved out of the larger Niagara County in 1821, gave Dr. Cyrenius Chapin a second opportunity to create a medical society. Records of the planning effort are sparse, but twenty-four physicians from the far reaches of Erie County gathered in January 1821 at the Buffalo establishment of P. M. Pomeroy. The original twenty-four included: Cyrenius Chapin of Buffalo, Daniel Allen of Hamburg, Lucius H. Allen of Buffalo, Thomas B. Clark of Buffalo, Sylvester Clark of Buffalo, Benjamin C. Congdon of Buffalo, Jonathan Hoyt of Aurora, Jonathan Hurlburt of Buffalo, Daniel Ingalls of Springville, Ebenezer Johnson of Buffalo, William Lucas of Buffalo, Charles McLowth of Buffalo, John E. Marshall of Buffalo, William H. Pratt of Eden, Chares Pringle of Hamburg, Elisha Smith of Buffalo, Rufus Smith of Aurora, Sylvanus S. Stuart of Buffalo, Ira G. Watson of South Wales, John Watson of Aurora, James Woodward of Buffalo, and Josiah Trowbridge of Buffalo (Potter, 1898, 1899; Rochester, 1861; Watt & ElBahtity, 2021; White, 1898).

Exercising all the fire and brimstone he practiced when giving his occasional Sunday sermons, Dr. Chapin rose at one early meeting of this new medical society to address his colleagues. He sounded an evangelic message as he railed against quacks who were doing "no end of harm." He denounced the "cold ingratitude" of the public toward the medical profession while slamming the public's inconsistency when frightened by disease. Chapin declared the medical profession "lax in maintaining the rank among the learned professions which it demands" and decried the community's habit of ignoring the physician's bill. "Nonpayment," he said, "is an insult and a hardship, compelling physicians to resort to an immediate collection at the time of service" like the common snake-oil salesman practicing at the back of a cart (Potter, 1898).

Chapin was on a roll; he followed his address with a public notice announcing, "It has too long been a prevalent idea with the public that the physician's bill is never to be paid and to call upon a patient, when restored to health and to the enjoyment of life by the skill and attention of his physician, for a reward for the services rendered is considered almost an insult and a hardship. . . . To relieve my own necessity, I am compelled to resort to an immediate collection and this I shall do without discrimination. Those, therefore, who think it a duty to save the cost of prosecution will find it expedient to bestow immediate attention to this subject" (Potter, 1898; White, 1898).

The offices of Dr. Dan and Dr. Cyrenius Chapin were both in Erie County, and they were now forced into an apparently successful collaboration. The first Erie County Medical Society officers included: president Cyrenius Chapin; vice president Daniel Chapin; secretary John E. Marshall;

treasurer Lucius H. Allen; and Board of Censors: Charles Pringle, Sylvanus S. Stuart, Benjamin C. Congdon, Lucius H. Allen, and John E. Marshall (White, 1898). Chapin would be reelected president in 1822 and 1823 (Samo, 1884). Tragically, Dr. Dan Chapin would never ascend to the presidency, as he died of exposure on that ill-fated walk home from a house call later in 1821.

Despite Cyrenius Chapin's emphasis on financial issues, economic hardship tainted the Erie County Medical Society from the beginning. The society charged a fee of $2 to join and annual dues of $1. The treasurer's end-of-year report for 1821 showed that only about half the dues had been collected, yielding receipts of $11 against disbursements of $8. By the end of 1822, the treasury contained six shillings and the county society carried debts amounting to $10.50. Impending insolvency prompted passage of a resolution stating, "Resolved, That the treasurer be directed to collect outstanding dues from members, peaceably if he can, forcibly if he must." The society raised the initiation fee to $5 and imposed a penalty of $1 for being absent at either of the semiannual meetings (White, 1898).

Enforcement did not go well. Meetings were held in January and June of each year and they were irregularly attended. By 1831, Buffalo was booming six years after the Erie Canal opened and doctors were being attracted to the boom town. However, only nine active medical society members were listed. Minutes of the society, housed at the Buffalo and Erie County Historical Museum, reveal little society activity between 1831 and 1834, when sixty-four-year-old Dr. Chapin again invested his energies to resuscitate the Erie County Medical Society.[2] This time another of Chapin's partners, Dr. Bryant Burwell, put the society on a secure path. Burwell also served as the delegate to the New York State Society (Potter, 1898). Burwell, like so many physicians new to Buffalo, had joined Chapin's practice for several years starting in 1825 and took an intense interest in the Erie County Medical Society's success. He convinced the Erie County chapter to lobby the state legislature for the establishment of a bureau of vital statistics. Burwell also spearheaded a campaign originally started by Dr. Chapin to vaccinate all willing residents of Erie County with cowpox. He chaired the county's Board of Censors and administered examinations to new applicants. Later, Burwell would help to form the American Medical Association.

---

2. The author reviewed handwritten minutes of the Erie County Medical Society at the Buffalo and Erie County Historical Museum.

After the 1834 rebirth, the Erie County Medical Society admitted five to seven new physicians every year. Regularly scheduled stagecoach service facilitated travel from the far reaches of the county, and Buffalo's shopping and entertainment spurred by the Erie Canal provided more reasons for doctors and their wives to visit downtown. The society meetings soon expanded beyond organizational business and unresolvable grumbles to include lectures and reviews of newly published medical literature.

Before long, another Chapin partner joined Burwell as a pillar of the Erie County Medical Society. Dr. Gorham F. Pratt served as the secretary from 1834 to 1840. Pratt had been born in Reading, Massachusetts, in 1804; attended medical college in Fairfield, New York; and was attracted to Buffalo to apprentice with Dr. Chapin, earning his license in 1833 (Potter, 1898). Pratt remained Dr. Chapin's partner until Cyrenius's death in 1838, a longer term than any other Chapin associate. Pratt built a very large practice among Buffalo's finest families and was elected the president of the Erie County chapter in 1841 (Devoy, 1896; Gram, 1898).

~

It will be late in the nineteenth century before licensure is taken out of the hands of individual county medical societies and their Board of Censors. Until then, Board of Censor responsibilities included reviewing the credentials of anyone wishing a license to practice medicine and performing an in person oral examination of each out-of-state candidate. Four conflicting issues confounded each county's Board of Censors. First, granting New York medical colleges the power to license their own graduates ignored the reality that some medical colleges admitted any student with the resources to pay lecture fees. Second, county medical societies depended on fees and member dues, a condition that put pressure on the Board of Censors to approve candidates. Third, large membership squeezed out quacks and sectarians who competed for patient fees. Fourth, allowing too many licensed physicians in a community increased competition between licensed doctors. In many counties, the censors simply canceled meetings, sometimes for years, rather than sort through these issues (Zimmermann, 1995).

The printing of the second edition of the American Pharmacopeia in 1830 revealed how complicated regular medicine was becoming. It listed over 100 herbal medicines and inorganic compounds in common use (Pharmacopoeia, 1830). There had been two medical journals widely circulated in the United States in the first decade of the nineteenth century:

the *Medical Repository* and the *Medical and Philosophical Register* (Horton et al., 1947). But as embryonic science inserted itself into medical practice, dozens more journals (and magazines) were distributed by 1825. Most articles were anecdotal case histories that described ever-increasing treatment options with little to back them other than the author's opinion. Soon, the expanding number of journals would give priority to large observational and experimental studies.

∿

Dr. Cyrenius Chapin was also involved in starting a separate Buffalo Medical Association, specifically for physicians practicing within Buffalo proper. The first meeting on July 16, 1831, listed the following members: Cyrenius Chapin, Judah Bliss, John N. Marshall, Josiah Trowbridge, Moses Bristol, Bryant Burwell, Henry R. Stagg, Alden S. Sprague, James N. Smith, Lucian W. Caryl, and Orson S. St. John. This group formed specifically to educate and inform its members, and Dr. Chapin was elected its president. Each meeting included a presentation by a member on a topic the group selected. The first paper discussed the circulation of blood and was read by Dr. Caryl with discussion by Dr. Trowbridge. The group met five times in 1831, but on two occasions the physicians assigned to discuss a paper came unprepared. There are no more meeting minutes after 1832, though a new Buffalo Medical Association was organized in 1845 (White, 1898).

By 1830, homeopathy was proving a significant challenge to regular medicine in Buffalo. Originally trained as a regular physician, Dr. Nash H. Warner began exploring the remedies promoted by Hahnemann's theory of homeopathy in his role as the chief attending physician at Buffalo's Marine Hospital. The more enamored he became with the doctrines of homeopathy; the more Dr. Warner castigated his colleagues who practiced "regular" medicine. His attacks could be bitter and often very personal, leading to his expulsion from the Erie County Medical Society. The expulsion brought him statewide notoriety, and his practice grew exponentially. He later founded the Buffalo Homoeopathic Society, which produced a widely distributed journal for several years (Hill, 1923; Potter, 1895).

∿

Returning now to nine o'clock in the morning of October 26, 1825, a marching band led a carriage carrying Governor De Witt Clinton down

Main Street. The crowd's enthusiasm nearly drowned out an artillery salvo that echoed through the village until the procession reached the western-most terminus of the newly completed Erie Canal. There, one climatic blast shattered the morning air. The governor boarded the *Seneca Chief* for a long voyage to the Hudson River. As Clinton departed, the massive 32-pounder cannon set off the echoing sounds of cannons stationed at intervals along the canal all the way to Albany. Public dinners and speeches at Rathbun's Eagle Hotel and Landon's Mansion House were followed by an evening ball. The *Seneca Chief* carried a barrel of Lake Erie water to New York that was ceremoniously emptied into the Atlantic. Once refilled with ocean waters, it was returned to Buffalo to mingle with the clear waters of Lake Erie.

Two years after the canal opened, on November 22, 1827, planning for a dedicated high school in Buffalo opened a meeting in the Eagle Hotel. The school was formally incorporated by year's end and Dr. Chapin was among those raising donations totaling $25,000. The new high school building was erected on Main Street, just northeast of the population center. Today it is the site of the Sisters of Charity Hospital.

In 1830, the village stretched north to High Street, eastward to Jefferson Avenue, southward to the Buffalo Creek Seneca reservation, and bounded on the west and northwest by Lake Erie and the Niagara River. Distinguished and well-known people lived in stately homes scattered throughout the village. The former secretary of war and congressman General Peter B. Porter lived on Ferry Street, at the time still in the village of Black Rock. He was the president of a new railroad connecting Buffalo and Niagara Falls. Orlando Allen, one of Dr. Chapin's first apprentices to find business more interesting than medicine, resided on Swan Street and not far from the Chapins. Dr. Josiah Trowbridge practiced out of a handsome brick dwelling and office on North Division Street. At the corner of Clinton and Washington, the Holland Land Company took occupancy of a two-story building close to the new Buffalo Savings Bank on Batavia Road, now renamed Broadway. Dr. Ebenezer Johnson lived on the Upper West Side, near Black Rock, in an ornate Italian villa (Welch, 1891).

Chapin's favorite haunt, the Park Coffee House, was on the east side of Main Street, between Park and Eagle Streets. Nearby, the Eagle Tavern took up nearly an entire block below Court Street, with a three-story brick building and adjacent stables. When General Marquis de Lafayette passed through Buffalo in 1826, General Peter B. Porter hosted a large public dinner in his honor at the Eagle Tavern (Welch, 1891).

By the early 1830s, Buffalo was home to 9,000 inhabitants. Thousands more traveled the waters of the Erie Canal and Lake Erie as commerce became king and provided the impetus to incorporate Buffalo as a city. Attorney Millard Fillmore was hired to draw up the papers leading to formal recognition in 1832 (Laux, 2014). Within nineteen years of being leveled by enemy flames, the community of independent frontiersmen — impoverished by war and burdened with debt — had reinvented itself. National newspapers said it reflected the perseverance, spirit, and energy of Buffalo's citizens. Specifically named were Granger, Forward, Townsend, Wilkeson, Coit, Allen, Tracy, Johnson, Walden, Samuel Pratt, Marshall, Trowbridge, Austin, Potter, Miller, Barton, Barker, Bennett, Heacock, and Dr. Cyrenius Chapin. These men were described as an "irresistible force" (H. P. Smith, 1884).

Chapter 18

An Agricultural Society and a Buffalo Boom

Wealth Depends on the Capacity to
Exchange One Thing for Another

It was wild game and fertile soils that supported a great Haudenosaunee culture in the fifteenth century. Creeks and rivers crowded with beaver, muskrat, and mink brought French trappers to the Niagara Frontier in the seventeenth century. In the eighteenth century, the British introduced administrative structure. In the nineteenth century, it was Americans and new immigrants who brought agriculture, business, and a canal. Men and women like Cyrenius and Sylvia Chapin shaped the region's rapid growth by fostering a culture of self-confident individualism. But for any culture to grow and improve, certain basic social infrastructure is essential. To understand the origins of another Chapin creation, the Erie County Agricultural Society, we need to return to 1819. Orlando Allen, the apprentice who found the skeleton for Dr. Chapin's office, sets that stage for understanding how Dr. Chapin came to lead agricultural change and improvement.

When Orlando arrived in Buffalo in 1819 at the age of sixteen, he wrote a detailed description of Chapin's postwar office:

> His dwelling was on [the] northeast corner of Swan and Pearl streets; his office was on the second floor of a wooden one-and-a-half story building, on the Main Street front of his lot, near the north line; this was a small building, . . . the first floor of which was at this time occupied by Mr. George Keese as a drugstore. John Wilkeson, Esq., then a lad of about my age, was the sole

clerk in the store. Our office, as I have said, was in the second story, reached by outside stairs, starting from the ground on the south side of the building, rising and winding around to the back end, through which was the door of the office. Immediately in the rear of the store, and some fifteen or twenty feet from it, was a small framed barn used for stabling the horse used by the doctor in his professional rides, together with his Boston gig, cutter, et cetera. On the south of the store were some small one-story buildings which occupied the remaining Main Street front of the lot, with the exception of some six or eight feet left for a passageway leading to the office. These offices, or small buildings, rested upon the front foundation wall of Dr. Chapin's dwelling, which was burned when Buffalo was destroyed by the British in December, 1813. Behind them was a wide passageway from Swan Street to the barn, which I have mentioned, large enough to form a very convenient and serviceable barn-yard. The office on the corner of Main and Swan streets was occupied by James Sheldon, Esq., the father of the present judge, Hon. James Sheldon. The one next north by J. Nash Bailey, Esq., as a justice of the peace, and the remaining one by the late James Sweeny as a tailor shop. (Bryant, 1877; Rizzo, 2010)

Young Orlando Allen describes Dr. Chapin's office/drugstore and home situation five years after Chapin's release from the British prisoner of war camp to be much like it had been prior to Buffalo's destruction in the winter of 1813–1814. During those five years, Dr. Chapin located his family living in Canandaigua, worked as a surgeon in the Buffalo military hospital, and practiced medicine with Dr. William Hortson in Geneva. It is unclear just when he returned to Buffalo permanently. His financial situation markedly improved with the promise of a government pension, and documents show he contributed to building Buffalo's Episcopal Church in 1817. Orlando Allen's note confirms that Dr. Chapin was fully reengaged in his Buffalo practice by 1819. By Orlando's arrival, Dr. Chapin and Sylvia would have been in the midst of building a larger home nearby at 55 Swan Street (C. W. Evans, 1903).

The postwar demands on Dr. Cyrenius Chapin would have kept most men busy, yet his restless energy pushed him to diversify his enterprises. As he recovered from his own near-total loss, Dr. Chapin grasped the opportunities the soon-to-be completed Erie Canal would bring to Western New

York families. Canada was securely British, but now the United States was expanding westward and attracting immigrants looking for land, needing jobs, and desperate for housing. The demand for lumber and agricultural products and the range of potential markets would soon expand. But most family farms used methods that were little changed from the earliest days of agrarian society. Chapin had also noticed on his many home visits that a few enterprising families were diversifying. Some were using in-home handlooms to create dyed cloth they could sell to neighbors and general stores. Improved farm and home production methods could bring much-needed cash to support his Western New York neighbors.

~

Dr. Chapin was confident the Western New York land was good. Before humans had tilled the soil, it had nurtured forests of maple, elm, cherry, beech, and black walnut, much of it remaining unharvested. Along the sandier soils of the lake shore, tall stands of pine, oak, and chestnut were also available for the cutting (Dunlop, 1833). He knew that by 1820, some farmers were already seeing their yields decline from crop after crop of wheat and wasting the potential for decomposed straw to nourish the soil by burning it off their fields. Nineteenth-century agricultural science had proven that yields were increased by alternating crops with clover or buck-wheat and by plowing under organic material, including the winter dung pile. But low literacy and social isolation left some families with little choice but to abandon failing farms and move farther west. Alternatively, many were moving into cities for subsistence wages (Dunlop, 1833). Their parents had departed New England a generation earlier when those soils gave out.

Chapin may have started buying land as an investment, but by 1820 he had become fascinated by agriculture and sensed opportunity as the ranks of Western New York farmers were being expanded by Irish, Swedes, and large numbers of German immigrants who were also unschooled in modern farm methods. Chapin found brotherhood with many of these new arrivals who were, like him, conservative and industrious. They had strong backs, little money, and a willingness to begin their American lives working for a landowner. Chapin figured that such a workforce, joined by improved farming methods, could create surpluses and profits, particularly with the canal promising lower freight costs and access to new markets.

When Dr. Chapin's family fled to a Hamburg farm the night Buf-falo burned, it was to the first farm he had purchased. The Holland Land

Company tried to keep down payments on land low enough to entice family sales, but for some, a couple of poor crops put them into foreclosure. Men with access to money, like Dr. Chapin, could pick up a foreclosed farm at a discount. Before the war, he had also purchased a foreclosed farm in Clarence, then added three more after the war. More purchases expanded the Hamburg farm to 300 acres on which he kept a considerable number of sheep, brood mares, and colts, as well as an imported stallion of pure lineage for breeding. His farms in Clarence were adjoining, totaling 250 acres and used mostly for raising sheep (Bryant, 1877). With little time to give them his personal attention, profitability in the early years was low. Then for several years, his apprentice, Orlando Allen, reorganized Chapin's property management and hired skilled foremen, including immigrants, to manage the farms. Farm profitability increased Chapin's interest, and he found himself intrigued with breeding horses and improving his stock.

~

The ever-confident Dr. Chapin knew just what Western New York farm families needed to improve their prospects, and New York State was ready to help. Through a series of legislative appropriations, the New York legislature passed a series of bills intended to advance agriculture by sponsoring county agricultural societies to teach farm families new methods. These new county agricultural societies would have skilled agents with the knowledge needed to improve the health and welfare of New York's farm families (Horton et al., 1947). Of course, better yields meant Dr. Chapin's farm-family patients could pay doctoring fees as well.

So, in 1820, the year before Niagara County split, Chapin organized the first Niagara County Agricultural Society, headquartered in Buffalo. He recruited leading farmers from each township to form a Board of Town Managers and got himself elected the society's first president. The board's strategy was to improve farm production by promoting education, encouraging domestic manufacturing, and fostering friendly competition. Dr. Chapin figured the best way to promote competition and communication was to hold an annual fair where goods and produce could be compared, judged, and discussed. Impulsive as ever, he pushed to stage the first countywide fair in the first year of the society's existence. He rented a Buffalo waterfront field for late summer 1820 where tents could be erected to house Niagara County's best animals and exhibits. Chapin made certain every Niagara County farm received an invitation to enter their prize stock, including sheep, cattle, pigs, and horses, as well as farm produce and home handcraft items (H. P. Smith, 1884).

As the date of the fair drew closer, it appeared that Dr. Chapin's vision for a grand fair was not widely shared. Most farmers were cash poor, deeply in debt, and well aware that they did not own prize stock to compete with that of gentleman farmers like Dr. Chapin. They considered their produce ordinary, their lives commonplace, and the roads difficult (H. P. Smith, 1884). These people had curiosity, but little to show at a fair.

Fortunately for Chapin and his plans, he had Orlando Allen, and Orlando was eager to please. By 1820, the seventeen-year-old Orlando was already an accomplished medical apprentice who shared his mentor's curiosity and budding energy. Though his interest in medicine had peaked about the time he had robbed the gravesite for Dr. Chapin's skeleton, his fascination with managing Dr. Chapin's business affairs had intensified. As the fair approached, Dr. Chapin rode the countryside, personally pleading with farmers to exhibit. Then, just one day before the fair was to open, he realized that even his own farm managers were not prepared to show.

The day before the fair was to begin, Chapin sent Orlando on horseback for the twenty-mile ride to his Hamburg farm, which was one mile south of today's Orchard Park. Upon arriving, he confirmed Chapin's worries: the superintendent had made no preparations for the fair. Orlando took it upon himself to select several sheep, a fine Merino Ram, and twenty head of cattle that he drove from Hamburg to Buffalo with the help of just one farmhand. The sheep and cattle trudged through mostly undeveloped roads, unfenced forests, and the Buffalo Creek Indian reservation to Buffalo, arriving at the fairgrounds at about three o'clock in the afternoon.

Orlando was barely off his horse when a pacing and nervous Chapin confronted him with the nonarrival of the sheep expected from his Clarence farm. Mounting a fresh horse, Orlando headed to the farm near today's Harris Hill, fourteen miles away. There, too, no preparations had been made to move the sheep to the fair. Orlando pressed the farm superintendent to help him select the forty best sheep and immediately began a return journey, driving the flock to Buffalo by lantern light. He arrived at Chapin's rented Buffalo fairground at sunrise.

Orlando wasn't finished. Major Miller, also from Clarence, had promised to enter his own prize ram, and Chapin desperately wanted the competition. The indefatigable Orlando hitched another horse to a wagon to retrieve Miller's ram. He found the ram uncooperative and disinterested in the exhibition, but with the help of at least one farmhand and considerable persuasion, he got the ram on the wagon and drove back to Buffalo (H. P. Smith, 1884).

Dr. Chapin viewed the fair as his personal accomplishment. Knowing that his family would attract public interest, he had a few of the best Niagara County farm seamstresses make clothes for every member of his family. He presented the dedicated young Orlando Allen with a brand-new suit of black cloth. In Orlando's words, "the day was fine, the entries quite numerous, and everything passed off to the satisfaction of all concerned." The festivities ended with a grand ball attended by most of Buffalo's high society (Bryant, 1877).

~

Most apprentices served their supervisor in multiple capacities, and Orlando Allen found he enjoyed doing clerical and business duties imposed upon him by Dr. Chapin. Like most apprentices, he undoubtably chopped his share of wood for the Chapin family, but, within months of his apprenticeship, he found his attention focused on the business of Chapin's many farms and managing his city property. To Orlando, keeping accounting books was more interesting than bloodletting and medical remedies.

Apparently, Orlando did enjoy people. He quickly became fluent in the Seneca language and gained enough medical knowledge to be of considerable assistance to Dr. Chapin. He was so popular with the Buffalo Creek Senecas that they requested Orlando and particularly liked the way he chitchatted while letting their blood. Dr. Chapin still struggled to gain command of the Seneca language and mispronounced the few words he knew, making his Seneca communication an exercise in pointing and shouting (Rizzo, 2010; H. P. Smith, 1884).

In fall 1821, an opportunity presented itself for Orlando to change career paths. Dr. Chapin opened a general-merchandise store in partnership with another of his former apprentices, Hiram Pratt. Ever since the death of Chapin's deceased friend, Samuel Pratt, Hiram had been close to the Chapin family. He had been Samuel's only son and was warmly welcomed by Sylvia and Cyrenius, who had lost their only son. Hiram and the Chapins were nearly inseparable after the thirteen-year-old Hiram had assisted the Chapin wife and daughters in their escape the night Buffalo burned. Orlando joined Hiram as the first, and for a while the only, salesclerk in the store named Chapin and Pratt. A year later, Pratt assumed full ownership of the enterprise and Orlando became his chief assistant. In 1822, Hiram opened a branch

Figure 18.1. Portrait of Orlando Allen as mayor in 1848. *Source:* Bryant, 1877. Public domain.

store in Detroit and sent Orlando there to manage it. Once the store was operational, Orlando returned to Buffalo to serve as Pratt's general manager with an annual salary of $1,000, about five times a clerk's salary. In 1826, Orlando married Hiram Pratt's sister and became a full business partner. Later, he was appointed the president of the Bank of Buffalo and guided the bank through the difficult recession of 1836–1837. In 1847, Orlando Allen was elected the mayor of Buffalo and would later serve in the New York State Assembly. Throughout his career, Orlando credited Dr. Chapin with modeling the courage and fortitude needed to channel his energies and be a useful citizen (Rizzo, 2010).

≈

With the creation of Erie County in 1821, Chapin found himself able to focus his continuing efforts to improve Western New York agriculture on behalf of a new Erie County Agricultural Society. Not quite starting from scratch, he convinced leading citizens from Hamburg, Aurora, Holland, Wales,

Eden, Boston, and Amherst to join this new society and support a fair just for Erie County. No doubt, Dr. Chapin had animals he was proud of, but he also remained convinced a fair brought people together and advanced farm- and home-based enterprise. When asking society members to finance a fair, his pitch was "[him being] one of the most influential men in the county" would assure the fair's success. But even pouring on the full force of his charm, he could not muster financing adequate to support another fair (H. P. Smith, 1884)

The idea of an Erie County fair finally took hold twenty years later, in 1841, when Lewis Falley Allen (no known relation to Orlando) would revive Dr. Chapin's legacy. Lewis Allen was born in 1800 in Westfield, Massachusetts, and arrived in Buffalo in 1827 as the financial manager for the Western Ensurance Company. His wife, the former Margaret Cleveland (1801–1880) was an aunt to the future United States president Grover Cleveland. The Lewis Allens purchased the rebuilt Black Rock home of General Peter B. Porter near the present-day intersection of Niagara Street and West Ferry. Lewis was also a gentleman farmer, owning twenty-nine acres of land on Williamsville Road (now Main Street), where he planted orchards and bred short-horn cattle. As Main Street prospered, Lewis sold the land and drove his herd to a new pasture along a well-worn path, today known as Allen Street. Another Lewis Allen hobby was planting elm trees throughout the Allentown neighborhood (H. P. Smith, 1884).

Lewis Allen reorganized Dr. Chapin's Erie County Agricultural Society, which held its first fair in October 1841. The next year, 1842, the fair started awarding prizes, and by 1850 the fair boosted 133 head of cattle, 89 horses, 73 sheep, and so many pigs that no one seems to have counted them. Following Chapin's model, awards were also given for food, crafts, and products produced by women. Horace Greeley spoke at the 1855 fair and an admission fee of 12.5 cents was established. In 1868, the fair moved to a permanent location on the grounds of the Hamburg Driving Park Association, where it continues its annual tradition today (Biniasz, 2000; H. P. Smith, 1884).

∾

Once the canal opened in 1825, Buffalo and Dr. Chapin welcomed an era of optimism passed between the hulls of canal barges and Lake Erie steamboats. The population of the city increased from 8,653 in 1830 to 15,661 in 1835, an 81 percent increase. Erie County's population grew from 35,719 to 57,504, a 61 percent increase. Politicians sang prophecies of greatness. City property selling for $4 an acre a generation earlier now commanded as much as $6,000 an acre with minimum down payment (White, 1898).

A railroad six miles long and pulled by horses was built between Buffalo and Black Rock in the 1830s at a cost of $15,000. But it was the Erie Canal that brought the good times, and almost immediately after completion it was widened and deepened. The Buffalo harbor end of the canal was expanded to a width of 80 feet and a depth of 13 feet. Thirty-two-year-old Millard Fillmore, in his ninth year of practicing law, was elected to fill one of three new state assembly seats Erie County gained in 1828. In 1832, Fillmore was elected to the United States Congress; the same year, populist Andrew Jackson won his second presidential term.

Good times brought a new Buffalo fever, this time one of speculation. Businesses of every kind borrowed to support almost any enterprise the human mind could imagine. In his war with the United States Bank, President Jackson withdrew all deposits of federal funds (about ten million dollars) in the fall of 1833, and the displaced assets flowed into state banks. They, in turn, expanded the availability of credit and sparked more speculation with little attention paid to capital reserves. Local governments undertook public works that competed for workers and made unemployment nonexistent, raising demand for newly arrived immigrants (White, 1898).

Buffalo's shipyards launched nearly a steamboat a month. At one 1833 launch, Dr. Cyrenius Chapin gave the following toast: "Buffalo and Black Rock—one and indivisible; may their citizens continue to be united in enterprise and deeds of benevolence as long as Lake Erie bears a wave" (Devoy, 1896; Shaw, 2012). Chapin foreshadowed a merger that would take place twenty years later, in 1853.

Though he enjoyed the hype, and loved to speak at public gatherings, there is no evidence that Dr. Chapin overextended his finances during the boom years. Detractors have suggested he overindulged in "malt and hard spirits" in the 1830s (Cruikshank, 1900). There is considerable evidence that alcoholic beverages loosened Dr. Chapin's tongue occasionally, but there is no solid evidence that spirits consumed him. With the only standard for safe water being whether a horse would drink it; hard cider, beer, and brandy were consumed by nearly everyone every day. Indeed, from 1790 to 1830, much of America had a drinking problem, consuming more alcoholic beverages per capita than ever before or since (Rorabaugh, 1979). In the 1830s, Buffalonians supported five breweries, the largest of which was the Jacob Roos brewery. The Roos brewery was located between Church and

Lock streets on the Erie canal, making shipping beer all over the northeast and Midwest possible. Roos made Buffalo a center for commercial beer distribution. (Devoy, 1896).

~

The pharmacy business also outgrew the doctor's black bag during those years. Mr. Le Couteulx, an agent for Joseph Ellicott and the Holland Land Company, had started the first small dispensary out of his home selling nostrums popular in the first decade of the nineteenth century. Once Dr. Chapin was established in Buffalo, he opened the first real drugstore on the first floor of his office building. It was a model that became common throughout upstate New York. Dr. Ebenezer Johnson in Black Rock copied it just a couple of years after Chapin. Jabez Allen, a physician practicing in East Aurora, kept his practice afloat with a pharmacy while waiting for the Erie County Medical Society to reorganize and grant him a license in 1838 (Lockie, 1968; T. Rosenthal, 2022). Practice-affiliated drugstores were a convenience for patients and assured a plentiful supply of the most commonly used remedies prescribed by the owner/doctor. For Dr. Chapin, it was another source of income and created the flexibility that allowed him to provide medicine gratuitously to needy patients.

The 1830s were a time for Dr. Chapin to lean on his reputation as a hero, emphasize his brand of Federalist statesmanship, and promote his vision for Buffalo. Through the first half of the decade, American banks issued paper notes based on rising land values and a few banks borrowed from London banks to expand their lending potential. Then, in 1836, land speculation played out its boom cycle and nervous London money markets began recalling their bank loans. American banks were forced to call in local loans, and a wave of business failures followed (Graves, 2001). Dr. Chapin may have avoided the worst of the speculation fever, but around him the economy of Buffalo faced major setbacks (Lockie, 1968).

~

Benjamin Rathbun exemplifies the business climate of the 1830s. He was the most prominent Buffalo investor of his day, and his downfall illustrates the impact of the 1836–1837 recession. After successfully running the Eagle tavern, easy money ignited a daring speculator side of Rathbun's nature. He started by building the American Hotel that quickly became the dominate structure on Main Street, offering nationally known entertainment like the ballad singer Henry Russell (White, 1898).

Rathbun wore a formal black suit that set off his square face and firm jaw, giving the impression of a confident clergyman. Initially, every business and transaction detail got his personal attention and his success attracted more capital that financed ever more enterprises. Within a few years, Rathbun was building houses, stores, factories, and public buildings while employing dozens of skilled workmen. His signature appeared on large contracts for building materials, stone quarries, brickyards, machine shops, and several stores. He even opened a private bank that issued unsecured notes signed "B. Rathbun," much like notes issued by more conventional banks (White, 1898).

Rathbun's trademark was a painted red wreath of flowers, with "B. Rathbun" in the middle. It appeared on his stagecoaches he operated between Albany and Buffalo and his local horse-drawn buses that moved residents up and down Buffalo streets (White, 1898).

One nephew in his overworked accounting office proved to have a natural talent for forging his uncle's signature. His forgery grew so pervasive that one day he signed his uncle's name in front of a creditor. An investigation followed that revealed not only many forged signatures but also the depth to which the economic downturn of 1836 had left Rathbun overextended. Unable to satisfy his creditors, Rathbun fled to Texas, but within weeks, he was brought home in irons and lodged in the Erie County jail. His nephew turned state's evidence and Rathbun was sentenced to Auburn Prison for five years. Upon his release, he opened a successful hotel in New York City (White, 1898).

Rathbun's pluck exceeded his grasp, but his boldness shows the determination shared by many Buffalonians as Buffalo transitioned from a thinly populated frontier town to a modern metropolitan city. Buffalo attorney Millard Fillmore organized a "panic meeting" in May 1837 that led to a new statewide banking law that would eventually renew confidence in Buffalo's business (White, 1898).

Chapter 19

Cholera, 1832

Numbers Embody People Who Shed the Epidemic's Tears

The 1830 United States census was the first to note that urban communities were growing faster than rural communities. Western New York employment was shifting from farm to shipping, manufacturing, and service. Most new jobs were for men, drawing immigrants and farmers exhausted by subsistence agriculture to cities. Many workers accepted the cheapest lodging they could find to maximize the wages they could send home, resulting in crowded living conditions, compromised sanitary accommodations, and intemperance. America's cities in the 1830s, including Buffalo, were ripe for an epidemic holocaust (Chudacoff, 1999).

Stories about Asiatic cholera, called the "plague of India" and "black vomit," began to appear on the back pages of America's newspapers in 1831. By the spring of 1832, communities in Europe were reporting an epidemic. Soon, cholera landed at the Port of Quebec on an Irish immigrant ship. It then spread among the French settlements up the St. Lawrence River through Lower Canada. One path continued along Lake Ontario's north shore to York (Toronto), through the newly dug Welland Canal to Lake Erie and on to Buffalo and Detroit. A second path came down Lake Champlain to Albany, where it once again split to the south along the Hudson River to New York City and westward at the speed of a barge, striking villages along the Erie Canal. Arriving from both directions, cholera struck Buffalo's 9,000 inhabitants in mid-July 1832. With no historical herd immunity, previously unexposed communities were devastated as cholera continued its relentless journey throughout America, traveling at the speed of nineteenth-century transportation (Rosenberg, 1962; Welch, 1891).

Buffalonians were suffering an unusually hot summer in 1832. The first cholera victim was described as "an Irish laborer, and habitual drunkard," who died eight hours after becoming ill. On the following day, there were two cases reported, one of whom died in eleven hours. A week passed, then six new cases were reported and one death. The next day, six more cases and two deaths (Hill, 1923).

It was July 19, 1832, when the *Buffalo Patriot* printed the first public notice of cholera. Within the week, it was clear to Buffalo's physician/mayor, Dr. Ebenezer Johnson, that the city was going to be severely afflicted. Two of the early victims were prominent lawyers, making it impossible to blame the epidemic on the squalid behavior of the laboring class. None of the Buffalo doctors had ever seen cholera and, like everyone, they did not understand what caused it. The prevailing opinion was miasma caused cholera and therefore it was not transmitted from person to person but carried through the air. By early August, 184 Buffalonians had been admitted to the almshouse and 80 had died. Untold others survived undocumented bouts of dysentery that were not recognized as cholera (L. F. Allen, 1896; Guthrie, 2007).

Mayor Johnson immediately appointed a Board of Health that included himself, Lewis F. Allen (Future Erie County fair organizer), Dr. John E. Marshall (city health officer), Loring Pierce (an undertaker), and Roswell W. Haskins (a printer and bookseller with a knack for accounting). The board was charged with cataloging the dead and interring their bodies. Mr. Haskins kept the death records and became the board's public face. He was naturally direct and possessed an inexhaustible nervous energy, even under normal circumstances. Now Haskins seemed to be everywhere at all hours. He brought order to cataloging the sick, removing patients to the almshouse when necessary, and seeing that burials were tracked. Haskins was a bull of a man with strong, broad shoulders. Residents told stories about Haskins carrying patients too weak to walk down the stairs of their home or tenement. His concern, and his courage, were the closest thing to reassurance anyone would receive (Hill, 1923; C. Johnson, 1876).

As the disease darted erratically up one street and down another, Mr. Pierce and Black Tony, a freeman Negro, found it best to pick up the dead after dark to avoid panicking neighbors. Every morning, Pierce and Black Tony reported to the mayor's Board of Health. Besides reporting the number of dead, the two men reviewed the daily case reports the city's physicians were required to submit (L. F. Allen, 1896).

Cholera's spread was fast and sharp. First, the majority of victims were poorly nourished and intemperate. But then, with equal unpredictability, it invaded the homes of Buffalo's aristocracy. The terrifying suddenness with which it carried off its victims frightened everyone, and those with means fled the city. In the process, they carried the disease to new families and communities. The spring waters near the village of Avon were one popular destination for the wealthy, but soon, like other rural communities, it too was overcome with death and disease. Coffin-makers and gravediggers worked continuously. Steamboats plying the Great Lakes were stopped on entrance to the harbor until passengers and crews had passed medical inspection. Stagecoaches and canal boats were met for inspection and clearance before entering the city limits.

Without understanding the nature of contagious disease, or how it spread, Buffalo borrowed on the public health directives of New York City, recommending water be avoided and beer, brandy, or hard cider be used to quench thirst. If water was to be consumed, citizens were advised to mix it with a generous amount of brandy. A special burial ground was opened on High Street to receive the steady stream of victims (L. F. Allen, 1896).

Figure 19.1. New York warning notice regarding cholera in 1832. *Source:* New York State Historical Society. Public domain.

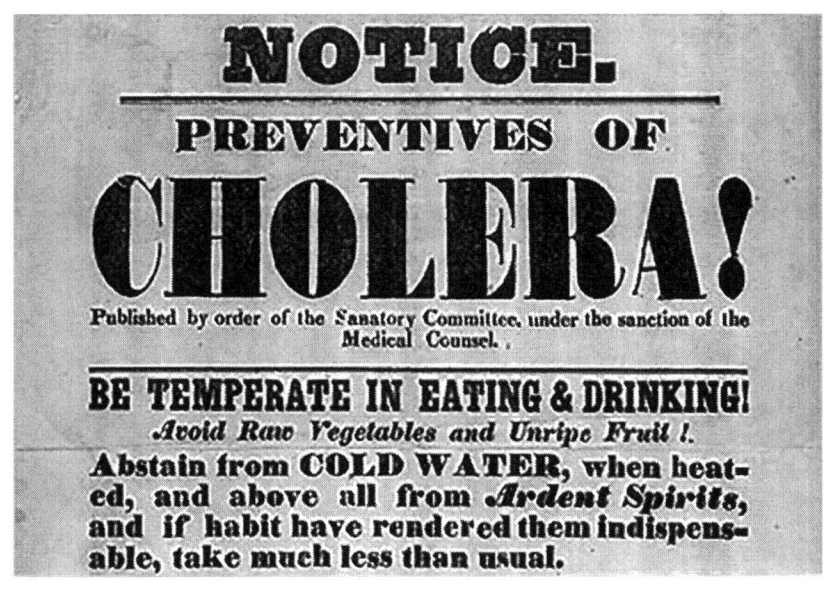

As the crisis unfolded, the Board of Health organized a special receiving house for destitute patients in the McHose House at Niagara and Ninth Streets with the already-busy undertaker, Mr. Pierce, in charge. Within days of opening, the cholera house's chief attendant joined the body count. He was replaced by a twenty-five-year-old Irish girl named Bridget who claimed she had no fear of cholera, but within a week, she too was carried to her grave (L. F. Allen, 1896).

∾

The leading physicians practicing in Buffalo in 1832 were Trowbridge, Marshall, the sixty-three-year-old Cyrenius Chapin, and Chapin's partner at the time, Dr. Bryant Burwell. Following his lifelong pattern of selectively following rules, Dr. Chapin cooperated with the Board of Health in all he thought useful and argued against all he saw as wasteful. Particularly, Chapin refused to submit the daily reports demanded by the Board of Health, declaring, "Why should I report my medical cases to a set of ignoramuses who don't know the cholera from whooping cough? No: I'll see 'em hanged first" (G. F. Pratt, 1869).

Mayor Johnson knew Dr. Chapin well and played along, describing Chapin's protest as "delightful" and altogether characteristic of the aging curmudgeon. Applying a bit of personal attention and charm, Johnson soon had Chapin providing daily reports. Chapin even assigned two medical apprentices to provide service to the Board of Health. One was Gorham F. Pratt, who in 1832 had just begun apprenticing with Dr. Chapin. The other apprentice, James P. White. would later gain international fame in women's health and medical education (Flint, 1882). The two apprentices made themselves available at all hours to see patients with an urgent need for medical advice, and White took up lodging at the Buffalo Creek pier to inspect all newly arriving vessels (G. F. Pratt, 1869).

One of Dr. Chapin's daily reports to the Clerk of the Board of Health in July 1832 has survived. The report describes seven patients under his care with "cholera morbus," the name used to describe deadly dysentery before cholera was understood to be unique. The report describes one thirty-seven-year-old man of intemperate habits; two women ages forty-four and twenty; and four men ages twenty-nine, twenty-three, twenty-five, and twenty-four. He describes all patients on that day's report to be convalescing (C. Chapin, 1832).

Fear gripped the city, and living another day seemed an uncertain prospect. Buffalonians took to wearing little bags of "gum camphor" around

Figure 19.2. One of Dr. Chapin's daily reports to the Board of Health in 1832. *Source:* Archives of the Buffalo and Erie County Historical Society. Public domain.

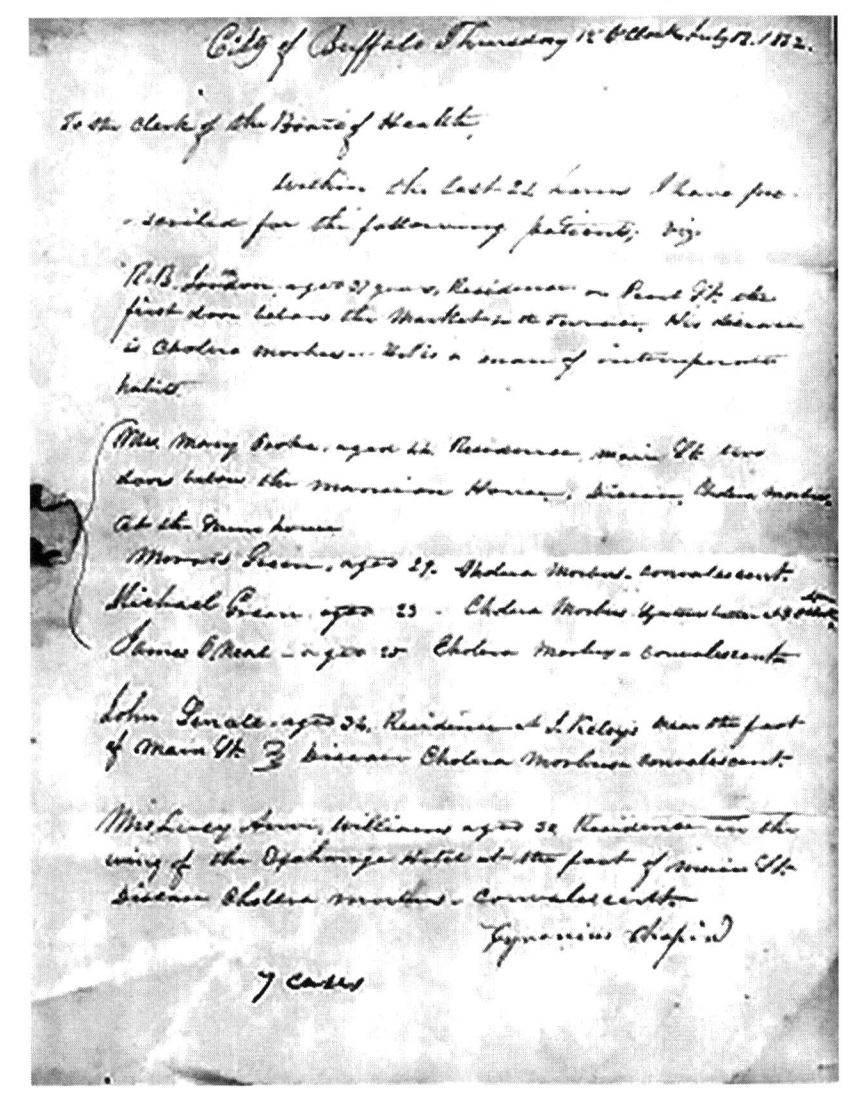

their neck while reported cases some days exceeded 100. Mr. Pierce's cry of "Bring out your dead!" interrupted the otherwise-deserted streets as he and Black Tony did their best to bury everybody within an hour or two of pickup (Hill, 1923).

After the first hard frost in late September, cases dropped to one or fewer a week. A few isolated settlements in the surrounding county were spared. Remarkably, no member of the Board of Health suffered an attack of cholera and Buffalo experienced fewer deaths than many cities of its size. Credit was given to the coordination of efforts provided by the Board of Health under Mayor/Doctor Johnson's leadership.

≈

Early nineteenth-century doctors viewed cholera as a new disease. Dr. David Hosack (1769–1835) had written a dissertation about severe dysentery using the term "cholera morbus" in 1791. It is one of the first references to cholera-like disease in American literature. He trained at the Medical College of New Jersey (today's Princeton) and Edinburgh and famously attended to the fatal injuries of Alexander Hamilton after his duel with Aaron Burr. Later, in his public-health work, Hosack made a distinction between contagious and infectious fevers. Infectious disease, he said, resulted from foul air (aka miasma) and contagious fevers spread by contact with a sick person. Though he declared "cholera morbus" to be contagious, Hosack's opinion was mostly ignored. It would be another fifty years before the cause was determined to be a bacterium in the victim's bodily fluids (Hosack, 1791).

The 1832 cholera epidemic disrupted society and forced American medicine into an age of scientific enlightenment that would mark the rest of the nineteenth century. Analysis of cases in Philadelphia suggested that homeopathic dilutions, consisting mostly of water, worked greater cures than bleeding and intestinal purging. Also, physicians realized that specific diagnostic labels could lead to specific remedies and more appropriate care. It became important to differentiate cholera from other dysenteries for prognostic reasons, if little else. Diagnostic specificity also facilitated experiments that compared remedies as medicine started on the long road to the germ theory. In 1832, Chapin relied on pure clinical observation for diagnosis, basing a cholera diagnosis on clinical course and the copious "rice water" stools patients produced. The only public-health tool available to Chapin was quarantine, which Hosack had calculated would prevent illness in twenty people for every index patient removed by quarantine (Anderson, 1831; Drake, 1832; Hosack, 1791, 1820; Rosenberg, 1962).

An unknown number of people exposed to cholera did not get sick, or they suffered only mild symptoms, and in the epidemic of 1832, Buffalo's prominent physicians all survived. As survivors, they gained lifetime immunity and protection from reinfection. Only a smoldering number of cases of cholera were observed in the summer of 1833, but the summer 1834 saw another cholera outbreak. A new Board of Health was put into action and several young men and women, previously exposed to cholera, volunteered to provide services to the sick (Hawthorne, 1848; Inglehart, 1877).

Lydia Harper was one of the 1834 heroes. She was described as a "fallen woman," though her presentation was that of a highly respectable middle-aged person with a "healthy look and intelligent features." Lydia volunteered as a nurse and willingly entered houses of all levels of society, providing food and medicines and attending to the needs of the afflicted, including administering baths. Grateful patients described her as a repentant Magdalen. Once the epidemic ceased, Lydia returned to her previous vocation, living out her long life in Buffalo (L. F. Allen, 1896).

Much of what we know about cholera's course in Buffalo comes from an undated presentation by two members of the Board of Health (Allen and Haskins) given before the medical society and available from the Cornell University libraries (L. F. Allen, 1896). Cholera's ability to spread rapidly and without regard to life station did much to force public-health issues. Villages responded more effectively when cholera returned in 1849 (Parkin, 1866; T. Rosenthal, 2022). The last major epidemic of cholera was brought home by Civil War soldiers following the war, but by then aggressive quarantine measures did much to limit cholera's impact. By 1870, few debated the contagious nature of cholera, and in 1883, the bacteria, *vibrio cholerae*, was isolated by Robert Koch (Lippi & Gotuzzo, 2014).

Chapter 20

The Patriot Wars, Dr. Chapin's Last Stand

Conflict Shares Much with the Tilting of Windmills

While Buffalo struggled through the financial crisis of 1836 to 1837, a segment of Canadians began expressing discontent with British governance. Remonstrations began in Lower Canada, where the French population wanted increased representation. Soon restlessness spread to the province of Upper Canada (today's Ontario). Many Americans were sympathetic to the plight of Canada's disgruntled citizens: some because they loved liberty and independence; some because they blamed English banks for the 1836 recession; and some because they hated all things British. Dr. Chapin was predisposed to join the "hate all things British" contingent.

Negotiations after the 1814 Treaty of Ghent clearly defined the United States–Canadian border, leaving only a small stretch in northern Maine still under debate (Graves, 2001). Still, most of the border was unmonitored and unenforced. The population of Upper Canada (Ontario) grew slowly. By the late 1830s, its population was about 500,000 compared to America's 16 million. Businesses and families crossed the border at will, and unhappy Canadians had little trouble finding sympathetic ears among their friends in America. A hardcore anti-British faction recruited like-minded Canadians and Americans into militant, vociferous, and raucous clubs that purposely ignored the border. They held their meetings in both countries, kept their membership lists secret, cultivated a militia-like structure, and called themselves Hunters Lodges or Patriot Societies (Graves, 2001).

In the twenty years since the end of the War of 1812, trade between Britain, Canada, and the United States had created an economy so interdependent that no government official wanted war. But the fractious Patriot Lodges saw the existing state of affairs differently and were so alienated that they initiated more than a dozen citizen-led, anti-British conflicts between 1837 and 1840. Variously called the Patriot Wars or the Hunters Wars, skirmishes occurred from the St. Lawrence River to Michigan. Citizen combatants called it a fight for freedom, but their efforts lacked consistent organization. The sixty-eight-year-old Chapin found it an insurgency he could not resist (Kinchen, 1956; McLaughlin, 2012).

∿

By the 1830s, the one-size-fits-all style of heavy-handed British rule had worn on segments of the Canadian populace. Across its empire, the British Crown long mandated a standard two-tiered legislative structure for its colonies, and the provinces of Upper and Lower Canada were no exception. Both provinces had a lower house, called the Assembly, that was elected by voters. But the real power lay with the upper house, called the Executive Council. Its members were nominated by the provincial governor and approved by the British Crown. Executive Council members held no obligation to consider legislation passed by the assembly. The result was a system of government controlled by oligarchs, large landholders, and high-ranking military officers who legislated according to their own preference and profit. Religion also played a part. By British law, the Executive Council in both provinces aligned with the Anglican Church. Most residents in Lower Canada were French Catholic, and most residents in Upper Canada belonged to a mix of non-Anglican churches. Common folk in Upper Canada referred to their Executive Council as the "Family Compact." Lower Canada referred to theirs as the "Château Clique" (McLaughlin, 2012).

William Lyon Mackenzie emerged as the self-appointed evocator of Canadian discontent in the province of Upper Canada. He was a fiery Scotsman whose unpaid debts from a failed newspaper forced him to leave Scotland for Canada in 1820. In Toronto, he opened a store and soon began publishing another newspaper that appealed to an anti-British, anti–Family Compact audience. Mackenzie's newspaper hurled such vitriol that his building was fire-bombed in an act that had the unintended consequence of propelling Mackenzie to even greater notoriety. Now a sought-after speaker, his blistering lectures thrust him into a successful run for the assembly in Upper Canada in 1829. As an assemblyman, Mackenzie gained a reputation for loud denouncements of the nepotism practiced by the Executive

Council and his popularity led to his election as the mayor of Toronto in 1834. When he failed to win a second mayoral term, he blamed members of the Executive Council for sabotaging his campaign. Makenzie's bitterness now added a scornful theme that audiences found entertaining, and soon Mackenzie was preaching revolution and Canadian independence from British rule (Read, 1896; Wilner, 1931).

In early December 1837, Mackenzie drew nearly 800 disgruntled Canadians from the rural hinterlands of Upper Canada to Montgomery's tavern, just north of Toronto. Most were farmers wishing to show their dissatisfaction with government land policy. Many thought they were attending an assembly of "Patriots" who wanted change. But in the gathering excitement, Mackenzie sharpened his rhetoric, and soon he was pushing for forceful rebellion (Lindsey, 1862).

The lieutenant-governor of Upper Canada at the time, Sir Francis Bond Head, dismissed Mackenzie as a hothead and minimized the threat. However, Head's militia commander, Lieutenant-Colonel James FitzGibbon, pushed for a more direct response. This was the same FitzGibbon who had captured Dr. Chapin at Beaver Dams in 1813. In the intervening twenty-four-years, FitzGibbon remained confident of his intuitions and wary of official government assessments.

By December 4, 1837, Mackenzie and his Patriot leadership decided seizing the city of Toronto was their best option for venting their grievances. The next day, they moved their ragtag citizen-army southward to take up positions just north of Toronto proper. Informants reported the Patriot movement to FitzGibbon, who, ignoring Head's orders, had positioned his militia at the city limits. Lacking any true battle plan, Mackenzie's uncertain militia rushed to engage FitzGibbon before either army was fully prepared. Then, almost immediately, Mackenzie's men broke rank and hurried back to Montgomery's tavern. Fitzgibbon, feeling it best to avoid bloodshed, waited two days before marching his militia to the tavern, where he ordered the remaining Patriots to return to their farms. His delay allowed the Patriot leadership to escape capture and flee to the United States (Groceman, 2017).

∽

Five days later, on December 11, 1837, William Lyon Mackenzie appeared in Buffalo in the company of Dr. Cyrenius Chapin. Dr. Chapin and Sylvia opened their home to the fugitive Mackenzie, who now had a $4,000 reward posted by Upper Canada for his return. Upstate New York newspapers cheered Mackenzie's courage and the "spectacular heroism" exhibited by the Canadian farmers. Their columns sensationalized Mackenzie's leadership in the Toronto battle, calling it a battle for freedom and nothing less significant than the 1776 American Revolution. Tabloid rhetoric reignited anger over the 1813 British burning of Buffalo, reviving the deep-seated rage still held by Chapin's generation (S. Evans, 2020; Groceman, 2017).

Dr. Chapin was also getting his share of headlines, leading him to organize a public meeting at a Buffalo theater for the evening of December 13, 1837. According to an account published in the *Buffalo Commercial Advertizer*, Chapin opened with preacher-style exuberance, exciting the standing room audience with, "Our neighbors in the North are at war, fighting for liberty. I have men now under my protection, at my house, on whose life a price is set, and whom I am bound to protect." In cadence, the audience shouted, "Who are they? Who are they?" (McLaughlin, 2012).

Figure 20.1. An 1838 poster advertising a Patriot Society (also known as Hunters Lodge) meeting in Buffalo. Codes were used to hide details from federal agents assigned to discourage American involvement in Canadian politics. *Source:* Archives of the Buffalo and Erie County Historical Society. Public domain.

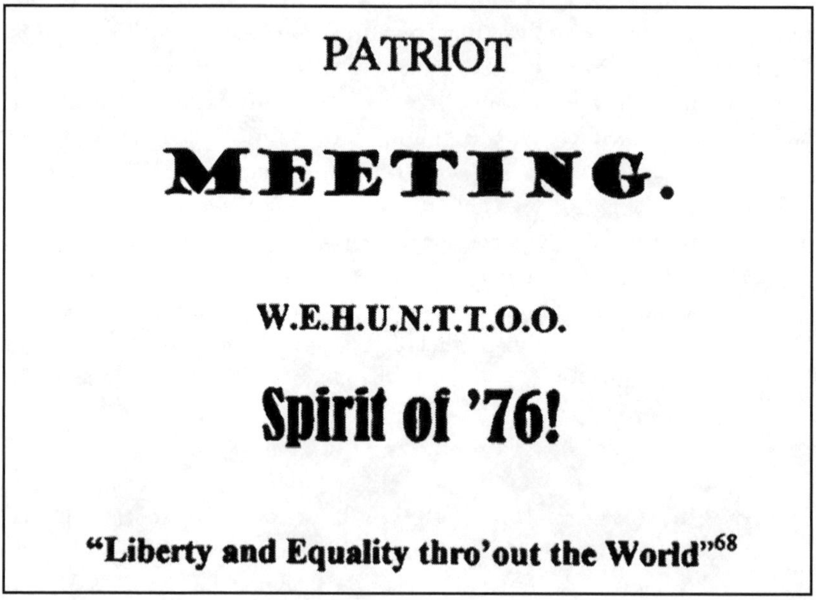

PATRIOT

MEETING.

W.E.H.U.N.T.T.O.O.

Spirit of '76!

"Liberty and Equality thro'out the World"[68]

At the podium and in his element, Dr. Chapin roared a reply, "One of them is William L. Mackenzie!" The *Advertizer* reported that "the vast assembly burst into a thunder of applause." The reporter claimed he had "never heard such a shout of exultation" (McLaughlin, 2012).

Minutes passed. Finally, the outburst subsided and Dr. Chapin continued. "Fellow citizens, Mackenzie's life is in our power—he has thrown himself upon our protection—will you protect him?" "We will" was the unanimous response. "To-morrow night, he shall address you. I am an old man; but at the hazard of my life, I will protect those who throw themselves upon my hospitality. If any scoundrels, for the sake of the $4,000 reward that is offered for him, shall undertake to get him, they must first walk over my body. I want six strong, brave young men, as good sons as God has got among us, to go to my house tonight, for fear of any attempt on the part of the loyalists" (McLaughlin, 2012).

Overcome by his own drama, Chapin waved a Bowie knife above his head as a symbol of the Texas martyrs who defended freedom at the Alamo just the year before. One hundred men rose to their feet to serve in Mackenzie's guard unit. Chapin picked the first six to mount the stage (McLaughlin, 2012).

As promised, William Mackenzie spoke at the same theater the next night. The audience was overflowing with nearly 3,000 people, or 1 in every 6 Buffalonians. Mackenzie was a practiced orator who understood an audience, and though short in stature, his rhetoric could deliver fire. He knew many in the audience were veterans of the War of 1812 and only a generation or two from America's own revolution. Mackenzie compared the suffering of Canadians to that which had caused the thirteen colonies to break allegiance with British "evils." He wove frontier kinship and revolutionary zeal into his vision of the Canadian Patriots, while carefully avoiding details of the bungled mess he left in Toronto (McLaughlin, 2012).

Next, thirty-six-year-old Thomas Jefferson Sutherland, an American, addressed the emotionally primed audience. Sutherland told them about his trip to Montgomery's tavern just before the Toronto raid when he delivered a letter signed by several Buffalonians that expressed support for the Patriot cause. Calling himself a colonel, Sutherland described the fanfare, energy, and enthusiasm he witnessed among the forces assembled at the tavern. The Buffalo crowd cheered when he described Mackenzie reading Buffalo's letter to his troops. Sutherland, fancying himself a natural-born leader, announced his willingness to be made a general in any force raised to support Canadian freedom. He closed with a request for ammunition, weapons, and men to form an army of liberation. The response was immediate, generous, and loud (Lindsey, 1862; McLaughlin, 2012).

Mackenzie appeared all over the city in the next few days. He spoke of taxation without representation, of stacked juries, of the British Crown's all-powerful upper house and its total disregard for the popularly elected assembly. He stirred crowds by asserting that Canadians and Americans were "the same people, having the same native energy, the same origin, and speaking the same language." Mackenzie promised audiences that a few thousand men could easily defeat the British troops, who he described as just a few pensioners waiting to return to Great Britain. Also overcome by his own rhetoric, Mackenzie began offering 300 acres of land for every soldier and a bounty of $100 in silver once his revolution succeeded. It was far beyond his reach, but the idea sold well to Western New Yorkers still suffering the effects of the 1836 recession (S. Evans, 2019).

≈

As December 1837 wore on, large grassroot gatherings built on the Hunters Lodge movement erupted in towns all along the American side of the border in Burlington, Albany, Rochester, Buffalo, Cleveland, and Detroit. Mackenzie was everywhere, stirring crowds and relying on the financial support of Dr. Chapin's friends and associates (S. Evans, 2019).

Buffalo's Eagle Tavern on Main Street became Mackenzie's headquarters and proudly flew the Patriot tricolored, two-star banner from its flagpole. Mackenzie pushed for an all-out invasion of Canada, and by mid-December he chose his leadership team. First and foremost was his wealthiest supporter, Rensselaer van Rensselaer, a member of the New York State militia who had never seen battle. Mackenzie named Van Rensselaer the commanding officer of his new Patriot army. Van Rensselaer's only credential, beyond money, was being a descendant of a long line of decorated military men, including Stephen Van Rensselaer of the Queenston battle. Van Rensselaer reasoned that being Canada's liberator would make him as famous as Sam Houston, who had recently liberated Texas. At that point in his life, Van Rensselaer's only notoriety was an abiding allegiance to hard liquor.

Rounding out Mackenzie's leadership team was the verbose Thomas Jefferson Sutherland who had told of delivering the Buffalo support letter to Montgomery's tavern, and Dr. John Rolph, who was a Mackenzie coconspirator at Montgomery's tavern. The ambitious Sutherland had experience in the US Marine Corps and was the editor of an anti-Masonic Democratic newspaper in Troy, New York. Dr. Rolph was a Toronto physician and Patriot who had made a separate escape to Buffalo following the failed Toronto uprising (S. Evans, 2019).

Plans quickly focused on the 300-acre Navy Island in the Niagara River that had been ceded to Canada as part of the Grand Island border negotiations following the War of 1812. Navy Island was just a quarter mile off the northwestern coast of New York's Grand Island and, being surrounded by strong currents in the Niagara River, casual access was difficult. Mackenzie brazenly declared Navy Island independent and convinced his coconspirators that his declaration would spark a rebellious call to arms throughout Canada (Groceman, 2017).

Soon, Van Rensselaer was strutting about the Navy Island camp with a cutlass in one hand and a brandy in the other. He welcomed newcomers and chatted with recruits. They were eager to fight, excited about the farms they planned on Mackenzie's promised land, and unprepared in matters of combat. So far, the 1837 to 1838 winter had been comparatively mild, but the crude huts that sheltered the hopeful liberators proved no match against even mild winter winds. Boredom and discomfort soon took their toll as it became increasingly clear that Van Rensselaer's most-developed skill was intemperance. Still, men kept arriving and the Navy Island Patriot army grew to nearly 600, half Canadian and half American (McLaughlin, 2012).

With the Niagara River mostly ice-free, a steamboat named the *Caroline* ferried men and essential supplies between Black Rock and Navy Island. On the night of December 29, 1837, the British sent a raiding party to the American shore at Black Rock where the *Caroline* was docked. Fifteen sailors slept on the boat, and some reports say all fifteen were killed before the British set the *Caroline* on fire and pushed it into the river currents that carried it over Niagara Falls. The body of Amos Durfee, a freed Black man who worked on the *Caroline*, lay on the dock, shot through the head. Later that day, Durfee's body was carried to Buffalo for burial, attracting a large and excited crowd (S. Evans, 2019).

The *Caroline* raid gave Buffalo newspapers plenty more fodder with which to stoke the tensions already set aflame by Mackenzie and Dr. Chapin. Many more unproven insults and accusations amplified the heroics as sympathetic Americans continued sending money and men to support Mackenzie.

Neither Congress nor President van Buren wanted war with America's two largest trading partners, Canada and Britain. Immediately after the *Caroline* raid, van Buren received a courier from Sir Francis Head, the

Figure 20.2. The burning *Caroline* nears the edge of Niagara Falls in December 1837. (Painting by George Tattersall, 1838.) *Source:* Archives of the Buffalo and Erie County Historical Society. Public domain.

lieutenant-governor of Upper Canada. Head apologized for the attack on the *Caroline* and admitted that the raid occurred on sovereign American soil and was therefore improper. van Buren readily accepted the apology.

Now it was up to van Buren to enforce peace. He sent General Winfield Scott to Buffalo with official orders to ward off further British intrusion, but his real mission was to enforce the Neutrality Act established after the War of 1812. Upon his arrival, Scott cut off new American reinforcements for the Patriots on Navy Island. Between Scott's presence, the boredom of winter, and the threat of no fresh supplies, the Americans on Navy Island began leaving for home.

By January 13, 1838, Van Rensselaer and Mackenzie also abandoned Navy Island and withdrew to Buffalo. As soon as Mackenzie stepped onto American soil, authorities arrested him for offenses under the Neutrality Act. His bail was set at $5,000, an amount his supporters quickly raised. In the several months it would take before Mackenzie went to trial, he continued to agitate for a Canadian invasion (McLaughlin, 2012).

Both Montgomery's tavern and Navy Island proved to be ambitious enterprises guided by chaotic and inadequate administration, with Mackenzie as the common element. However, the many Hunters Lodges were not inclined to relinquish their enthusiasm easily. Their focus shifted from one massive invasion to skirmishes at multiple locations from Detroit to the St. Lawrence. At the same time, General Scott organized his efforts to discourage American participation in any operations against Canada. In Buffalo, he appointed militia Captain Amon N. Clapp, then the newspaper editor of the *Aurora Standard*, to organize a body of American regulars and volunteers to patrol the eastern shore of Lake Erie (Kinchen, 1956; T. Rosenthal, 2022).

As January 1838 progressed, winter assumed its more-usual frigid temperatures and Lake Erie quickly froze over. Sensing an opportunity, a band of Hunters Lodge enthusiasts, supported by Dr. Cyrenius Chapin, commenced plans for an invasion of Canada in mid-February. To prepare the way, forty men departed from Bayview, a hamlet on the Lake Erie shore south of Buffalo, to set up a staging camp on the lake ice. Several newspapers, including the *Aurora Standard*, attached Dr. Chapin to this effort, and some reports place him on the ice with the staging party. The staging party built several shanties and gathered hemlock boughs for bedding. They also arranged a line of pine boughs across the ice to guide the expected invading force to a landing on a secluded Canadian beach (S. Evans, 2020).

An informant passed word to General Scott that an illegal raid was in the works. Scott ordered the interruption of a Buffalo Hunters Lodge meeting and confirmed the invasion plans, including the staging party. Scott immediately sent troops to disperse the para-militia training camp set up in Bayview to ready men for the cross-ice invasion. Captain Clapp's unit was sent out onto the frozen Lake Erie in sleighs where, four miles out, they found the staging camp, pine boughs, and makeshift shanties. The interlopers promptly surrendered as Clapp's men demolished the shanties and confiscated all their firearms, including a large quantity of crude pikes fitted with a spear and hook to be used by men who had no access to a gun. Once back on the American shore, the would-be invaders were allowed to return to their homes, provided they promised no further participation in military actions against Canada (S. Evans, 2019; White, 1898).

Cyrenius Chapin, just days past his sixty-ninth birthday, had contributed much in the way of leadership, money, and energy to support Mackenzie's mission. The lake-ice invasion would have been his third personal effort to liberate his Canadian friends from the British yoke. It is impossible to confirm rumors that Chapin was in the staging party, but present or not, the winter winds had turned bitter for Cyrenius Chapin. He took a chill that developed into a fever, and within a few days of the Lake Erie ice debacle, Dr. Chapin took to his bed, likely with pneumonia. On February 20, 1838, Dr. Cyrenius Chapin died in his home on Seneca Street (C. Johnson, 1876; White, 1898).

~

The last week of March 1838, Sir Francis Bond Head resigned from his position as lieutenant-governor. In his hurry to return to England, he saddled a horse to rush across New York State, intent on boarding a ship in New York City. While staying a night in Watertown, New York, he was recognized and a posse from a local Hunters Lodge chased him for several miles. Head, however, was an accomplished horseman and made his way to New York City without ever coming close to capture (Bonnycastle, 1852).

The week following Clapp's breakup of the Lake Erie ice raid, Stephan Chase, a young law student from Rochester, New York, was arraigned before a Buffalo Judge. In short order, he was convicted of leading the rogue Buffalo militia group and planning the Lake Erie invasion that Chapin had supported. Charges included conspiring to invade Canada and conducting several other sorties into Canada that included the burning of several buildings (Editor, 1838b).

Isolated skirmishes were all that remained of the waning Patriot war, but civilian dissatisfaction with the British parliament was deep-seated, leading to passage of the North America Act in 1840. That act began a reform process in the Canadian provinces that eventually lead to the creation of a Canada dominion within the British Monarchy in 1867. The United States passed the Remedial Justice Act in 1842, which firmly placed foreign relations as the sole responsibility of the United States federal government and made it illegal for states or individuals to claim any such authority.

Mackenzie's eventual conviction for breaching United States neutrality laws resulted in eleven months in a Rochester, New York, jail. To support his family, he published a fallacious book telling his version of the rebellion. After release, Mackenzie traveled around the United States raising money and making inflammatory speeches (Dent, 1885). In 1840, he started a British hate newspaper he called *Mackenzie's Gazette*. Nonetheless, in 1849, the government of Upper Canada pardoned Mackenzie and allowed him to return to Toronto. In 1851, he was elected to the provincial legislature, serving from 1851 to 1858. During World War II, his grandson, William Lyon Mackenzie King, served as Canada's tenth prime minister.

Rensselaer van Rensselaer did not fare so well. He spent six months in jail for his role in the Navy Island camp. Twelve years later, on January 1, 1850, he committed suicide.

Canadian historians blame the hostilities of 1838 to 1840 on Hunters Lodges and Patriot Societies located mostly on the American side of the border. Most maintain that a few Canadian refugees financed by American enthusiasts urged the combatants on, resulting in the death of several dozen innocent Canadians (Read, 1896). One last attempt to wrestle control of Canada away from Britain occurred in 1866, the year before Canadian independence. The Fenians, an arm of the Irish Republican Army joined by several hundred Irish Americans and Civil War veterans, assembled in Buffalo and crossed the Niagara River at Black Rock. After planting their flag on the Canadian shore, the Fenians were forced to return to Buffalo (Bohen, 2012; Groceman, 2017).

~

There was little official ceremony over the death of Dr. Cyrenius Chapin. American support for the Patriot wars, though widespread, was officially illegal. Some detractors suggested that Dr. Chapin was drunk and incapable of making sound decisions at the time of his death (Cruikshank, 1900). There is ample evidence to support Dr. Chapin's appreciation of distilled spirits, but there is no existing reference to his appearing drunk in public. Nonetheless, the sum total of one short obituary appeared in the *Buffalo Gazette* and it was obliged to mention "foibles." It follows:

> Dr. Cyrenius Chapin—The brave old soldier, the consistent and true patriot, the useful and esteemed citizen, is no more. He expired at his dwelling after a short illness on Tuesday last (2/20/38), in the 66th [sic] year of his age. On Thursday, the birthday of Washington, his body was followed to the grave by an immense concourse of citizens, and consigned to its last home with military honors. There let him rest, and his foibles with him, for he had them; while his private worth, his real virtues, and his eminent services shall long rest in the memories and hearts of our citizens. (*Buffalo Gazette* February 26, 1838; Editor, 1838a)

Chapter 21

The Legacy of Cyrenius Chapin

Deeds Performed by Broad Shoulders, and Capable Hands, Cheat Death of Its Finality

Contemporaries said Dr. Cyrenius Chapin's personality was defined by his passions. He often seemed blind to controversy, yet controversy stuck to him like a burr. He was self-assured and held to his opinions with little regard for the chaos that might result. As he applied these same traits to his work as a doctor, patients felt like he was fighting for them, and he was always fighting. In Dr. Gorham Pratt's biography, prepared in 1868 for the Erie County Medical Society, he reviewed the ten years he spent associated with Dr. Chapin—first as an apprentice, then as a partner. He described Chapin's restlessness as "perseverance driven by an indomitable and aggressive spirit" (G. F. Pratt, 1869). Pratt may have captured the most-concise description of Chapin's life.

William Ketchum (1798–1876) was a contemporary of Dr. Chapin's and a Buffalo mayor in 1844. He wrote several biographies of Western New York people. According to Ketchum, in the last few years of his life, Dr. Chapin lapsed into "a disregard of Christian duty" by "too free use of ardent spirits." He makes no mention that Americans, in general, were consuming more hard liquor per person in the 1830s than any time before or after (Rorabaugh, 1979). Several anecdotes confirm that Dr. Chapin enjoyed his drink; however, only Ketchum and a few Canadian historians suggest that drinking got the best of Dr. Chapin. Even Ketchum concedes that Chapin's fellow Buffalo pioneers held the doctor in high esteem, both as a citizen and a soldier in the War of 1812 (Ketchum, 1865).

Another nineteenth-century historian and Cornell faculty member, Crisfield Johnson, summarized the obituary carried in the *Buffalo Bulletin*, adding, "Old Dr. Chapin had been prominent during the winter [1837–1838], making speeches at the meetings of the [Canadian] sympathizers, and feeling all his youthful fires revive at the prospect of another war with England. But his waning power was unable to keep pace with his feelings, and in February he sickened and died" (C. Johnson, 1876).

A Rochester, New York, newspaper published the most-extensive tribute to Dr. Chapin a few days after his death. The *Monroe Times* obituary read: "From a somewhat familiar knowledge of the public services of Dr. Chapin as one of the founders of Buffalo, as a man of exalted character and high enterprise, as one of the most patriotic and daring defenders of our frontier during the late war, as an eminent physician and truly philanthropic man, we cannot withhold (now that he is gathered unto his fathers) our testimony of his worth, and our regrets at his decease. . . . Dr. Chapin possessed of eminent generosity of heart and energy of character, probably accomplished more than any other individual in alleviating the hardships and improving the condition of the first settlers of the Holland Purchase, and in promoting the prosperity of Buffalo" (Ketchum, 1865).

Cyrenius Chapin died surrounded by family in the stately Seneca Street home he and Sylvia had built after the War of 1812. He was the last person buried in the "New Amsterdam" Franklin Square Cemetery bounded by Franklin, Church, Delaware, and Eagle Streets. It was only a few steps from the spot where, in December 1813, he defended Buffalo using the makeshift cannon he likely stole off a British frigate the year before. The cemetery was the one that he, Samuel Pratt, and Joseph Ellicott had carved out of Holland Land Company holdings in 1805. By 1838 it had fallen out of use, but a special permit was obtained to allow Dr. Chapin's burial. The graves would later be moved to Forest Lawn Cemetery to make way for a new Erie County Hall, today known as the "old county hall." Dr. Chapin's gravesite was directly beneath the present Church Street entrance to that old county hall. His wife, Sylvia, was the doctor's sole heir and was awarded a continuation of the government pension that her husband had received for his sacrifices during the War of 1812. She died on October 1, 1863, and both Cyrenius and Sylvia now rest in Forest Lawn Cemetery in Buffalo (C. Chapin, 1838; Kohler, 2010).

≈

Figure 21.1. Old Erie County Hall on the site of Buffalo's first cemetery. Dr. Chapin's original grave was near the front doors. *Source: Buffalo Evening News*, 1908. Public domain.

By the time of Chapin's death in 1838, Buffalo had begun its long embrace of architecturally magnificent buildings, wide streets, city squares, and parks that Frederick Law Olmsted would retool after the Civil War. By 1840, politicians proclaimed their city of 20,000 people to be *the* hub for Great Lakes trade, a financial center of growing importance, and a cradle for the arts (Ketchum, 1865). In 1840, the lot Dr. Chapin purchased in 1803 at the corner of Main and Swan Streets for $346 was estimated to be worth $150,000, which would be about $4 million in twenty-first-century currency. The property remained in possession of the Chapin family for several more decades (G. F. Pratt, 1869). Eventually, the offices of the Erie County Medical Society would be located on the site of Dr. Chapin's office at the Main and Swan site. The society continued at that site for most of the twentieth century.

Figure 21.2. Building at Buffalo's Main and Swan Streets, former site of Dr. Cyrenius Chapin's office and drugstore. This building was the home of the Erie County Medical Society for much of the twentieth century. *Source:* Kohler, 2010. Used with permission.

Cyrenius and Sylvia Chapin anchored their lives around Dr. Chapin's medical practice and their success in the areas of investments was remarkable, but they suffered tragedy and loss at home. Only one of the couple's five children was alive in 1838. Their first child, Sylvia, was born on February 7, 1796, and died at age thirty-six on December 1, 1832, as the cholera epidemic swept Buffalo and the United States. She had married the son of Reverend Elkana Holmes, Buffalo's first regular pastor and a frequent guest in the Chapin home. The Chapins' second child, Royal, lived only six weeks. Their third child, and only son, was born in 1800, though no specific birthdate can be confirmed. He was named Cyrenius Burnham

Chapin and died of unknown causes on April 1, 1811. The Seneca Chief Red Jacket had taken an interest in young Cyrenius and joined the Chapins in mourning the child's death. He attended the funeral and presented a series of gifts to commemorate the boy's spirit. Their fourth child was born on January 13, 1801. She was named Amelia and died at age seventeen on August 15, 1818, cause unrecorded. A fifth child, Louise, was born in 1803. She would match her parents' contribution to Buffalo's continued development. All family members are now buried in Plot Section 5 of Forest Lawn Cemetery in Buffalo (Burr, 1927).

Louise Chapin Weed died on July 20, 1894, at age ninety-one. She married Thaddeus Weed on October 9, 1823, and proved a credit to her parents' belief that daughters need to "learn more than how to make a good shirt and cook a tasty pudding." At the time of her death, she was the oldest member of St. Paul's Parish and had lived in Buffalo longer than any other person. She was the last person to remember Buffalo being called New Amsterdam and told vivid stories of fleeing the fiery village at age eleven. (Illustrated, 1906–1908).

The well-read Louise proved a valuable confidant to her husband, who she survived by many years. When Thaddeus Weed arrived in Buffalo by stagecoach in 1818 from Troy, New York, he made two observations: first, the 842 whites and 1,200 Native Americans were mostly dirt farmers who could not raise 5 dollars cash if they had to, and second, the closest place to purchase a shovel or a hoe was 35 miles away in Batavia. Weed set about opening the very successful Weed Hardware Store on the northwest corner of Main and Swan Streets, next to Dr. Chapin's office. A young Louise may have admired the purposeful newcomer from the windows of her father's office. In those early years, Weed understood that a large part of his success would depend on the support of the Senecas. So, when Red Jacket wished to trade three panther hides for an ax and a bridle, Weed accepted, securing Red Jacket as a steady client for years.

Both having harkened from New England Puritan stock, Thaddeus and Louise Weed patiently allowed several years for their mutual admiration to blossom into courtship. They married in the autumn of 1823 and raised three children: DeWitt, Louise, and Hobart Weed. After his father's death in 1846, Hobart helped his mother run the hardware business for the rest of the nineteenth century (C. W. Evans, 1903).

⁓

Two years before his death, Buffalo presented Dr. Cyrenius Chapin and Sylvia with a silver setting of two massive pitchers and twelve goblets. An ad-hoc committee led by General Peter Porter planned the 1836 tribute after Chapin's partner, Gorham Pratt, expressed concern that the then sixty-six-year-old doctor might be slowing down a little. The planning committee included Hiram Pratt and Chapin's competitor and former mayor Dr. Ebenezer Johnson, as well as several other Buffalo dignitaries. The city council passed a proclamation that read: "From a somewhat familiar knowledge of the public services of Dr. Chapin, as one of the founders of Buffalo—as a man of exalted character and high enterprise, as one of the most patriotic and daring defenders of our frontier during the late war—as an eminent physician and truly philanthropic man—we cannot withhold our testimony of his worth" (Ketchum, 1865; G. F. Pratt, 1869). The pair of silver pitchers and goblets were represented as a gift from the citizens of Buffalo and are in the possession of the Buffalo Historical Society. Dr. Chapin continued to practice medicine after 1836, though the dependable and well-liked Gorham Pratt carried much of the burden for urgent work.

Figure 21.3. Pitcher presented to Dr. Chapin in 1836. *Source:* Kohler, 2010. Used with permission.

Hiram Pratt, the son of Chapin's friend Samuel Pratt and a partner in the Chapin and Pratt general store, added to the 1836 accolades by describing Dr. Chapin as "one of the most remarkable men of western New York. Few men have led a more useful life, and still fewer have woven into their career so many romantic and exciting incidents." Hiram Pratt was like a son to the Chapins. He was the same age as their deceased son and his father, Samuel, had joined Dr. Chapin in the effort to secure land for the Franklin Square Cemetery. When his father died prematurely, Hiram became a regular in the Chapin household. As the British burned Buffalo, Dr. Chapin trusted the thirteen-year-old Hiram to escort his wife and daughters on the wintery eighteen-mile walk to the Chapin farm in Hamburg. After Buffalo's destruction, Hiram Pratt and his mother joined the Chapins in Geneva, New York. Dr. Chapin and Hiram's mother both encouraged Hiram to become a doctor, but Hiram viewed himself as a businessman, a vocation that attracted another Chapin apprentice, Orlando Allen (Letchworth, 1874). Hiram and Orlando became close friends, so when Dr. Chapin offered the two young men an opportunity to assume management of his store, they started what would become a lifelong collaboration. Hiram went on to build a fleet of Great Lakes steamships, construct the Frontier Mills at Black Rock, and found the Bank of Buffalo. The Common Council elected Hiram Pratt mayor in 1839, though the recession of 1837 had shattered his optimism and his spirit. He died on May 1, 1840, at age forty and is buried in Forest Lawn Cemetery.

Like so many others, Orlando Allen also adopted his mentor's habit of melding professional and community work. Any telling of Dr. Chapin's life story requires several mentions of Orlando Allen. He was born in the village of New Hartford, New York, on February 10, 1803, to parents who knew the Chapins in Oneida County. In 1819, at age sixteen, he came to Buffalo to enter apprenticeship training in Dr. Chapin's office. He, too, was a descendent of the New England Puritan culture with little formal schooling, but he was possessed by a fondness for reading. Dr. Chapin and his partner at the time, Dr. Congdon, provided professional services north into Canada's Niagara peninsula and as far south as Erie, Pennsylvania, covering all of it on horseback. Orlando quickly picked up the Seneca language, but his talents gravitated to accounts receivable generated by his supervising doctors. In the process, he found an aptitude for numbers and was quick to appreciate that poor farmers existed in a mostly cashless culture. Seeking payments from the practice's few wealthy families was essential to achieving the mission both his preceptors espoused. Orlando was a curious young man. He quickly read all of Dr. Chapin's extensive medical library and acquired the skeleton that hung in Dr. Chapin's office. But his genius was his straightforward approach to commerce and administration. By his second year, he took on the management of Chapin's farming operations and improved the marketing strategies for their products (Bryant, 1877; Rizzo, 2010).

Chapin's struggles with the Seneca language were well known, but Orlando loved to listen to and retell stories about Native American culture. He was a skilled mimic, and the drama in his presentations revealed a sensitivity for people and traditions. When Orlando joined Hiram Pratt in managing Chapin's new general store, he obtained permission from the Senecas to market mineral oil derived from Native lands near French Creek. It was a big seller and profitable for the Senecas and for the store. In 1831, Orlando married Hiram Pratt's sister, Marilla, and later became the president of the Bank of Buffalo. From 1848 to 1849, he served as the eighteenth mayor of Buffalo and later as a New York State assemblymen endorsed by the Whig party (Bryant, 1877; Rizzo, 2010).

Bryant Burwell, a native of Herkimer County, became Dr. Chapin's apprentice in 1824. Dr. Burwell was a graduate of Fairfield Medical College near Utica, New York, and completed additional training in Philadelphia. He served as the vice president of the Erie County Medical Society in 1832 and a delegate to the state society in 1833. He was a consultant to the state legislature about issues of physician licensure and a permanent member of the State Medical Society. Dr. Burwell represented the Buffalo Medical Association at the initial convention held in New York City in 1846, and he was a delegate to the first and second meetings of the American Medical Association held in Philadelphia (1847) and Baltimore (1848). Dr. Burwell died in 1861 (White, 1898).

The aforementioned Gorham F. Pratt was born in Reading, Massachusetts, in 1804 and came to Buffalo in 1830 at age twenty-six. He entered the office of Dr. Cyrenius Chapin as a medical student and took his doctorate degree at Fairfield Medical College near Utica, New York, in 1831. Soon afterward, he formed a partnership with Dr. Chapin and continued as a partner until Dr. Chapin's death. Dr. Pratt became a member of the county society in 1833; served as its secretary from 1834 to 1840; and was elected the vice president in 1840, becoming president in 1841. Pratt acquired a large practice among Buffalo's best families and was considered one of the most-distinguished physicians of his time. He died April 5, 1851 (White, 1898).

In the 1868 Erie County Medical Society tribute to Dr. Chapin, thirty years after his death, Gorham Pratt wrote: "He [Dr. Chapin] was not a man to tamely submit to adversity, but by it stimulated to greater activity." Like Chapin, Dr. Pratt was noted for his charities, his hospitalities, and as a friend of the poor. In all business transactions, both men were strictly honest, but according to Pratt, Chapin was particularly intolerant of deceit or duplicity and blunt to a fault. Like his mentor, Pratt took a lively interest in public affairs and carried on the tradition of active support of the Buffalo community (G. F. Pratt, 1869).

Another of Dr. Chapin's apprentices, Dr. Jacob Jemison, was a grandson of Mary Jemison and raised in the Seneca Buffalo Creek village. He trained with Dr. Chapin from 1820 to 1823. Historical documentation is contradictory, but it seems that Dr. Chapin became familiar with Jacob in 1811 after Jacob's father, Thomas, was killed by Jacob's uncle. The Jemison brothers, Thomas and John, were no strangers to alcohol, but John had a history of abusing his wife. Thomas confronted John one day and the two men took to an angry fight that ended with Thomas's death by tomahawk. The act was declared self-defense and John was acquitted at trial. At some point, Dr. Chapin took an interest in Jacob, eventually helping him get admitted to Dartmouth College in 1816 and later may have helped him enroll in a "medical college near Albany." Jacob would have been one of Chapin's most-educated apprentices. He later became a surgeon's mate in the Navy and died of fever on a ship in the Mediterranean. He was buried at sea (Seaver, 1860).

~

In 1836, General Peter B. Porter wrote a letter to Dr. Chapin, his friend and fellow soldier. Porter reflects on their shared experience during the War of 1812 and his respect for Chapin: "I know of no individual who was on all occasions more open and decided in the expression of opinions, approving the justice of the war on our part; none who displayed more patriotic zeal and enthusiasm in encouraging and aiding its efficient prosecution; none who was more ready to embark in every emergency, and who actually did embark in almost uninterrupted succession of enterprises against the enemy, involving imminent personal hazard, as well as great fatigue and privation, none more liberal of his purse and I think I may safely add, measuring the merits by the number and importance of the various commands and commissions which were confided to you, and the limited means furnished for their execution, none who rendered more valuable service to the army and country than yourself" (Samo, 1884).

Today, there is a street in Buffalo named Chapin Parkway. Several writers, including an article in the 1941 *Courier Express* newspaper, claim that the residential street is named after Dr. Cyrenius Chapin. Such attribution ignores the street marked the southern boundary of Dr. Daniel Chapin's farm, making it more likely to have been named for Dr. Daniel Chapin, not Cyrenius (Anonymous, 1941). Given their on-again, off-again relationship in life, it is only appropriate that the naming of Chapin Parkway carries on their quarrels.

∼

Five stalwart physicians must be credited with establishing a proud tradition for medical practice and community service in Buffalo, New York. As physicians, their work depended on an accommodating bedside manner that combined knowledge, common sense, kindness, and confidence. Other than a few minor surgical procedures, they offered little more than comfort and encouragement for families and patients while natural immunity won or lost its fight. In the process, they came to understand their community and its broader needs.

Of these physicians—Cyrenius Chapin, Daniel Chapin, Ebenezer Johnson, Josiah Trowbridge, and John E. Marshall—none stand out more than Dr. Cyrenius Chapin. His contributions were local, but he identified himself as a physician, a citizen, and an American patriot willing to risk his life and treasure. He seemed predisposed, and at times eager, to bear the burden of a soldier. He could be demanding and difficult but was absolutely honest in his dealings with patients and fellow pioneers. Chapin could not say no to calls upon his skill, sympathy, or charity. Though personally entrepreneurial, he made great sacrifices in defense of his country and its interests, as he believed them to be. His was an age of revolutions at a time when independence not only referred to a national government, but also meant individual self-determination. Chapin was Western New York's version of a local influencer, vital to shaping the postrevolutionary American experiment.

Acknowledgments

·

Viewing history through the life of one particular person requires accepting conditions and attitudes that might be considered problematic in today's culture. The most obvious is the use of "Indian," common to Dr. Chapin's day but mostly replaced by a more respectful Native American or Indigenous people today. Because attitude drove so much of Cyrenius Chapin's life, the term "Indian" is often retained here to reflect the relationship between white settlers and Native Americans in nineteenth-century Buffalo. Most references to Britain, or Great Britain as it was called after 1707, indicate actions and policies of the unified England, Wales, and Scotland.

The War of 1812 lasted two and a half years. Britain's resources were stretched by its battle with Napoleon, and the United States was challenged by its own lack of preparation and inconsistency of leadership. The accounts of the war given here are centered on Dr. Cyrenius Chapin and gloss over many of the details described by more extensive works. Background is given to understand Dr. Chapin's role, but it is not a complete account of the war, nor of its effect on the maturation of the "American Experiment." In the citations, readers will find several excellent books with much greater detail about the War of 1812. Readers are encouraged to read the cited works by Benn, Berton, Cruikshank, Elting, Hickey, Taylor, and others.

There were several treaties that have gone down in history as the *Treaty of Paris* because they were signed in Paris. One such treaty in 1763 ended the war known as the Seven Year War in Europe and the French and Indian War in North America. Another *Treaty of Paris* marked the formal end of the American Revolution in 1783, and still another *Treaty of Paris* ended the Spanish-American War in 1898. I have used dates to specify which *Treaty of Paris* is being referenced.

Wherever possible, two or more references have corroborated historical accounts described in the book. Many times, historical accounts contradict each other. Interpretations of intent by historical figures and even specific dates can vary. This is most obvious when reading accounts of the battles fought on the Niagara Frontier. For instance, Canadian historians treat Laura Secord as a hero and credit her with saving Canadian independence. American historians tell the same story but suggest that she betrayed her friendship with Dr. Chapin. This story, and others, are told here with respect for both viewpoints, focusing on the roles of individuals within the context of their situation.

The reader is likely frustrated that there is little coverage of Dr. Chapin's family in the text. It is a frustration shared by the author. I intended to tell a very personal story of Dr. Chapin, but years of research and chasing down official archives revealed little more than a very few cryptic references in church documents. Louise, the youngest daughter, had a long life and contributed significantly to the success of the Weed Hardware enterprise. Yet, as was the custom of the time, her husband and son received most of the headlines.

I am indebted to my beta readers who read the early versions of this book. They include Georgia Rosenthal, Stephanie Cooper, and Dr. "Joe" Lanigan. SUNY Press acquisition editor Richard Carlin has patiently supported the project. His discipline and expertise made the book better, more readable, and more accurate. SUNY Press used a panel of peer reviewers who, while anonymous to me, contributed several valuable suggestions, making for a more readable text. The production staff at SUNY Press include Michael Campochiaro, Julia Cosacchi, Ryan Morris, and James Peltz. They proved not only capable, but also talented. My copy editor, Alexandra Hoff, painstakingly fixed my typos and improved my phrasing. Thank you all.

Georgia Rosenthal, my wife, has been a steadfast supporter throughout this project and read every chapter well before they were polished. Amazing!

Bibliography

Abrams, J. E. (2013). *Revolutionary Medicine: The Founding Fathers and Mothers in Sickness and in Health*. New York: New York University Press.

Adams, C. K., & Trent, W. P. (1909). *A History of the United States*. Boston: Allyn and Bacon.

Adams, F. (1886). *The Genuine Works of Hippocrates*. London: Sydenham.

Aigin, J. (1814). Reminiscience. Retrieved from https://nyheritage.contentdm.oclc.org/digital/collection/VTP005/id/244/rec/6

Allen, L. F. (1896). First appearance, in 1832, of the cholera in Buffalo. With incidental notices of the late Roswell H. Haskins. Extract from paper read before the society. In B. H. Society (Ed.), *Ithaca, New York: Cornell University Library* (pp. 245–46). Buffalo, NY.

Allen, R. S. (2006). The British Indian Department and the Frontier in North America, 1755–1830. *Canadian Historic Sites: Occasional Papers in Archaeology and History No. 14*(14).

Anderson, T. A. (1831). *The Practical Monitor for the Preservation of Health and the Prevention of Diseases*. Philadelphia: Z. Jayne.

Anonymous. (1941, November 9). Chapin Parkway. *Courier Express*.

Arabaci, B. (2023). Pearls' of the Nineteenth Century: From Therapeutic Actors to Global Commodities, Medicinal Leeches in the Ottoman Empire. *Medical History, 67*(2), 128–47.

Assembly, N. Y. (1812). Thirty-Fourth Session. *Journal of the Assembly of the State of New York*.

Atkins, B. (1898). *Sketches of Early Buffalo and the Great Lakes*. Buffalo: The Courier Company.

Auchinleck, G. (1972). *A History of the War Between Great Britain and the UNited States of America During the Years 1812, 1813 & 1814*. Toronto: Pendragon House Limited.

Ayers, E. L. (2023). *American Visions: The United States, 1800–1860*. New York: W. W. Norton.

Barbuto, R. V. (2014). *Staff Ride Handbook for the Niagara Campaigns, 1812–1814*. Fort Leavenworth, Kansas: Combat Studies Institute Press: US Army Combined Arms Center.

Benn, C. (1998). *The Iroquois in the War of 1812*: University of Toronto Press.

Berton, P. (1981). *Flames Across the Border: The Canadian-American Tragedy, 1813–1814*. Boston: Little, Brown.

Biniasz, M. (2000). *On Behalf of the Erie County Agricultural Society, Erie County Fair, Hamburg, New York*. Dover: Arcadia Publishing. Retrieved from https://www.google.com/books/edition/Erie_County_Fair/wMTFAwAAQBAJ

Bogue, D. (1852). *The Etiquette of Courtship and Matrimony: with a Complete Guide to the Forms of a Wedding*. London: Savill and Edwards.

Bohen, T. (2012). *Against the Grain: The History of Buffalo's First Ward*. Buffalo: Bohane Books, LLC.

Bonnycastle, R. H. (1852). *Canada, as It Was, and May Be* (Vol. 1 & 2). London: Colburn and Co.

Borneman, W. R. (2006). *The French and Indian War: Deciding the Fate of North America*. New York: HarperCollins.

Brands, H. W. (2018). *Heirs of the Founders: The Epic Rivalry of Henry Clay, John Calhoun and Daniel Webster, the Second Generation of American Giants*. New York: Doubleday.

Broadwater, R. P. (2012). *American Generals of the Civil War: A Biographical Dictionary*. North Carolina: McFarland Incorporated.

Brown, D. S. (2022). *The First Populist: The Defiant Life of Andrew Jackson*. New York: Scribner.

Brown, J. B. (1812). Case in which the Oil of Turpentine was employed with success in Taenia. *New England Journal of Medicine, 1*, 269–70.

Brown, T. (1824). *Lectures of the Philosophy of the Human Mind*. London: William Tegg.

Bryant, W. C. (1877). Orlando Allen. Glimpses of life in the village of Buffalo. Read before the society, April 16, 1877. Reproduced by Cornell University Library, 1993. Retrieved from https://babel.hathitrust.org/cgi/pt?id=coo.31924067076806&seq=4

Buchan, W. (1826). *Domestic Medicine: A Treatise on the Prevention and Cure of Diseases by Regimen and Simple Medicines* (27th ed.). London: A. R. Spottiswoode.

Burnham, J. C. (2015). *Health Care in America: A History*. Baltimore: Johns Hopkins University Press.

Burr, K. (1927, June 26). Dr. Cyrenius Chapin. *Buffalo Times*.

Carpenter, L. (1823). *Unitarianism: The Doctrin of the Gospel*. Bristol: Parsons and Prower.

Cassedy, J. H. (1986). *Medicine and American Growth 1800–1860*. Madison: University of Wisconsin Press.

Cathell, D. W. (1882). *The Physician Himself and What He Should Add to the Strictly Scientific*. Baltimore: Cushing & Bailey.

Chapin, C. (1832). *Letter to Buffalo Board of Health Listing Cholera Cases*. Buffalo: Buffalo History Museum.

Chapin, C. (1836). *Chapin's Review of Armstrong's Notices of the War of 1812*. Black Rock, NY: B. F. Adams.

Chapin, C. (1838). *Cyrenius Chapin: Last Will*. Buffalo: Buffalo and Erie County Public Library: Archives.

Chapin, G. W. (1924). *The Chapin Book of Genealogical Data Volume 1*. Hartford: Chapin Family Association.

Chazanof, W. (1970). *Joseph Ellicott and the Holland Land Company: The Opening of Western New York*. Syracuse: Syracuse University Press.

Chudacoff, H. P. (1999). *The Age of the Bachelor: Creating an American Subculture*. Princeton, NJ: Princeton University Press.

Clay, H. (1959). *Papers of Henry Clay*. Lexington: University of Kentucky Press.

Combe, G. (1851). *A System of Phrenology*. Boston: Benjamin B. Mussey and Company.

Congress, E. (1824). *Report: Property Captured, or Destroyed by the Enemy, 1812–14*. 18th Congress Second Session, pp. 1–53. Retrieved September 29, 2024, from https://archive.org/details/propertylostcapt00unit#:~:text=Property%20 Lost,%20Captured,%20or%20Destroyed%20by%20the%20Enemy%20 1812-14.%20by

Council, N. L. (2017). *The Devil for Us All—Dr. Cyrenius Chapin*. Retrieved from http://discover1812.blogspot.com/2014/09/the-devil-for-us-all-dr-cyrenius-chapin.html

Cozzens, P. (2024). Brutal Reckoning in the Creek War. *American Heritage, 68*(8). Retrieved September 29, 2024, from https://www.americanheritage.com/ brutal-reckoning-creek-war

Crawford, M. J. (2021). Cinchona. In M. Thurner & J. Pimentel (Eds.), *New World Objects of Knowledge* (pp. 241–46). London: University of London Press.

Cruikshank, E. A. (1888). *The Battle of Lundy's Lane, 1814*. Welland: William T. Sawls.

Cruikshank, E. A. (1896). *The Documentary History of the Campaign on the Niagara Frontier in 1814*. Weland. Retrieved September 29, 2024, from https://hdl. handle.net/2027/aeu.ark:/13960/t2p55wp0w

Cruikshank, E. A. (1900). Immigration from the United States into Upper Canada, 1784–1812—Its Character and Results. Proceedings of the thirty-ninth annual convention of the Ontario Educational Association held in Toronto on the 17th, 18th and 19th April 1900: 263–83. Retrieved September 29, 2024, from https://archive.org/details/ldpd_14439773_000#:~:text=Immigration%20 from%20the%20United%20States%20into%20Upper%20Canada,%20 1784-1812%20-

Cruikshank, E. A. (1912). *A Study of Disaffection in Upper Canada in 1812–5*. Ottawa: Royal Society of Canada.

Davies, J. D. (1955). *Phrenology, Fad and Science: A Nineteenth Century American Crusade*. New Haven: Yale University Press.

Dent, J. C. (1885). *The Story of the Upper Canadian Rebellion Vols. 1&2* (Vols. I & II). Toronto: C. Blackett Robinson.

Devoy, J. (1896). *A History of the City of Buffalo and Niagara Falls*. Buffalo: The Times.

Drake, D. (1832). *A Practical Treatise on the History, Prevalence, and Treatment of Epidemic Cholera*. Cincinnati: Corey and Fairbank.

Duffy, J. (1993). *From Humors to Medical Science: A History of American Medicine* (2nd ed.). Urbana: University of Illinois Press.

Dunlop, W. (1833). *Statistical Sketches of Upper Canada for the Use of Emmigants* (3rd ed.). London: John Murray.

Eberle, J. (1831). *Treatise on the Practice of Medicine*. Philadelphia: John Grigg.

Ebert, M. (1952). The Rise and Development of the American Medical Periodical, 1797–1850. *Bulletin of the Medical Library Association, 40*, 243–76.

Editor. (1812, February 19). Who Shall Decide When Doctors Disagree. *Buffalo Gazette*.

Editor. (1832). Remains of Dr. Spurzheim. *Boston Medical and Surgical Journal*.

Editor. (1838a, February 26). Obituary: Dr. Cyrenius Chapin, Obituary. *Buffalo Gazette*.

Editor. (1838b, February 26). The Patriot War. *Buffalo Bulletin*.

Eisenhower, J. S. D. (2008). *Zachary Taylor, The American Presidents Series*. New York: Times Books.

Elliot, J. (1896). *The Debates in the Several State Conventions on the Adoption of the Federal Constitution as Recommended by the General Convention at Philadelphia, in 1787, Second Edition, 5 Vols*. Philadelphia: J. B. Lippincott & Co.

Elting, J. R. (1991). *Amateurs, to Arms! A Military History of the War of 1812*. Boston: Da Capo Press.

Evans, C. W. (1903). *History of St. Paul's church, Buffalo, N. Y., 1817 to 1888*. Buffalo: The Matthews-Northrup Works.

Evans, P. D. (1924). *The Holland Land Company*. Buffalo: Buffalo Historical Society Publications.

Evans, S. (2019). *The Patriot War: 'Remember the Caroline.'* Retrieved from newyork almanack.com/2019/07/the-patriot-war-remember-the-caroline/

Evans, S. (2020). Patriot Games: William Lyon Mackenzie and the Upper Canada Rebellion. *WNY Heritage*(Winter), 8–17.

Faragher, J. M. (1992). *Daniel Boone: The Life and Legend of an American Pioneer*. New York: Henry Holt and Company.

Filson, J. (1784). *The Discovery, Settlement and Present State of Kentucky*. Lincoln: University of Nebraska.

Finger, S. (2020). Dr. Oliver Wendell Holmes on phrenology: Debunking a fad. *J Hist Neurosci., 29*(4), 385–98. https://doi.org/10.1080/0964704X.2020.1733909

Fischer, J. R. (2007). *The Sullivan Campaign Against the Iroquois, July–September 1779*. Columbia: University of South Carolina Press.

Flint, A. (1882). *A Memoir of Professor James Platt White, MD*. Buffalo: Commercial Advertiser Press.

Fox, D. R. (1919). *The Decline of Aristocracy in the Politics of New York*. New York: Columbia University.

Fried, S. (2018). *Rush: Revolution, Madness, and the Visionary Doctor Who Became a Founding Father*. New York: Crown.

Fuller, M. (1845). *Woman in the Nineteenth Century*. New York: Greeley and McElrath.

Glenn, D. P. (2013). "Savage Barbarities and Petty Depredations": Supply Shortages and Military-Civilian Conflicts in the Niagara Theater, 1812–14. *New York History, 94*(3–4), 182–204. Retrieved from www.jstor.org/stable/newyorkhist.94.3-4.182

Goldman, M. (1983). *High Hopes: The Rise and Decline of Buffalo, New York*. Albany: State University of New York Press.

Goldman, M. (2007). *City on the Edge: Buffalo, New York*. Amherst, NY: Prometheus Books.

Gram, F. C. (1898). Historical Sketch of the Medical Society of the County of Erie. 1821–96. *Buffalo Medical Journal*.

Graves, D. E. (2001). *Guns Across the River: the Battle of the Windmill, 1838*. Toronto: The Friends of Windmill Point.

Graves, D. E. (2024). Memorable in the Annals of the United States, The Curious Case of General Alexander Smyth, 1812. *Western New York Heritage, 26*(4), 50–61.

Graymont, B. (1972). *The Iroquois in the American Revolution*. Syracuse: Syracuse University Press.

Greenhous, B. (1970). A Note on Western Logistics in the War of 1812. *Military Affairs, 34*(2), 41–44.

Greenstone, G. (2010). The History of Bloodletting. *BC Medical Journal, 52*(1), 12–14.

Groceman, R. M. (2017). *The Patriot War and the Fenian Raids: Case Studies in Border Security on the U.S.-Canada Border in the Nineteenth Century*. Fort Leavenworth, KS: Truman State University.

Guthrie, G. (2007). Summary of Known Deaths from 1832, 1849 and 1854 Cholera Epidemics, Buffalo New York. Retrieved from https://drive.google.com/file/d/1AWuzrS1i-tGpm8fEk4w16yaSHVPKpqgp/view?usp=drive_link

Haller, J. S. (1982). The United States Pharmacopoeia: Its origin and revision in the 19th century. *Bulletin of the New York Academy of Medicine, 58*(480–92).

Hannings, B. (2012). *The War of 1812: A Complete Chronology with Biographies of 63 General Officers*. Jefferson, NC: McFarland & Co.

Hauptmann, L. M. (1999). *Conspiracy of interests: Iroquois dispossession and the rise of New York State*. Syracuse: Syracuse University Press.

Hawthorne, G. S. (1848). *The True Pathological Nature of Cholera, and an Infallible Method of Treating It*. Liverpool: John Churchill.

Hertzler, A. E. (1938). *The Horse and Buggy Doctor*. New York: Harper & Brothers.

Hickey, D. R. (2012). *The War of 1812, A Forgotten Conflict*. Urbana: University of Illinois Press.

Hill, H. W. (1923). *Municipality of Buffalo, New York, A History 1720–1923* (Vol. 1). New York: Lewis Historical Publishing Company, Inc.

The History of Grand Island. (2022). Retrieved from Isledegrande.com/Giecom.net

Hodge, W. (1885). *The Late William Hodge, Senior*. Buffalo: Bigelow Brothers.

Hollister, F. M. (1913). *Some Early Buffalo Characters*. Ithaca, NY: Cornell University Library.

Horton, J. T., Douglass, H. S., & Williams, E. T. (1947). *History of Northwestern New York: Erie, Niagara, Wyoming, Genesee and Orleans Counties*. New York: Lewis Historical Pub. Co.

Hosack, D. (1791). *An Inaugural Dissertation on Cholera Morbus*. New York: Samuel Campbell.

Hosack, D. (1820). *Observations on the Means of Improving the Medical Police of the City of New York*. New York: Elam Bliss.

Ikeda, M., Tanaka, S., Saito, S., Ozaki, N., Kamatani, Y., & Iwata, N. (2018). Re-Evaluating Classical Body Type Theories: Genetic Correlation between Psychiatric Disorders and Body Mass Index. *Psychol. Med., 48*(10), 1745–48.

Illustrated, B. A. G. (1906–1908). *Memorial and Family History of Erie County, New York* (Vol. 1). Buffalo, NY: The Winthrop Press.

Inglehart, F. M. (1877). Buffalo's first mayor, Dr. Ebenezer Johnson. Paper read before the society, February 12, 1877. In *B. H. Society* (Ed.). Ithaca, NY: Cornell University Library.

James, W. (1818). *Full and Correct Account of the Military Occurrences of the Late War between Great Britian and the United States of America*. London: Black, Kingsbury, Parbury, and Allen.

Jasanoff, M. (2008). The Other Side of Revolution: Loyalists in the British Empire. *The William and Mary Quarterly, 65*(2), 205–32.

Jenner, E. (1802). *An Inquiry into the Causes and Effects of the Vario-lae Vaccinae, a Disease Discovered in Some of the Western Counties of England, Particularly Gloucestershire and Known by the Name of the Cow Pox* (2nd ed.). Springfield: Ashley and Brewer.

Jennings, F. (1988). *Empire of fortune: crowns, colonies, and tribes in the Seven Years War in America*. New York: Norton.

Jobst, K. A. (2005). Homeopathy, Hahnemann, and The Lancet 250 Years On: A Case of the Emperor's New Clothes? *The Journal of Alternative and Complementary Medicine, 11*, 751–54.

Johnson, C. (1876). *History of Erie County, New York; Being its annals from the Earliest Recorded Events to the Hundredth Year of American Independence*. Buffalo: Matthews & Warren.

Johnson, J. R. (1816). *A Treatise on the Medicinal Leech*. London: Longman, Hurst, Rees, Orme, and Brown.

Kane, M. E. (2022). *Shirts Powdered Red: Haudenosaunee Gender, Trade, and Exchange Across Three Centuries*. Ithaca, NY: Cornell University Press.

Kennard, T. (1858). Medicine Among the Indians. *St. Louis Medical and Surgical Journal, 16*, 392–93.

Kennedy, J. (2023). *Pathogenesis: A History of the World in Eight Plagues*. New York: Random House.

Kenyon, C. M. (1955). Men of Little Faith: The Anti-Federalists on the Nature of Representative Government. *The William and Mary Quarterly, 12*(1), 3–43.

Ketchum, W. (1854). *An Authentic and Comprehensive History of Buffalo* (Vol. 2). Buffalo: Rockwell, Baker & Hill.

Ketchum, W. (1865). *History of Buffalo with Some Account of Its Early Inhabitants, Both Savage and Civilized* (Vol. 2). Buffalo: Rockwell, Baker & Hill.

Kinchen, O. A. (1956). *The Rise and Fall of the Patriot Hunters*. New York: Bookman Associates.

King, L. S. (1982). III. Medical Sects and Their Influence. *JAMA, 248*(10), 1221–24.

King, L. S. (1982). IV. The Founding of the American Medical Association. *JAMA, 248*(14), 1749–752. https://doi.org/10.1001/jama.1982.03330140059036

King, W. H. (1905). *History of Homeopathy and Its Institutions in America*. New York: Lewis Publishing Company.

Klingaman, W., & Klingaman, N. (2013). *The Year Without a Summer: 1816 and the Volcano that Darkened the World and Changed History*. New York: St. Marin's Press.

Knollenberg, B. (1954). General Amherst and Germ Warfare. *Journal of American History, 41*(3), 489–94. https://doi.org/10.2307/1897495

Kohler, C. D. (2010). Colonel Cyrenius Chapin: The Brave Soldier, The Good Citizen, The Honest Man. *WNY Heritage, 12*(4), 28–36.

Landis, H. R. M. (1901). *The History and Development of Medical Science in America as Recorded in the American Journal of the Medical Sciences, an Historical Study*. Philadelphia: Lea Brothers and Co.

Landis, H. R. M. (1912). Austin Flint: his contributions to the art of physical diagnosis and the study of tuberculosis. *Bull Johns Hopkins Hosp, 23*, 182–86.

Laux, W. (2014). The Village of Buffalo 1800–1832. *Adventures in Western New York History, 3*. Retrieved from https://issuu.com/tbhm/docs/the_village_of_buffalo_1800_1832/22

Letchworth, W. P. (1874). *Sketch of the Life of Samuel F. Pratt with Some Account of the Early History of the Pratt Family*. Buffalo: Warren, Johnson & Co.

Lindsey, C. (1862). *The Life and Times of William Lyon Mackenzie*. Toronto: P.R. Randall.

Lippi, D., & Gotuzzo, E. (2014). The greatest steps towards the discovery of Vibrio cholerae. *Clin Microbiol Infect, 20*, 191–95.

Livingston, E. B. (1910). *The Livingstons of Livingston Manor*. New York: Knickerbocker Press.

Livsey, K. E. (1991). *Western New York Land Transactions 1804–1824, 1825–1835*. Baltimore: Genealogical Publishing Co., Inc.

Lockie, L. D. (1968). *Pharmacy on the Niagara Frontier: The Past and Present*. East Aurora, NY: Henry Stewart Incorporated.

Louis, P. C. A. (1836). *Researches on the Effects of Bloodletting in some Inflammatory Diseases and on the Influence of Tartarized Antimony and Vesication in Pneumonitis* (C. G. Putnam, Trans.). Boston: Hilliard, Gray, & Company.

Manley, H. S. (1947). Buying Buffalo from the Indians. *New York History, 28*(3), 313–29.

Manley, H. S. (1950). Red Jacket's Last Campaign: And an Extended Bibliographical Note. *New York History, 31*(2), 149–68. Retrieved from www.jstor.org/stable/23149773

Marquis, A. N. (1902). *Men of Buffalo: a collection of portraits of men who deserve to rank as typical representatives of the best citizenship*. Chicago: A. N. Marquis & Company.

Matthews, A. (1909). Uncle Sam. *Proceedings of the American Antiquarian Society, 19*, 21–65.

Maude, J. (1826). *Journal of a Visit to the Falls of Niagara in 1800*. London: Longman, Rees, Orme, Brown & Green.

McKenzie, R. (1971). *Laura Secord: The Legend and the Lady*. Toronto: McClelland and Stewart.

McLaughlin, S. J. (2012). *The Patriot War Along the New York-Canada Border*. The History Press.

McWilliams, J. (1976). The Faces of Ethan Allen: 1760–1860. *The New England Quarterly, 49*(2), 257–82. Retrieved from https://www.jstor.org/stable/364502

Meeks, E. (2022). Urchins of New York and Elsewhere: Remembering the Sky Parlor for Lost Children and the Public's Fascination with Those Who Went Astray. *JSTOR Daily*. Retrieved from https://daily.jstor.org/daily-author/elly-meeks/

Mohr, F., Redwood, T., & Procter, W. (1849). *Practical Pharmacy: The Arrangements, Apparatus, and Manipulations of the Pharmaceutical Shop and Laboratory*. London: Taylor, Walton & Maberly.

Morgan, L. H., & Lloyd, H. M. (1904). *League of the Ho-dé-no-sau-nee or Iroquois*. New York: Dodd, Mead.

Mt.Pleasant, J. (2016). Food Yields and Nutrient Analyses of the Three Sisters: A Haudenosaunee Cropping System. *Ethnobiology Letters, 7*(1), 87–98.

Munro, R. (1799). *Settlement of the Genesee Country, in the State of New York in a Series of Letters from a Gentleman to his Friend*. New York: T. & J. Swords.

Murphy, L. R. (1991). *Enter the Physician: The Transformation of Domestic Medicine 1760–1860*. Tuscaloosa: University of Alabama Press.

Nimura, J. P. (2021). *The Doctors Blackwell: How Two Pioneering Sisters Brought Medicine to Women and Women to Medicine.* New York: W. W. Norton & Company, Inc.

Olmstead, F. L. (1856). *A Journey in the Seaboard Slave States: Slavery in the years before the American Civil War.* San Francisco: Dix and Edwards.

Parker, A. C. (1909). Secret Medicine Societies of the Seneca. *American Anthropologist, 11*(2), 161–185.

Parker, A. C. (1923). *Seneca Myths and Folk Tales.* Buffalo: Buffalo Historical Society.

Parkin, J. (1866). *The Antidotal Treatment of the Epidemic Cholera* (3rd ed.). London: John Churchill & Sons.

Percival, T. (1803). *Medical Ethics; or, a Code of Institutes and Precepts, Adapted to the Professional Conduct of Physicians and Surgeons.* Cambridge: Cambridge University Press.

Pharmacopoeia, G. C. f. t. F. o. t. A. (1830). *The Pharmacopoeia of the United States of America, Second Edition.* New York: S. Converse.

Potter, W. W. (1895). Fifty Years of Medical Journalism in Buffalo. *Buffalo Medical Journal, 25.*

Potter, W. W. (1898). A Century of Medical History in the County of Erie, 1800–1900. *Buffalo Medical Journal, 37*(9, 10, 11).

Potter, W. W. (1898, 1899). A Century of Medical History in the County of Erie, 1800–1900. *Buffalo Medical Journal, 38*(1, 3, 4, 6, 7, 10).

Pratt, G. F. (1869). Biographical Sketch of the late Cyrenius Chapin of Buffalo. *Buffalo Medical and Surgical Journal, 8,* 1–8.

Pratt, J. W. (1925). *Expansionists of 1812.* New York: The Macmillan Company.

Quaife, M. M. (1913). *Chicago and the Old Northwest 1673–1835.* Chicago: The University of Chicago Press.

Rayback, R. J. (2017). *Millard Fillmore: Biography of a President.* Buffalo: Buffalo Historical Society.

Read, D. B. (1896). *The Canadian Rebellion of 1837.* Toronto: C. Blackett Robinson.

Richards, L. (2003). *Shays's Rebellion: The American Revolution's Final Battle.* Philadelphia: University of Pennsylvania Press.

Riedel, S. (2005). Edward Jenner and the history of smallpox and vaccination. *Proceedings (Baylor University. Medical Center), 18*(1), 21–25. Retrieved from http://www.ncbi.nlm.nih.gov/pmc/articles/PMC1200696/

Rizzo, M. F. (2010). *Through the Mayors' Eyes: Buffalo, New York.* Buffalo: Old House History at Smashwords.

Rochester, T. F. (1861). History of the Origin, and Transactions of the Medical Society of Buffalo. *Buffalo Medical and Surgical Journal, 1*(2), 33–49. Retrieved from https://babel.hathitrust.org/cgi/pt?id=hvd.32044103052619&view=1up& seq=72&q1=Rochester

Rorabaugh, W. J. (1979). *The Alcoholic Republic: An American Tradition.* New York: Oxford University Press.

Rosenberg, C. E. (1962). *The Cholera Years: The United States in 1832, 1849, and 1866*. Chicago: The University of Chicago Press.

Rosenthal, T. (2022). Jabez Allen, MD, and the March from Bloodletting to Germs. *WNY Heritage, 23*(4), 6–13.

Rosenthal, T. C. (2020). *Bloodletting and Germs: A Doctor in Nineteenth Century Rural New York*. Philadelphia: BookBaby.

Ross, S. (1962). Scientist: The story of a word. *Annals of Science, 18*(2), 65–85. https://doi.org/10.1080/00033796200202722

Rush, B. (1774). *An Inquiry into the Natural History of Medicince Among the Indians of North-America and a Comparative View of Their Diseases and Remedies, with Those of Civilized Nations*. Paper presented at The American Philosophical Society, Philadelphia.

Rush, B. (1794). *An Account of the Bilious remitting Yellow Fever as it Appeared in the City of Philadelphia in the year 1793*. Philadelphia: Thomas Dobson.

Rush, B. (1812). *Medical Inquiries and Observations Upon Diseases of the Mind*. Philadelphia: Merritt, Printer, No. 9, Watkin's Alley.

Rush, B. (1815). Defence of Blood-Letting, as a Remedy for Certain Diseases. *Medical Inquiries and Observations, 4*.

Rutkow, I. (2022). *Empire of the Scalpel*. New York: Scribner.

Samo, J. B. (1884). The Medical Profession of Erie County. In H. P. Smith (Ed.), *History of the City of Buffalo and Erie County* (vol. 2, pp. 414–44). Syracuse: D. Mason & Co.

Seaver, J. E. (1860). *The Life of Mary Jemison: DEH-HE-WA-MIS* (6th ed.). New York: C.M. Saxton, Barker & Co.

Shaw, R. E. (2012). *Erie Water West: A History of the Erie Canal, 1792–1854*: University Press of Kentucky.

Sleeper-Smith, S. (2018). *Indigenous Prosperity and American Conquest: Indian Women of the Ohio River Valley, 1690–1792*. Chapel Hill: North Carolina University Press.

Smelser, M. (1958). The Federalist Period as an Age of Passion. *American Quarterly, 10*(4), 391–419.

Smith, C. (2017). Native American History: A Tale of Medicine. Retrieved from http://www.thedifferentialdx.com/native-american-history-a-tale-of-medicine/

Smith, D. S., & Hindus, M. S. (1975). Premarital Pregnancy in America, 1640–1971: An Overview and Interpretation. *Journal of Interdisciplinary History, 5*(4), 537.

Smith, H. P. (1884). *History of the City of Buffalo and Erie County* (Vol. 1). Syracuse: D. Mason & Co.

Smith, P. (1812). *The Indian Doctor's Dispensatory: 1812* (Bulletin No. 2). Cincinnati: Brown and Looker.

St. John de Crevecoeur, H. (1793). *Letters from an American Farmer*. Philadelphia: Project Gutenberg.

St. John Skinner, M. (1905). Reminiscence, by Martha St. John Skinner, of the burning of Buffalo by the British during the War of 1812. *Buffalo Historical Society Publications, 9*. Retrieved September 29, 2024, from https://buffaloah.com/h/stjohnmarg/source/2.html

Starr, P. (1982). *The Social Transformation of American Medicine*. United States: Harper Collins Publishers.

Stearns, J. (1827). Origin of the Medical Society of New York. Retrieved from https://brianaltonenmph.com/6-history-of-medicine-and-pharmacy/hudson-valley-medical-history/the-post-war-years/the-early-medical-profession-in-new-york/part-4-the-dutchess-county-medical-society/john-stearns-sept-17th-1828-origin-of-the-law-to-incorporate-medical-societies/

Stearns, S. (1801). *The American Herbal or Materia Medica*. Walpole: Thomas & Thomas.

Stephenson, K. (2004). "The Quarantine War: The Burning of the New York Marine Hospital in 1858." *Public Health Reports 119*(1): 79–92.

Strum, H. (1980). New York Federalists and Opposition to the War of 1812. *World Affairs, 142*(3), 169–87.

Sugden, J. (1985). *Tecumseh's Last Stand*. Norman: University of Oklahoma Press.

Tannenbaum, R. J. (2002). *The Healer's Calling: Women and Medicine in Early New England. Cornell University Press*. Ithaca, NY: Cornell University Press.

Taylor, A. S. (1866). *A Manual of Medical Jurisprudence* (8th ed.). Philadelphia: Henry C. Lea.

Taylor, A. S. (2010). *The Civil War of 1812: American Citizens, British Subjects, Irish Rebels, and Indian Allies*. New York: Knopf.

Thompson, J. H. (1897). *Jubilee History of Thorold: Township and Town from the Time of the Red Man to the Present*. Thorold and Bever Dams Historical Society.

Thomson, J. L. (1818). *Historical Sketch of the Late War Between the United States and Great Britain* (5th ed.). Philadelphia: Thomas Desilver.

Thomson, S. (1835). *New Guide to Health; Or, Botanic Family Physician*. Boston: J. Howe.

Toner, J. M. (1878, June 4, 5, 6, 7). *Transactions of the American Medical Association Annual Meeting*. Paper presented at the AMA Annual Meeting, Buffalo, New York.

Trowbridge, J. (1869). *Biographical Sketch of the Late Josiah Trowbridge, M.D. of Buffalo*. Buffalo: The Courier Company.

Turner, O. (1849). *Pioneer History of the Holland Purchase of Western New York*. Buffalo: Jewett, Thomas & Co.

Viewed in scrapbook at Buffalo and Erie County Library without further citation. (1909). *Courier Express*.

Vogel, M. N., Patton, E. J., Redding, P. F., & Foy, E. (2009). *America's Crossroads: Buffalo's Canal Street/Dante Place; the Making of a City*. Acorn Books LLC.

Warner, J. H. (1987). Power, Conflict, and Identity in Mid-Nineteenth Century American Medicine. *Journal of American History, 73*(941).

Warner, J. H. (1997). *The Therapeutic Perspective: Medical Practice, Knowledge, and Identity in America, 1820–1885.* Princeton, NJ: Princeton University Press.

Watson, P. A. (1992). The 'Hidden Ones': Women and Healing in Colonial New England. In *Medicine and Healing, Dublin Seminar for New England Folklore.* Boston: Boston University.

Watt, S., & ElBahtity, A. (2021). *Images of America: Medical Society of Erie County.* Charleston, S. Carolina: Acadia Publishing.

Welch, S. M. (1891). *Home History: Recollections of Buffalo During the Decade from 1830–1840 or Fifty Years Since.* Buffalo: Peter Paul & Bro.

Whewell, W. (1837). *History of the Inductive Sciences, From the Earliest to the Present Times.* London: John W. Parker.

White, T. C. e. (1898). *Our county and its people: a descriptive work on Erie County, New York.:* The Boston History Company.

Willius, F. A., & Dry, T. J. (1948). *A History of the Heart and the Circulation.* Philadelphia: W. B. Saunders Company.

Wilner, M. M. (1931). *Niagara Frontier: A Narrative and Documentary History.* Chicago: S. J. Clark Publishing Co.

Wollstonecraft, M. (1792). *A Vindication of the Rights of Women.* Boston: Peter Edes.

Wood, H. C. (1875). Medical Education in the United States. *Lippincott's Magazine of Popular Literature and Science, 16*(96), 703–11.

Zimmermann, A. K. (1995). The Journal of an Upstate Physician: Medicine in the Life of Alexander Coventry, MD; 1785–1831. *The Hudson Valley Regional Review, 12*(1). Retrieved from www.hudsonrivervalley.org/review/pdfs/hvrr_11pt2_zimmermann.pdf

Index

Saint (St.) Paul's Episcopal Church, 61, 76, 143, 168

Scott, Winfield, 103, 135, 194–95

Secord, Laura, 114–15, 210

Sectarians, 48, 64–65, 153, 155, 157, 162

Seneca(s), 6–8, 11–13, 15, 28, 36, 51, 67–69, 71–74, 80, 94, 98, 101, 117–18, 143, 164, 172, 203, 206–207

Language, 69, 71, 172, 205–206

Shays Rebellion, 9, 31–32, 35

Sheep, 140, 170–71, 174

Smallpox, 13, 43, 49–50

Smith, Elisha, 160

Smith, James, 163

Smith, Michael, 92–93, 95

Smith, Peter, 50

Smith, Rufus, 160

Smyth, Alexander, 107–108, 144

Stagecoach, 143–44, 146, 162, 177, 181, 203

Stearns, Samuel, 18, 48, 62, 156–57

Stearns, John J., 155

Steamboats, 144, 146, 175

Sthenic, 47, 51, 151

Strong, Nathaniel T., 74

Sullivan, John, 11–12

Suspenders, 36

Sutherland, Thomas Jefferson, 191–92

Syracuse, 78

Taylor, Zachary, 102–103

Tecumseh, 85–87, 102, 119

Thames River, 118–19

Thomson, Samuel, 53, 63–65, 155–56

Tippecanoe, 85, 87, 103

Tompkins, Daniel D., 88, 96, 101, 140

Tonawanda Creek, 59, 73, 75, 146

Tories (Tory), 123

Toronto (York), 24, 110, 179, 188–91, 193, 196

Treaty of Ghent, 136, 187

Treaty of Paris

Revolutionary War: 1783, 7, 24, 209

Seven Years War (French and Indian) 1763, 6, 24, 209

Trowbridge, Josiah, 60–62, 66, 110, 147, 159–60, 163–65, 182, 208

Troy, New York, 108–109, 193, 203

Tuberculosis, 52

Tuscarora, 6, 36, 125

Vaccination, 49–50

Virginia, 37–38, 108

Walden, Ebenezer, 75, 109, 132–33, 165

Warner, Nash, 163

Washington, D.C., 14, 86, 89–90, 102, 109, 120

Washington, George, 4, 11, 14, 17, 33–34, 39, 49, 68, 117, 197

Waterhouse, Benjamin, 50

Weed, Louise Chapin, 77, 203

Weed, Thaddeus, 77, 203

Welch, Samuel, 41, 69

Wilkinson, James, 111, 113, 117, 120–24

Williamsville, 126, 132, 148, 174

Willink, Wilhelm, 13

Winney, Cornelius, 7, 12

Wollstonecraft, Mary, 77–79

Yellow fever, 20, 4`6, 49

York. See Toronto

Youngstown, 134

About the Author

Dr. Thomas C. Rosenthal, Emeritus Professor of Family Medicine, University at Buffalo, practiced patient-centered medicine while authoring over 100 scientific papers. He edited the *Journal of Rural Health* and the textbook *Office Based Geriatrics*, and he received awards for medical curriculum innovation. His previous book, *Bloodletting and Germs: A Doctor in Nineteenth Century Rural New York* (2020), received the 2022 Gold Medal for cultural fiction.